Time to Grieve: Daily Devotional Essays

David J. Crowley

ISBN: 1484017501
ISBN-13: 9781484017500

DEDICATION

In honor of the departed in my life

For our daughters, Saralyn and Jocelyn

This project has a long inception. I was an altar boy during Vietnam. Too many flag draped coffins appeared in church. Too many mothers couldn't bear to receive the flag from the stricken member of the service assigned that hard duty. I've officiated at too many funerals and not enough baptisms and weddings. Early in ministry, I saw firsthand the awful pain of grief in close encounter. Part of its impetus came from my frustration that pastoral care resources were very strong on therapeutic aids but not so strong on the religious resources that make a distinction between therapy and pastoral care. Later, I came across a book by Burton Cooper where he said that we need to mine different veins or seams of the Bible, as we may well have exhausted the small number of passages we keep returning to. Over the years, a projected book of grief turned into a series of brief looks at biblical passages that changed into trying to make a year's worth of biblical reflections. Part of this was written after the death of my mother at 92. When I was about halfway through the draft, I was diagnosed with an aggressive prostate cancer.

Grief has a random aspect to its course. So, these devotional essays move in a fairly unpredictable pattern. Toward the end, they do emphasize hope more. These essays stress thought as well as emotion and spirit. They also touch popular culture as illustrations a good bit. I can imagine someone flipping through these essays, or going through them one at a time for a year.

1) I Cor. 10:13-We hear familiar bromides at times of loss. "God had a job for your loved one." God wanted your loved one to be in heaven." So many pat phrases pour out from us, out of a sincere desire to be polite and also to try to help ease the pain and anxiety of the moment. I don't know if it comes from us or others, but I notice a profound sense of discomfort among others when they realize that you have lost someone to death recently, as if you have a contagious disease. This passage often gets changed to "God doesn't give us more than we can stand or can take, or bear." I have heard it far too many times during funeral visitations. I have gotten to the point where I warn families to expect the standard phrases and even keep track of the most annoying ones. To my ears, it sounds as if it is a test to measure our breaking point; it skates close to the sadistic. One would wish to respond that in that case, we wish we would be much weaker, so the test would not come. I was told after a funeral in church by a member of the congregation that God was testing me with my cancer. My unvoiced response was that I would rather skip the course than be subjected to this method of evaluation. The flaw in the cliché is the assumption that God is giving us the loss or travail on purpose. I do not see the image of God as one of a Zeus hurling thunderbolts at us to see how we will respond. I don't see this as the image of the God of Jesus Christ. The quote from v. 13 is "God will not let you be tested beyond your strength." The Greek word ranges from test to tempt. I mentally and sometimes verbally respond with a passage from James 1:17. "Every good and perfect gift comes from above." I don't see God as taking our loved ones in the first place. I don't see God using those losses as a test of our faith. If that is the case, it is a poor lesson plan. I also hear an echo of a more punitive view of God than many of us share. Would God use a death to "teach us a lesson?" How would that possibly meet the demands of proportional justice? The Greek word could be tempt or try or test. I don't know if that makes it any better. Perhaps we could hear it as God does not place us in a situation beyond our capacity. It pushes us to consider where is God's hand direct or indirect, no? Ken Haugk, the founder of Stephen Ministry, did a survey where the vast majority of respondents were not comforted by those of us trying to be God's mouthpiece with the typical religious clichés we offer for them to we hear. Perhaps we do better to

not try to speak for God, but to try to be the listening ear of Christ.

2) Response to Job 38-42- Many read the end of Job and think that God has simply overwhelmed Job and dismissed his complaints. In a new and different way, God responds to Job's challenge of how God works with the world. First, God gives Job a tour of the universe. Years ago, people at the cusp of adulthood received a grand tour of Europe. We used to speak of trips as a chance to get away from it all. (See Road to Wellville). It has the sense of a vacation package, where we get away from it all and explore. It's a distraction from the heavy concerns that afflict him, a break from all the pain. It shows him that the world does not revolve around him and his issues. Job gets to see the immensity of creation. Yes, God responds to Job, but God has other concerns. God wants Job to grasp that he exists in a world of relationships, intersections, and contacts. The world is not made for him and is not to be judged according to whether it enhances or defeats Job. Second, its cosmic sweep moves him out of his inward gaze. He is able to move beyond his pain and see more than only pain in the universe. God is seeking to enlarge his perspective. Third, he sees the complexity of the the creation. This is an important point. In creation the wild and the tame exist together; so do birth and death. In its sublimity, creation does contain uncontrolled things. We are not the center of the universe. In The Poet's Gift Donald Capps writes (99) "it was God who did not give reasons but extended Job an invitation to take renewed interest in the world around him." At the end of the section (42:6) it is commonly translated as Job taking a humble posture in repenting in dust and ashes. We have multiple translations for this. In the NIB Newsom gives us a list, including: "I repent of dust and ashes, or changed my mind about dust and ashes, or even comforted concerning dust and ashes." Instead of being beaten into submission, these different translations would point to Job coming to a new understanding. Today let's select repent of dust and ashes. Job is going to start to live again. He has struggled long and hard to come to grips with reasons for his losses.

3) Lk.13:1-9- We have another example of Jesus refusing to blame people's moral failings as the proximate cause of their suffering. Jesus does not blame victims. Jesus will not say that we deserve evil to befall us. We even get two types of evil, the natural evil of an accident and the malevolent evil of Pilate. Jesus won't compare the relative moral worth of victims or those outside the tragedy. Jesus will not blame victims for their plight from either cause. He does not place either form of suffering as the responsibility of a divine design. He even goes so far as to say not to gloat in a righteous feeling that one has been protected from calamity due to some intrinsic special worth. In other words, tragic events are part of the situation where we find ourselves. Please notice that he does not listen affirmatively but challenges their religious assertion. Of course some deaths are the direct result of a poor decision, sets of decisions, or carelessness. By and large, fault cannot be attributed to the one who has died, nor family and friends. We may want to assign fault and blame, but it is rarely on point. A new form of the blame game is raising its head with the new wave of positive thinking promotions. We hear comments such as he just quit fighting; she had a bad attitude. Positive thinking may be a worthwhile, even brave, response to trouble, but I have trouble understanding it as some sort of protective shield or magic elixir to banish trouble. Christians do not see "mind over matter" as much as they see us seeking to transform from within. (See the models in H. R. Niebuhr's Christ and Culture). We look for some sort of scale that balances our deserving suffering.

4) Jacob's grey head (Gen. 42:38) -Jacob never gets over the loss of Joseph. for that matter, he has also been widowed from Joseph's mother, Rachel. He has borne the grief too many years already. He cannot face the loss of his youngest son, Benjamin. He will grieve until he himself dies. he has not found the closure that is sometimes promised to the grieving. Maybe he has gotten to the point where grief seems his destiny, and he can find a way to pull out of its hold. We speak too much of closure. Even if the wounds of grief heal, the scars remain. On the other hand, people do get stuck in grief for long periods of time. It is as if the wound is forever

fresh. It is an act of healing to seek counseling and medication in the face of persistent grief that last years. Sometimes, people get stuck in grief if they fear that they will forget the loved one. It may be a fear of coming to grips with reconstructing life in the face of death. At times, it can be a sense that not moving along in grief may be a sign of the depth of one's love. Sometimes, the grief is complicated by a variety of factors: the type of relationship, the type of death. Joseph was a dreamer, an interpreter of dreams as well. I don't put a lot of stock in dreams, but some do. Recurrent dreams may afflict us after a loss. Sometimes we dream what is forbidden for us to say or feel or think. Voklan and Zintl report that dreams can change during therapy, and that change can well be a sign of processing the loss in a deeper, healthier way. The important German pastor and theologian, Friedrich Schleiermacher delivered a sermon at his son Nathanael's grave. He quite bravely dispenses with the offers of solace given him and his family that his son was able to avoid the temptations of this world. The "stooped father" for he saw the world as "as an unending development of all that is good and Godly," so he had no reason to believe that the light of faith could be extinguished in his beloved son. He turns away from the proffered joys of heaven, because he says as a bookish thinker, it raises more questions than answers. He knows the pain of Jacob: " my heart clung full of love, is now ineradicably stricken through, the friendly, refreshing picture of life is suddenly destroyed, and all the hopes that rested upon him lie here and shall be buried with this coffin. What should I say?" In a most generous move, he turns to his wife and children and thanks them for the love shown to the boy. He turns to his teachers to praise them for their attentions and training. Whom do you need to thank for the life of your loved one?

5) Joseph-Gen 50. Sometimes loss brings fear of retribution within families. Bickering over the estate can cause new areas of resentment. Recently, at a graveside service a family was bickering over respective shares of the funeral director's bill. Sometimes the terms of the will are attempts to continue control or resentments from beyond the grave. The Redford movie an Unfinished Life is a look at how family dynamics can be

poisoned for years by reactions to loss. Not only was the son's life unfinished, but his spouse, daughter, and father are also caught up in their own unfinished responses to grief and their own life as a family. Joseph demonstrates the healing power of forgiveness. It is difficult for the brothers to realize that he has indeed forgiven them. They feared that he was biding his time until their father would die. Then he would exact his vengeance. After all, they had considered killing him and then sold him into slavery. They led their father to believe that he had been killed by a ravenous beast. The reader cannot know if the brothers have concocted the story of Jacob's dying wish, or if it were a reality. At the same time he utters a powerful Biblical truth. "Am I in the place of God? You meant it for evil, but God meant it for good." (see p. 673 NIB on guilt and status)Notice that he calls their actions evil. He does not gloss over them. He has remembered their wrongs, but he will not retaliate in kind. Finally, in reconciliation he says they will be cared for. Do you think that you need to forgive your loved one? I realize that it is odd to speak of forgiving the dead. At the very least, you can renounce a active desire for revenge. You can seek to come to an understanding of the way they were. You can relinquish the hold the hurts have on you. At some point, we can stop ceding power to their actions and perceptions and claim self-responsibility and self-care. Many of us collect and nurture our hurts as if they were a precious garden. Others collect them and place them in a treasure box or a n emotional backpack. When angered, we open them up and let their contents spill out. Did your loved one withhold forgiveness from you?

6) Ruth and Naomi-(see Trible's God and the Rhetoric of Sexuality) ch. 1 Death stalks this passage; death soaks this passage. Naomi and her family fled famine, but now, after some years, Naomi loses her husband and their two sons. Moab natives Ruth and Orpah are widowed, with no adult children to provide for security. So, three women are in difficult circumstance. Still, the focus is on moving toward life in the face of death. No mention, as yet, is made of a punishment from above. After all these years, we are unsure about treating widows properly. They are perhaps the best examples of secondary losses, where their social network gets

disrupted, as they are no longer part of a couple. Ruth and Naomi create an unlikely community. Ruth decides to now become an alien in Judah, as her mother-in-law decides to return to her town, Bethlehem (house of bread).At the same time Orpah (back of the neck) makes a good decision to stay at home, but Ruth makes a noble, proper decision as well. Both decisions are respected; here the Bible does not say that one and only one way can lead to a good and proper decision. It does indicate in relations, blood relations are not the only relations that matter to us. In ch. 2 Naomi lets fly with her feelings to God. She disclaims her name, joy or pleasantness, and claims the name Marah, bitterness. She calls God by two different names but lays her troubles directly at God's doorstep, especially as El Shaddai carries a sense of being almighty. Gerald Janzen explicitly links Naomi and Job by calling them soulmates. Naomi's restoration will very much be a human product, not the wave of the hand that signals the return of Job to a new life. Still, they are on the road home, for Naomi, at least, to Bethlehem, the house of bread, a good name for people in need of sustenance, at all levels. Shakespeare (Richard II) said "each substance of grief has twenty shadows." It puts all sorts of pieces of a life in the shade.

7).Mary at the cross-We picture this in art as much as in our own imagination. (see some other famous examples) Perhaps Mary represents all mothers who lose a child. I think of the Pieta of course, but it was a standard representation in religious art. I was raised in pre-Vatican II Catholic grade school. Mary was indeed the feminine face of the faith, the face of compassion, protection, and solace. To be a parent at the foot of the cross seems beyond belief. Take a look at her face. Is it possible that she is praying? Look at the TV movie, Jesus, and see how Mary recreates the Pieta setting but then goes to wash the bloody face of her son in the tomb. Did she hear the words of the Annunciation again (Lk. 1:35)? In Luke's gospel one goes back to the brave words of the Magnificat and hears them thrown back. Did she hear echoes of Simeon's prophecy in the temple with the infant Jesus, or did she recall the shepherds' rep[ort of the angel chorus? Compare the Pieta to the manger scenes. Luke, remember, says that she meditated on them in her heart. Surely, she did much soul-searching after the Crucifixion. In a way, Mary represents those who lose a child to injustice. As I reflect on this, perhaps picture therapy, art therapy, is a practice for the grieving, to go through representations of suffering and loss could open our eyes to different dimensions and interpretations of loss. Our Orthodox sisters and brothers use icons as a focus for their prayer life. Consider going through some images of grief and note your reactions. Try to put into words what you think the person is experiencing that is captured by the image. You may consider making a grief scrapbook. As you go through photographs, what are the striking ones for you? Do you find particular artistic images touching you? As the time passes have you found that different images mean more or less to you?

8) Peter's reaction to cross in Mk.8 is one most of us share. Three times Jesus will announce that he is on the road to suffering and death. Surely another way would have to be found. Indeed, he suspects that a demonic force has entered Jesus in order for him to speak in this way. For in this instance Peter rebukes Jesus. Rebuke is the same word used when Jesus heals people of demonic possession. Notice that this segment is directly after Peter has declared Jesus to be the Messiah, the anointed one, the Christ. Surely the anointed one cannot be subjected to cruel suffering and death. Peter has just found the long awaited One. Now that same person is going to suffer and die? I often say that it is a difficult thing to be American and Christian, In part, I mean that our cultural optimism, our expectation of progress, makes it difficult to deal with suffering. Jesus is warning Peter that his mission of being messiah will not be triumph, but tragedy. In Last Temptation of Christ, the great temptation is to avoid suffering and to embrace a normal life. By extension, we do not want to face it ether. Jesus responds brusquely to Peter, in part at least, as Jesus himself feels the pull of avoiding suffering. Recall that the temptations in Luke and Matthew's account center on avoiding suffering. Jesus will not avoid the path that leads to suffering. He will work through its terrors. He does not embrace suffering for suffering's sake, but he does face suffering

for a cause of salvation. After all, the image is the cross, a result of state execution, not generalized troubles. I am of two minds when we speak of carrying the cross as part of our human burden or is it a specific response when the powers that be are threatened? The great demonstration of solidarity with humanity is suffering with us, as well as for us. Could Jesus have been Emmanuel, God with us, and avoid human suffering? Some mystics engage Jesus through their suffering or in meditation on the sufferings of Jesus. They make a spiritual gateway out of what is a bolted door for many of us.

9) Romans 8:28 almost brought me to blows more than once in seminary. How could a suicide be God at work for good? Did his suicide mean that God did not regard him as loving the Holy One? How could God possibly mean to utilize a tragedy for good? After my brother's suicide, well-meaning folks quoted that verse to me a number of times. If I had not taken Prof. Neuger's class on grief with its reminders that we speak out of anxiety when facing the grieving, I would have been knocking heads. Is it a gospel word? Yes. Is it helpful to many in the shocked moments of early loss? No, it may not be a gospel word in the early days of grief. In time, we may be able to see some threads of good being woven into a loss. That is hindsight, maybe even only a view from heaven. Indeed that may be a way at the passage. As James Fowler wrote, God is always reweaving the new creation. Notice it is reweaving. He imagines a responsive, relational God who works with what we do. This is not the God of decree and command. That weaving may well take more than a lifetime. That reweaving is always aimed at bringing the good, maybe even the best, out of a complex set of situations. We cannot expect anyone to discover good in the immediate aftermath of a loss. It only increases their burdens. In part, my interest in grief stems from my brother's suicide over twenty years ago. Maybe some good has emerged out of that tragic end in my own pastoral work. Even if it has, it is not worth the cost. We do well to be careful about pushing Easter moments on to a Good Friday time. At the same time, Romans 8 goes on to tell us that nothing can separate us from the love of God in Jesus Christ. I used that as a mantra for a while, both in terms of his

suicide and my own grief. It was a piece I held on to for dear life while feeling adrift, before I could even get the energy to start a lover's quarrel with God. In hindsight, we can perhaps perceive some good that God has drawn out of tragedy. It is a sin to impose that future perspective on someone in the throes of early grief. To foist a sentence of Scripture on someone without any sense of what they are going through is judging a person's condition. It has a sense of one size fits all. Where do you seem to fit and not fit with conventional notions of grief?

10) Lament psalms (examples. 13, 22,)-When I was a child, I learned that prayer was "talking and listening to God. The prayer I was taught was to ask for blessing for my family. I quickly learned that we could pray for help, for good things to happen, for help in trouble, prayers of intercession, maybe especially for knowledge to help me get through a math test or how to untangle a knotty diagramming exercise for a sentence. While I found it easy to ask for things or to ask for help, I did not find it so easy to find words for spiritual, emotional, or mental hardships. Lament prayer gives words to pain and talks them out with God in a structure that we can learn from that great prayer book, the Psalter. While we may think of the 23rd psalm first, a plurality of the psalms is in the lament vein. Any pain can be placed in the envelope of prayer. Here, this prayer textbook shows that the lament form is worthy prayer, not mere whining to God. Lament prayers pour out questions and pain and lay it before God. We don't have many cultural tools to form and frame our feelings of loss. Emily Dickinson wrote of "the hour of lead." To counteract that leaden feeling, I like the lament form, as it is candid prayer before God. It allows us to open ourselves up before God. It is not concerned about polite and careful address. These are cries of the heart. Usually, laments end in a resolution. In one sense, this is due to catharsis, where one gets it off the chest in prayer. In another deeper sense, the form gives hope for resolution even when hope seems distant. Jesus himself prayed the beginning of the lament Psalm 22 at the cross. I've heard people say that he used it as a shorthand to get at its conclusion, but I don't believe it. On the cross Jesus felt forsaken and he prays that sense in all of his

anguish. Since Jesus could share that pain, so can we. If Jesus could quote a psalm of lament in a time of deep distress, so can we. An inability or refusal to be able to be candid with God about our troubles seems then to lead to only partial prayer. Worse, it could lead us to see prayer as formal only, or sugar-coated positive bromides that do not touch the varied elements of our experience. A Biblical scholar, Walter Brueggemann, has written of the "costly loss of lament." It is religiously costly; we lose this structure to our detriment. Failure to be able to use this prayer form diminishes the depth of our relationship with God. Instead of casting about when we need some way to structure our thoughts and feelings about loss, we are given this biblical model of prayer.

11) Ritual-Leviticus 1-4-The funeral directors had a slogan recently that "ritual heals." Primal indigenous religions are full of rituals so one can try to properly address the spirit world and its impact on this one. We have a ritual deficit in contemporary culture, as we move to a do it yourself ritual, instead of having expected, socially understood methods. Amid the chaotic swirl of thoughts and feelings, it helps to have a pattern, to know the steps of the mourning. Being part of a pattern demonstrates that we are not alone in this human drama. Unable to learn to steps, it give us a familiar pattern to follow. Even though we are demanding individualized funerals, they are starting to take on a dispiriting sameness. Years ago, mourning clothes had social significance. I admire the Jewish practice of pinning a black piece of cloth on a lapel, itself a change form the days when clothing was rent in a public display of grief. . In Victorian times, we had mourning clothes set out for a year and a day. Then, slowly to "lighten' it, one slowly brought color back into one's wardrobe. On the other hand, Queen Victoria wore mourning clothes for the rest of her life after she was widowed from Prince Albert. I realize that as soon as many of us hear the word, ritual, we immediately jump to the epithet, ritualistic. The very patterns of ritual keep some proper distance, so it can translate joy or pain into a social framework. Practice of a method does not make something devoid of meaning. For our eldest daughter's wedding, she asked me to learn to waltz. Already I am on the wall of the studio in the

hall of fame/same of uncoordinated, self-conscious helpless dancers. Still, once one gets the steps, things fall in to place, at least for most people without two left feet. So, ritual can help us learn the steps. To be personal, a ritual does not have to start from scratch. Indeed, it can be intensely personal but still draw on a variety of ideas and traditions. We are perhaps too quick to dismiss riutals, without allowing ourselves the time and trouble to allow the rituals to function and to seep into our own consciousness. Prayers can be rote, but I have seen too many people crave to recite the Lord's Prayer or the 23rd psalm as they lay dying. A short prayer of remembrance (yizkor) in some Jewish circles promises to make a contribution to charity on the first religious holiday after the death of someone. In our family we always set out an extra place setting for Jesus on Christmas Eve. It also served, I think, to remind of us those in the family, especially our father, who would be forever absent from our table due to his early death at sea.

12) Lamentations and acrostic-Eugene Peterson-In his book Five Smooth Stones, Eugene Peterson has a chapter on Lamentations. He notices that it uses a multiple acrostic form. In other words, it goes through an A to Z listing. Sometimes the opening letter get repeated. The sense of it is that you have your say. It pushes us to be able to say, enough. In grief, people find it hard to listen to our repeated stories of loss and pain. When you get to read or pray of grief in an A to Z format, it gives the sense of completeness, but it also gives structure when grief seem so chaotic and formless. It also gives a sense of when to stop. For a while at least, one can close the book on lament. In other words, it serves to place a frame around grief, so it doesn't appear so open-ended and overwhelming. The changes come at us in waves, and it is hard to distinguish one from another. our minds are so beset with option and decisions that we cannot seem to think straight. Anna Brenner said: "the only feelings that do not change are the ones ignored"(Mourning and Mitzvah). She also notes that pain does acquire a virtual size and shape inside. Physical symptoms often occur in mourning. Sleep gets disturbed, and appetite may dwindle or expand. Some can't catch their breath. After my brother died, I felt a

consistent pain in the middle of my chest, and then I caught pleurisy. Emotional hurt is mirrored by physical pain. Look at how Lamentations is willing to touch on varieties of pain. Country music and blues both are willing to face pain. When Cole Porter was struggling to become a popular song writer, he was urged to find the blue note, a note that Jewish popular songwriters had adapted from their own cultures catch in the melody. Indeed, Lamentations itself has a "limping" meter, one that has the break of a sob in it. Usually that sob also ends on a note of hope, somehow. In his remarkable sermon Alex's death, the late William Sloane Coffin moves through a lament in a powerful series of brushstrokes, as he spoke of the death of his son, at 24, in a car accident. He lashes out as those who call an accident, God's will. "nothing so infuriates me as the incapacity of seemingly intelligent people to get it through their heads that God doesn't go around this world with his fingers on triggers...his hands on steering wheels."

12A) The middle of Lamentations has hope in its very center at 3:19. In the midst of all of that destruction and pain, its center is a kernel of hope. Grief without hope can destroy. In early grief we move numbly, one day after another. In the Middle Ages we spoke of two spiritual maladies that have some relation to grief, acedia and tristitia. Acedia is not being able to care, of being burned out, of compassion fatigue. Tristitia is a deep spiritual sadness, an inability to see joy or feel joy when it is presented, when it can be appreciated. It is a sadness that turns its back on life, or maybe is unable to see the goodness in life, a partial spiritual blindness, perhaps. Hope is a prescription for both maladies. This passage is a signal flare that new mercies are given day after day. In the midst of grief, we can hope, are urged to hope, even if it seems faint and weary. At some point, we are able to see color amid all of the grays. At some point, we can hear a sweet song again. Eventually, we can laugh again without feeling guilty. As we stumble through, our backs start to straighten and our blurry vision starts to clear enough to look beyond just this day. In time, we can recognize new mercies and not replay the past. Even in the midst of heartache, we can notice some grace notes. It insists that new every morning are God's mercies. Hope is not necessarily rational. It ignores the lines of a trend. Against evidence, it looks for a brighter horizon line. Having hope at its center prevents us from falling into despair. How do we "keep hope alive?" Have you been able to detect "new mercies" sometimes, if not every morning? May the wings of hope fly you into a future. Hope has wings as it lifts us above the pain and confusion on the ground. Hope has wings as it lifts us into a new perspective, one that can take more in, without getting too caught up in details.

13) Lk. 7:11-17 -Let's assume that Joseph's disappearance from the narrative in Luke indicates that he died before Jesus began his mission. The 199 TV movie, Jesus, imagines such a scene. Maybe that is why Jesus is moved by her grief. In john's gospel Jesus creates a new family with Mary and the beloved disciple. Of course, treatment of widows was at the heart of Hebrew ethics, along with the orphan and sojourner. Over and over, they are the test of the soul of society. Still, this almost impetuous miracle goes far beyond caring for her basic needs. It seems to me that this is an almost impulsive act of compassion by Jesus. This does not seem to be the same motive as the Jesus who said "let the dead bury the dead."(see I Kings 17:20, presented is the same as in v. 23 or 2 K 4:32) (felt compassion in LXX has mercy extended in Prov.17:5., as in 6:36.??) No only is she widowed, but this is her only son. What will become of her? Why would Jesus tell her not to weep? "Do not weep" makes sense only in what follows. Maybe all it meant was the soothing phrase we will tell a child, don't cry. (Is there a poem on the raised son? widow poem by Merton) Maybe Jesus was moved so by her weeping that he felt compelled to act. Maybe it was more spontaneous, as Jesus felt the pain of the mother and was moved to act without a lot of pondering the issues. In the raisings by Jesus one is soon after death, one at the funeral, and one some days after the burial. In this sequence, or spread of miracles, we are in the face of the new age, the apocalypse, the revealing of a new way in the world. The age of death is drawing to a close, even as it appears it has dominion. These raisings are trumpets like those of Jericho that the seemingly impregnable fortress of death has been breached.

14)I Thes.4:13-5-Early in Paul's ministry, maybe twenty years after the death of Jesus, the people in the town are worried that the new age has not arrived in time, and they have lost loved ones to death. My sense is that they expected the Second coming, the parousia, to occur quickly, but now the familiar hand of death has struck again. What will become of them and us? I don't want to get into an argument of "the rapture" here, at least, but do want to lift it up for another purpose. It seems the emphasis is placed on this point: that we will be with Christ. Instead of the raptor of death snatching us up, the loving arms of Christ will capture us. Community and continuity with the Risen One will persist. If I understand him correctly, the point is that at the end, both the living and the dead will be alive in Jesus Christ. "We will be with the Lord forever." Another important piece is the declaration that we should not grieve as those who have no hope. Some misread it as saying that the Christian should not grieve. No, it expects grief but that it will differ from those who have no hope. Hope in what, exactly? It sounds to me as if this is not all there is to human existence in this realm. In life and in death we rely on the God of life. What is it to grieve as those without hope? Without that hope, memory is all that keeps the traces of a life together. Our lives are more than footprints in the shifting sand on the beach. to grieve with hope allows

15) Gen.32 Jacob at the creek. Waterways are good symbols of a boundary, liminal experience. Jacob is at a crisis point. He is wrestling with sides of himself, wrestling with his future v. his past. It may well be an identity crisis dream. Jacob battles all night with a stranger. Is it a dream, or not? In grief sleep can be an issue, especially sleeping too much, too little, or having disturbed sleep. Some are afraid to fall asleep out of fear of what dreams may come into play. It is hard enough trying to maintain some control, and sleep removes that control eight hours a day. Here in this nighttime struggle, is the stranger human, angel, divine? At the close of the struggle, Jacob will not let go until he receives a blessing. He does, but the struggle gives him a limp from a damaged hip. Grief work is

difficult work. Even when we emerge from the worst battles, we may limp. We are dislocated from a former way of being ourselves. It is a struggle to battle with all of the conflicting feelings and random thoughts. It is a real battle to face things about ourselves we would much rather not face. A spiritual side of grief is wrestling with our image of God and wrestling with different sides of ourselves. We may not leave it unscathed, even if we emerge with a blessing. We worship a God who engages us where we are. We may realize that our image of God has not grown with us, and we expect the image carried by a six year old to handle the journey of an adult. God realizes that faith changes in struggle. Faith works in and through doubts and struggles. It is not static, nor rigid. So, part of the spiritual struggle of grief may well be a battle with contending views of God, a battle with how we think the world should work, a battle with thoughts and feeling usually kept well below the surface. For years after the death of a friend, Tennyson worked on a poem, In Memoriam, AHH. " I stretch lame hands of faith and grope/and gather dust and chaff and call/to what I feel is Lord of all/ and faintly trust the larger hope." That struggle will not leave us unchanged. I am loath to suggest that one should aim for a different image of God, but I have seen many people have a profound shift in their image of God in a variety of directions. Some move a a more deterministic God, while others move toward a more sympathetic God. In grief we may not have Luther's reckless trust, but we can find the faint trust of the poem, perhaps. As with faith the size of a mustard seed, just a little is plenty. In Kaddish, the author is in the small group at prayer. "Their faith is an irreducible quantum. They are here because they believe, and I am here because they believe (114)."

16) Heaven is not described in much Scriptural detail, so it becomes a repository for our projections. After the Civil War, we witnessed an explosion of interest in describing it, with so many young men killed in the prime of life. Heaven took on a picture of blissful domesticity. Look at material such as Acres of Diamonds. Interest in spiritualism also flourished, as we could see in Mary Todd Lincoln. Cemeteries continued a change from the churchyard to area resembling public parks (See Garry

Wills in <u>Lincoln at Gettysburg</u>).The move toward romantic ideas wanted people to be able to experience nature to facilitate going to a cemetery as a place of peaceful contemplation. If death lead directly to an idyllic heaven, then those in repose would be in a place reflecting just that. I like the lyrics of Mary Chapin Carpenter's In My Heaven. "Nothing shatters nothing breaks...no one's lost/ no one's missing/no more partings/ just hugs and kissing...by the time you're here/we've all we've got." John 14:4 says in my father's house are many rooms. Maybe the rooms will be "decorated" to fit our particular needs, or maybe that will be washed away in the great transformation. My mother, in bitter moments, would say that heaven had better be pretty great to make up for this life. Bruce Springsteen sings of "searching for my beautiful reward." I knew a woman, now departed, who knew that heaven would provide her with the 'Barbie legs" her 5 foot frame was denied. A retired farmer told me that part of heaven for him would be an empty medicine chest, and his pill reminder box would have shots of Kentucky whiskey in it. For me, I prefer to use the resurrection appearances as my pointer to heaven. Jesus is recognizable, but also recognizably different. He has not left his life back here. He knows his friends, and he bears the scars of the cross. Wendell Berry, in part of his series on Port William gives us this from Jayber Crow: "This is a book about Heaven. I know it now. It floats among us like a cloud and is the realest thing we know and the least to be captured, the least to be possessed by anybody for himself. It is like a grain of mustard seed, which you cannot see among the crumbs of earth where it lies. It is like the reflection of the trees on the water."

17) 2 Cor. 5:1-5 has a good sense of our earthly body with something better to come. Surely anyone grieving knows about sighing and groaning within this tent. Anyone in the presence of a grievously ill patient has heard those groans. Those in the difficult vigil groan inwardly as well, as the minutes and hours tick by. Death does not always come easily, as the body fights for life. I think of a tent as a temporary affair, even a makeshift affair, some shelter, but not a house. No matter how much attention we

pay to this temporary dwelling, we hear a promise of a "building not made by human hands, eternal in the heavens." My baby boomer's generation obsession with youthfulness will result, in the end, with youthful looking corpses. Deluxe tents are still tents. Even though our sojourn here may seem far too short, a spiritual structure awaits. The eternal reigns over the temporal. Paul develops his ideas with a remarkable, poetic set of images. He speaks of an inner v. outer, visible or unseen, earthly and heavenly, at home or away from home, or temporary v. eternal, as he makes a polarity of being clothed or naked here as well the images pile on top of each other, interact with each other, to give more heft to his point. Instead of saying that we slough off this mortal coil and reveal our inner essence, the soul, he says that we put on life, perhaps a reference to the baptismal garment. Then he speaks of life swallowing up mortality. Usually death, that snake, was thought to be the one that consumed life.

Our eldest daughter was a big fan of the TV series <u>Buffy</u>. Few programs ever showed the blinding confusion of grief better than an episode, "The Body." Few touch on the inarticulate stammers of those who are with the grieving and have no clue how to act or what to say. Buffy's mother dies suddenly, of natural causes. Even the usual soundtrack was absent from the show's presentation. The crew can fight demons, but they have no training how to begin to comfort their friend. Buffy is a superhero; her foes are hideous creatures of darkness. Here, her mother falls prey to her own body's weakness and dies without being able to point a finger at a monster, unless the monster is Death itself. Even with her powers, Buffy gets sick to her stomach in the face of raw grief. The monster of death does wound her. The tent of grief holds sighs, but it, too, is a temporary dwelling. 2 Cor.5 is a good choice to be in the <u>BCW (Book of Common Worship</u> of the Presbyterian Church, USA) for funerals. Around our passage, it contrasts this world with the next, but it does not denigrate our mortal existence.   Anyone seeing someone ravaged by illness sees the image in an instant. I love the idea that we may see this flesh and blood decay, but that we are part of a divine edifice, not built with human hands that will last, "eternal in the heavens." It is one thing to call something built Ford tough, it is another entirely to call it God-built, built to last. In a way it tells us that life is transitory, like a tent, and not to be seen as a stable, completed project. When John Adams was widowed form his beloved, if he had already started an exchange of letters with his old friend and nemesis Thomas Jefferson. Jefferson had been long-widowed. I'm not sure if he believed in heaven, but he warmed to the task to try to comfort his old friend. He even imagined a gathering of the young revolutionaries in a reunion at the close of their long lives. God can build securely what cannot last in this life. While we may come to imagine these bodies, these tents, as being permanent structures, they provide but temporary shelter. We may feel betrayed by them when they show themselves to be unable to stand up against some of the storms or the long haul of our journeys.

18) Phil. 2 speaks of the emptying of Christ, kenosis. (See Lewis, <u>Between Cross and Resurrection:168-75</u>). It does push us to consider what it means to be human, or divine, for that matter. In the very nature of creation God makes space for existence, a great scrabble word here, zimzum. In some Jewish thought, one speaks of a contraction of God's power to allow the free space for existence itself.. When necessary, love expands or contracts the scope of power. The willingness to give some space for us could indeed be a sign of the fullness of the love of God. That selfsame love seems to some of us to preclude control over the creation given space by the Designer. Whether it is a self-limitation or the brute fact of a creation, God made a world with some significant degrees of freedom. Part of that love knows the emptiness of loss. We rail against Death, as we cannot control it. Loss has a way of emptying out our basket of illusions, so we enter into a sense of emptiness. How many times one hears the grieving say that they feel empty inside. It is said that nature abhors a vacuum. Maybe we need to empty ourselves of some of our pretensions about control, about a world that makes perfect sense, in balance. One of the questions grief will then raise is how we will fill the empty space? Loss forces us to examine how unstable and weak our attempts at control can be. Quite simply, being emptied of some of our baggage allows God to filter through, to course through our lives more readily.

Of what did Jesus empty himself? What was retained? What obstacles to your grief need to be emptied? Perhaps, we do well to empty ourselves of our pre-suppositions about loss and the proper coping tactics for it.

19) Phil 4 gives us a good reminder on dealing with difficulty: be aware of what thoughts fill our minds. Cognitive therapies realize that our thoughts can affect our emotions as well as the commonly assumed reverse. In other words, feelings are not ultimate. They can be influenced by our thought processes and habits. We can get on a train of unhelpful thoughts just as surely as we can get into an emotional spiral. Grief becomes a prism for thoughts and feelings. Some could suggest giving oneself the assignment of grieving for a selected amount of time each day. Distracting dark thoughts with noble ones can be a technique for coping with the flurry of difficult thoughts constantly intruding on the mind and heart. If unable, as yet, to think of the sterling qualities of a loved one, we could look to other ennobling things. Consider having handy a list of ten easy to do things that tend to give you a lift. it could be some favorite movies or songs. Consider a list of future projects that would help the public while memorializing your loved one. Self-control is not the virtue it once was. The new cognitive therapies that seek to develop healthy ways of thinking return some of its tools for us. What are ten movies that usually give you a lift? Do you have a number of favorite songs? Recuperating in its root sense looks toward taking or grasping. That's a word we use for physical recovery, but not that often for emotional recovery. Its root would lead me to think that it means grasping health, taking back some charge of life, taking in good again. Recuperation rarely comes in a flash. We see we are on the road to recovery, but ti can be a slow process. I realize that for some of us, reading uplifting things only makes us feel more depressed, so listening to the blues or reading sad stories seem to fit our mood and lift spirits. Others require infusions of positive, upbeat material to get a psychic jolt. Anyway, Paul's long list of virtuous thoughts does not preclude either upbeat or downbeat material. Quality lies at the heart of the list. We need material and thoughts that nourish the spirit, so fast food thoughts just will not provide enough nourishment.

20) Dt. 34 looks to the death of Moses. In time the rabbis could not bear the thought of his death, so they filled in the story and had Moses assumed in heaven, since no burial spot was known. Perhaps, it was thought that no mere gravesite could encompass the memory of the great man. Memory does not require a shrine. Moses would indeed be unforgettable. The death of the great can affect us. for Americans that does not only mean death by assassination, but of great public figures: TV stars, politicians, humanitarians, athletes. No one lives a fully completed life. I must say that his view of the Promised Land without getting to enter it is particularly poignant. He has been with the people for a generation. Now at the gates of the Promised Land, Moses is denied entry.(see another entry)The death of Moses is heartrending, as he does not live to set foot in the land he worked so long to find. All of those years, to be on the very edge of the goal, and then to be denied it, seems so unfair and futile. Even though a transition with Joshua was assured, I wonder if the people thought they could make it without Moses, the only leader they had known. On the other hand, few of us feel as if we have completed the bucket list, let alone the tasks of our lives. As Dennis Olson notes in Deuteronomy and the Death of Moses, no shrine was erected for Moses. Shrines can turn idolatrous. Perhaps that is one reason why we buried Osama Bin Laden at sea, to prevent an easy shrine. The freed slaves will not set up their lives around the figure of Moses. It is God that leads them from slavery to freedom. No, their goal is the Promised Land, not a shrine to the past in Egypt or the wilderness. Moses will be the great liberator, but a shrine would look to the past, and their future would be the Promised Land. Do you have a vision of the Promised Land? What did your loved one finish or leave unfinished? What regret of unfinished work do you think they may have had? What would you like to finish and what do you fear that you will leave unfinished? Have you tried to emulate someone? Who is in your personal shrine or Hall of Fame? How do you handle a hero who reveals imperfections? Have you had moments when you thought you could not go on without a loved one? How did you learn to do so?

21) 2 Sam. 1:17-27-My sense is that David's lament works at two levels: for public consumption, public relations, if you will, as well as a sincere personal recounting of loss for the leaders of Israel. The refrain is: "how the mighty have fallen." While he speaks, he enjoins victors and even nature itself to close, in silent deference to the fallen. He notes that Saul and Jonathan perish together, even as he threatened to tear the family relationship apart. He admits to an extraordinarily close tie with Jonathan. Notice that he grieves for Jonathan but does not mention the same for Saul. Public figures are distant from us, but television has created a sense of intimacy. They are not friends and family. Nonetheless, we do mourn the death of leaders. When JFK was murdered, the reactions of the nation were similar to those of a death in the family. We tend to put forward the good points of a loved one. Maybe we are healing when we are able to admit some of their faults. Here in Indiana, we honor RFK's words to a crowd in Indianapolis when Martin Luther King was murdered. No stranger to grief, he recalled, with some accuracy, words of Aeschylus, "in our sleep, pain which cannot forget falls drop by drop upon the human heart, until in our despair, against our will, comes wisdom through the awful grace of God." I remember Ted Kennedy saying that "my brother need not be idealized in death beyond what he was in life a good and decent man who saw suffering and tried to heal it...saw war and tried to stop it." When his nephew John was killed in a plane crash he recalled an Irish saying that he hope that he would live to comb gray hair...he had every gift but length of years." What losses of public figures have touched you over the course of years?

Part of me resents that death is a public affair, as the private needs of family and friends seem paramount. That circle of intimates is hard to manage of course. What has been the most moving public eulogy you have seen? What were some moving moments for you in the eulogies of a family member or friend? What would you like to be said about you at your own funeral? Have you spoken a eulogy at a service, even with a brief memory?

22) Judges 11-I was not particularly interested in this book, but

Presbyterians had to take a Hebrew-based Bible class, and our Lutheran Old Testament professor, Dennis Olson, was kind enough to offer us chance to work on it while he was working on a commentary on the book. My main paper was on Jephthah's daughter. She is condemned to death because of her father's rash vow for victory. Religion is not only the tie that binds us together (its root meaning), but it can be an instrument of pain when misused or poorly understood. Before the end, Jephthah's daughter bewails her virginity (Judges 11:38-40). (This story is so unbearable that some read it as an exile, a a vow of virginity, instead of her being put to death). I am sure that her father did too. Part of the story points to people making religious errors, even lethal ones, when they are not properly taught. For that matter, the Christian religion of life has been a bulwark for the death of so many people, under the rubric of following the Prince of Peace. In our do it yourself-start from scratch religious culture, this is a warning. It is so hard to think of all the things that a child will miss when death closes their future here. Every year brings thoughts of a page not turned, another milestone missed. I read recently of Elizabeth Edwards speaking of the future and wondering how long she would be dead when that expected event occurred, such as an upcoming Olympics. The passage notes that she was remembered by the women of Israel. The way we know of her is Scripture, as hers was a private life. After centuries, her untimely death is remembered. We may be concerned that lives are erased by the passage of time. It seems a weak reed to hope that our passage through life lives on the frail memories of those who follow us. Already I look at some pictures of our children as babies and have no idea who else is in the photograph. I am consoled by the notion that our memories are within the memory of God. Part of our difficulty stems from the issue of memory and forgetfulness. We get concerned that we won't remember a loved one and then feel guilty when they aren't on our mind and heart. We also are concerned at a deeper level that they have forgotten about us.

23) Elisha and the Shunammite woman (2 Kings 4:11-37) A foreign woman was gracious to Elisha. He promised her that she would have a son. When

the son grew, he grew ill and died in her arms. She sought out Elisha. She goes out to meet Elisha. In her confusion, she tells his servant that all is fine with her and her family. She then grabs Elisha and his servant protects him. Elisha realizes that she is in 'deep distress (v. 27). Elisha sends his servant ahead and then goes to the child himself. For Christians, this movement in the narrative certainly has a sense of resurrection, as Elijah breathes the breath or spirit of life into the boy. (The words are the same in Hebrew and Greek). She had been granted a son, as he had promised when she offered him hospitality. How could a gift be given then yanked away, especially the gift of the life of a child? Later (ch.8) she appears to be widowed. She has already suffered too much. In other words, what more could she lose? Some think that he may be risking his own life in placing himself over the boy. He is embodying a battle between life and death, a struggle between the forces of life and the demonic. Could he be transferring some of his own life force to the boy? Yes, this may being up the thought of why do I have to wait for heaven to be with my loved one? Why couldn't my family be recipients of such a spectacular healing? Of course, we do bring back people with the paddles after a heart attack. Some people certainly have more than their share of loss. With Rabbi Kushner, I see some of it as reflecting the randomness, the free space, the relinquishing of control within creation. I am not speaking of a deistic deity who has started the clockwork and then let it go its own way. I see God more in a process theology vein in this instance. (See Epperley for an introduction to process thought). God is not above what happens to us, as if the Healer is at a distant remove from us. No, God is involved and responds to evils in the world, always laboring to work toward some good over time.

24) Elijah and Elisha (II Kings 2). The mantle is a good symbol of carrying on the work of one to another. Sometimes we do not want to receive the mantle. We want to live vicariously through our progeny at times. I know someone who has not quite recovered from being asked to return to the family farm and another person who felt called away from his vocation as a writer to take care of the farm. Sometimes the inherited mantle doesn't

fit. A legacy can turn in to a burden at times. I know a man who felt that guilt pushed him into taking over a farm after the death of his father. for some legatees, the term family business is a curse. when we grow up hearing the sacrifices made for the family business is for us to carry on its proud tradition, that can be an unwanted mantle, a heavy one. When we project on to children some of our uncompleted goals, then we may be trying to place a mantle in their shoulders that never will fit properly. I think of those parents who try to mold their children into being a future NFL quarterback and that alone, such as Todd Marinovich. Some of us sense that we can never live up to the mantle that has been placed over our shoulders. Others are pleased and proud to take on the responsibility. We all carry the tapes of our family of origin's interactions in our hearts and minds like a continuous loop of tape. When our buttons get pushed, as often as not, the play button on family tapes has been pressed. Sometimes the torch is passed from one generation to the next, and it may well be a shock to realize that we may be the matriarch or patriarch of the family all of a sudden. At times, we may want to carry the torch for unfinished projects of the deceased. Those who inherit the running of a family business will speak of the tradition they uphold. What legacies do you carry from your family?

25) John 14 continues this gospel's theme of the difficulty of bridging the physical and the spiritual. It certainly gives hope for the continuing presence of the Spirit after the death of Jesus. For many, it also gives but a hint of heaven. What is that place prepared for us, what sort of dwelling? It seems an expansive place, a place with plenty of room. (That place can be internal or beyond, or both, of course). I remember my uncle used to tell us to "eat, eat, there's plenty more where that came from." The sense of preparation sounds as if we prepare a room for a guest. Growing up, I recall that the most sacred object in our home was the guest towel, never to be touched. Perhaps, heaven can be imagined as a place of divine hospitality. I imagine it to be a place of hospitality toward our whole lives, not just a piece of them. After all, we are "enmattered souls" as Wendy Farleycould designate us (see Wounding and Healing). Maybe it will be hospitable to our potential to grow as well. Mary Chapin Carpenter sings

of "My Heaven" where "nothing shatters; nothing breaks" where a favorite dog appears, just as in the movie with Robin Williams, "What Dreams May Come." Some of us imagine that we cannot imagine a paradise without family members and friends, a prized pet and a cherished memory. If required, heaven can be a place of uniformity or variety for us. Eph. 3:10 speaks of the wisdom of God in its variety. At any rate, the place could well refer to the continuing presence of Christ in our existence together. One of the ways we come to grips with loss is that we still need to locate our loved ones somewhere, and heaven is the locale we can place them and see them as happy, safe, and well. In the notion of the communion of saints, those houses/mansions have windows. The doctrine admits that love does bridge the gulf between earth and the other side of life. God has plenty of room for us within that capacious heart.

26) Gen. 4-Abel, in Hebrew, sounds similar to the word for meaningless in Ecclesiastes. It comes from the word for mist, for vapor. The thought would be that life is evanescent, that it is too short, and that it disappears like the morning mist in a low area. (It is also a word for meadow, a good name for an early shepherd.) This is certainly a feeling of the grieving. The writer of Ecclesiastes knows from experience that life is hard. When we feel that we shouldn't even bother when life is so fleeting, we capture the sense of the name. Can it then be an accident that the name shows up so early in the primeval history? East of Eden, life does seem short. J.K. Rowling in the Harry Potter books has creatures called dementors who "drain away every though of joy, hope, and happiness" out of people leaving them with only their worst memories to relive, so they are driven mad. Even being near them chills the blood. Vampires may drain the lifeblood, but Dementors drain us of the lifeblood of our positive emotions. These terrible creatures are as good an image of the effects of being depressed as I have seen.
Why bother? What's the use? It does seem that life is in vain at times, "meaningless, meaningless, all is meaningless." It is so hard to find meaning in a loss, especially an unexpected one. for no good reason,

Abel's life seemed to be a vapor, its number of breaths too short. He is the initial symbol of violence, in this case religious violence over the acceptance of a sacrifice. Remember that grief too, especially intense grief, will soften and fade in time, itself a vapor. It also raises up the issue of justice. Abel's blood cried out for justice. God did not choose capital punishment for Cain, but the mark of Cain served as both protection and warning for him.

27) Ecclesiastes takes the persona of someone who has seen it all as they grow older. Wealth, fame, power all seem insignificant as the years have passed. What is promised in being the ultimate key to happiness fails. "Been there, done that." They all seem like mere vapor, wasted breath, chimeras. Big answers to big questions seem to elude us, or prove wanting. We expend so much effort and energy on things that prove to be fleeting, transient. So, he looks to smaller things in life as the antidote to despair. We are told to work at the tasks we have with all of our might. Later (9: 7) we can enjoy sharing a bed, wearing good clothes, being able to celebrate, So often, the big targets in our dreams are unreachable. As Fred Craddock said (Interpretation Comm. Luke 16) we may not be able to christen a boat, but we can offer a cup of cold water, not able to write a book today, but we can write a note to someone who could use some cheering up or encouragement. Small acts are more easily rendered concrete than grand visions. Consider making a list of small things that tend to give you a lift. I knew a therapist who would go to cash a check for five dollars in the bank, as it made her feel better that she had some money in her pocket without feeling that she was being profligate with her spending. I've suggested something similar to folks, and they have responded with everything from going dancing, to listening to some favorite songs, to having a piece of pie, well make that a big piece of pie to renting a movie. Maybe a big resolution seems to forbidding at this time. Perhaps you can find the will and energy to try some small steps.

28) When 9/11 hit, we invited folks into church. As I waited, I read Psalms 55 and 109, cursing psalms. These too are prayers. We do not act on the

curses, but it is a relief to expose the fury that elicits such feeling in prayer. Scripture is an expansive envelope that can hold all sorts of prayers. Ellen Davis has a great chapter in Getting Involved with God where she describes the emotional and spiritual changes within her as she prayed these psalms after heartbreak. God realizes that it is good for us to translate our often inchoate feelings into prayer. God is no stranger to our most negative thoughts and feelings. Those too may be communicated in prayer. God, like a great therapist, won't judge us harshly just because those feelings are present. Indeed, acknowledging them may well be the first step in robbing them of their latent power over us. When we face forces far beyond our control, then maybe lashing out with curses helps us to cope. Our feelings of rage against a drunk driver, against the torture of failed cancer treatments can be forged into prayer. These prayers can be cathartic. It's probably good not to make a steady diet of them. They do take violent or untoward action out of our hands and put those notions into a safe place. Go further and design some prayers to curse death and suffering themselves. (I find it helpful to occasionally personify those awful forces in life). What safer place can we place those feelings of rage and impotence than into the lap of God? Yes, Jesus does say that we should bless those who persecute us, to turn the other cheek, to go the extra mile. I am suggesting that we who are not saints can find it in ourselves to do just that only after we have let our passion for revenge out with some good old-fashioned cursing psalms.

29) Thanksgiving psalms are a guide into praying for the blessing God has given us in the life we have lost. Thanksgiving is not the first thing that enters our mind in grief, but it is an important start in our healing. It helps us organize our thoughts about where we are grateful for where their lives have touched ours. It surely will happen that some thanksgiving prayers will provoke a flood of grief because we can't have what we so miss in the deeds and qualities that made up their personality, their way of being in this world. As we move through grief, it may be a good idea to organize some prayers around thanksgiving for the life that is gone to us. As the BCW puts it, for "all in them that was good and kind and faithful." Be

specific in taking the time to name good qualities, countless good deeds, moments of falling in love with them again. A good deal of work is being done on the virtue of gratitude. The practice of it seems to correlate with all sorts of healthy habits and attitudes. Its opposite, ingratitude, promotes a bitter, disappointed self-curved life. Robert Emmons is making a career in examining gratitude as a virtue in our day to day lives. He writes that " ingratitude leads ...to a confining, restrictive, shrinking sense of self." Even if a relationship was a troubled one, surely one can recall some facets of the relationship for which to be grateful. As we have become more involved as consumers instead of citizens, we find it harder to say thank you. Instead, we delude ourselves into thinking we can demand and have a right to more and more. Coming to the point where we can be grateful for a life that has touched ours and that we have touched is a good sign for coming to terms with loss. No, being thankful does not somehow balance the scales. Thanksgiving does give us the crucial perspective that life is a gift. We respond to the gift of a life with gratitude, but not a sense of possession.

30) Mt. 2:13 and holiday loss- According to Matthew, what became Christmas and Epiphany was the start of a massacre in Bethlehem. Death does not take a holiday. Of course, is there a better time for a death than others? Most of us hold a picture of holiday bliss in our minds. Even in the best of times, we rarely achieve even a semblance of its sheen. Most of us dread facing the first holiday, indeed any holiday after a loved one has died. My mother died last Christmas night. this year, I have been slow in sending out my Christmas cards. In part, other than my laziness, it may well be that it's a stark reminder that I won't be signing her name to our Christmas cards any longer to the family. The almost imposed feeling of good cheer collides with our opposite set of emotions. It's similar to the feeling that we almost want the weather to look gloomy when we are feeling down. The shiny decorations serve as a blinking contrast to the decidedly undecorated, bare way our hearts feel. All of the cheer points an accusing finger at our dread of the days ahead. "Our holidays were in a plain brown wrapper"(105: Beyond Tears). Anyone who faces the first

holiday without a loved one knows that Scrooge is not the only one who faces the ghosts of Christmas past. Especially in the first holidays, the empty place at the table looms large indeed. In facing a holiday in the face of loss, one does well to acknowledge missing the absent. If we try to always have the family together, the absence is palpable. Mentioning the loss during grace but not having mourning dominate the entire grace is a good start to face down the pain. Some may leave a place setting empty. In Polish families, at Christmas Eve, we always set a place for Jesus. Some Jewish families set a place for Elijah. Some families may well choose to rearrange the old seating arrangements. Sometimes it is hard seeing the cards come in with intact families smilingly displayed. In the middle of the civil war, Longfellow's journal was empty in 1863. In 1864, he wrote "Christmas Bells." "And in despair I bowed my head/there is no peace on earth, I said/for hate is strong/and mocks the song of peace on earth, goodwill to men." Making a holiday ritual is often helpful, a new ornament on the tree. Reaching out to others removes the Scrooge in us. I know someone who delivers meals for local churches on Thanksgiving and Christmas as a good work but also to help stave off feelings of loneliness. This horrible story extends the threat of the Pharaoh to the firstborn Hebrew males. Still the feast day of the Magi is called Epiphany, as in manifestation, letting light shine all around. Making a special end of the year present ot an organization that fights a problem of importance to you: against disease, political oppression, economic scarcity, you name it, can be a salutary way to mark the holiday. Part of the epiphany moment for me was realizing that the presence of the Christ Child shines light on a darkened world, but it is still a darkened world.

31) Is. 40 is thought to mark a departure in the book of Isaiah, as it shifts its locus from Jerusalem under siege to the exile community. Its first word is command to the heavenly court for them to comfort, comfort my people." Enough of punishment, comfort is now needed. Comfort has a sense to us of soothing, but the word's roots evoke a sense of powerful strengthening, of being emboldened to face the day and the challenges ahead. The phrase, speak tenderly, tells us to more literally "speak to the

heart." Even with this message, an answering voice has a sense of the transient nature of life. Even though time is often short, God adorns nature with beauty. All of life may well seem ephemeral in the sweep of time. As Springsteen sang 'everything dies baby; that's a fact." Beauty is often fleeting; nature is rarely evergreen. Nonetheless, the transient is beautiful, has worth; it is valuable; it is priceless. Life is indeed a fragile gift. So many astronauts who were on the moon were astounded not only of the "magnificent desolation" of the moon" (Aldrin) but the awareness of the precious fragility of the Earth when seen from the moon. Every living thing has its limits. Mortality is the rule. Our time here is temporary indeed. It is especially poignant when a young person dies. It is all the more poignant when the blossom of youth is cut off, but any age life seems to cut off too soon most of the time. Still, the passage starts out with the double imperative to comfort, comfort my people, as a verb. That is not a word we hear often placed in the imperative mood, is it? Just being in the great outdoors or being in a tended garden offers solace for some. A rabbi once said that we should write a book, raise a child, and plant a tree for they affect life far beyond our days here. I've always rejected the image of footprints in the sand as a mark of a life to be washed away or burned up like dried up grass clippings. Everyone dies. The cable show Six Feet Under ended its run with an ending montage of the deaths of its main characters as a young woman drove off to find a new life in New York, but even the beautiful young girl will die, as she does full of years, at 102. What sort of legacy do you want to leave? If you asked others, especially your family, what would they say you bequeathed them? I am especially thinking about character lessons, ways of being, and words of wisdom.

32) Ezekiel's muteness (3:25) seems to me appropriate. It can be viewed as an enacted prayer or prophecy. At times, we are stunned into silence. Silence can be the stony chill of contempt, but it can be a nodding agreement; it can be the silence of being overwhelmed, awestruck, and speechless. In the face of loss, what can we say? Silence can be golden. When we speak it is often some reflex of old words or some mumbled

inanity borne of anxiety. Silence often seems the wisest course. I think of the unease and silence that mark Agee's memory in <u>A Death in the Family</u>. When we read it in college, remarks were made that they were disappointed that it lacked eloquence. I replied that grief was not a time to expect a soliloquy worthy of Hamlet, himself a mourner. Hauerwas has a book, <u>Naming the Silences</u> with valuable insights into our struggles. Naming them may give the illusion that we can capture and overcome them. Silence is the initial, maybe permanent response appropriate to the magnitude of an event. At the very least silence keeps us from saying something untoward. . Job's friends sat shiva, a period of a week in silent mourning. In a way, even trying to put the inexpressible into words seems to cheapen the experience. On the other hand, words are what we have. It is different than the enforced conviviality of a visitation in a funeral home or a wake. When we do speak, it is often out of anxiety and we stammer or say something conventional that we do not mean. Sometimes, a hug says more than any words. Words are inadequate, but they are our tools to communicate. Silence can speak. Even mute nature "speaks." In Corrina, Corrina, a housekeeper takes care of a family where the father watches home movies over and over, and the little girl has become mute. Bit by bit, she helps the girl see that her mother's death was not her fault or responsibility and that her mother is waving at her from heaven if the girl would only open her eyes and look. As Dumbledore says in Harry Potter, "words are...our most inexhaustible source of magic... capable of causing injury or remedying it."

33) Hos. 11 is a fine look at the feeling attributes of the love of God. It stands against our easy words that God "takes" our loved ones. God recoils from the thought of inflicting punishments, or giving up on us. Still, we are reminded that God is different from us, no mere mortal exalted to a high degree, no idol, but God. Transcendence is part of the divine nature, even if it does not encompass the whole of God's relation to the world. Instead of considering that God has power as control to the nth degree, making God a heavenly emperor, one could consider seeing the fundamental difference in the capacity of the Related One to love. Love

does indeed include feeling, so a loving God is acquainted well with a divine version of it. It does seem that God cannot bear the very thought of losing a people when God remembers their childhood. We often think back and say what a good kid someone was. Indeed, I sometimes wonder if we have heaven as place for us as God says to us, "how can I give you up?" It seems that God does not wish to face eternity without us either. As in Is. 42, the first of the servant hymns, God goes back to childhood, to taking us by the hand. God see a people and individual as good kids all, it seems. God views us through the prism of a loving parent, it seems. Here God sounds like a parent going through the baby books and photo albums when the child is leaving home or off to marry. I keep going back to its images of us being tied together to god: cords of human kindness and bands of love. God's love is shown, in part, through our human bonds. We mortals are incapable of facing the reality of the divine. For Christians, the closest vision we get is the narrative of Jesus. I do not get a sense of Jesus as inflicting punishments; indeed, he received them. The image of the Good Shepherd is one of walking to guide us, or the road to Emmaus account is one of walking with the grieving.

34 Joel 1:8-10- Mourning is linked to that of a young woman. As we grow older, we acknowledge, even if we keep it in the back of our minds, that we will multiply our losses. Death seems an alien invader in the bloom of life. In a traditional culture, the young woman has lost her security. She has lost her imagined future. Nature too reflects the inner emptiness and the threat of privation that widowhood must have brought in those days. We resent the alteration of the imagined future that death brings. Death seems in its proper place for the very old, who have lived out rich and full lives. Death robs the young of dreams of the future. It violates our sense of the natural order of things. What seemed to be a wide open future not seems constricted and closed. We push it to the back of our minds, but we realize that we may well bury our parents. Parents do not bring children into the world with the thought that they may have to bury them. How did you handle loss when young? Did you have some significant losses? What did you learn about yourself in the midst of them?

35) In Isaiah, Widow Zion is a character of sorts to personify the ruined Jerusalem, as opposed to Dame Zion. She is a twin to the suffering servant.More than that, it uses the feelings of abandonment and social vulnerability. One primary metaphor for the love of God for Israel was the marriage metaphor. Prophets even likened idolatry to adultery to get at the utter sense of heartbroken betrayal that God knows from our fragile religious commitments. So it is understandable that they would then reach out for the dissolution of a marriage in the tragedy of death. The image takes a familiar personal, painful circumstance and applies it to a public sense, really stretching its zone of meaning. The widow metaphor asks if God could be dead to them. That strikes me as a bold, insightful image to apply. I suppose it could bring up the flip side, if they seemed dead to God as well. It certainly captures a sense of riding high and being brought low, economically, in power, and in spirit. It captures the image of loneliness, of a sense of being abandoned. As we live in a marriage, our lives may not become fused, but they certainly grow intertwined. Our lives take on an expectation of their presence. Still, we can be lonely in a crowded room as well as in solitude. Loneliness is a symptom of missing someone with whom we shared our lives. It is also a symptom of the basic human need for intimacy, for connection, for relationship. Later, the image changes to the fresh future of a new marriage. Even images do not remain frozen in time.

36) The story of the family of Abraham after the primeval history in Genesis, from chapter 12 through 50, is one of God staying faithful to a dysfunctional family across the generations. In the Claypool book, God the Ingenious Alchemist, the Episcopal priest writes: "Jacob, the deceiver, was deceived by his own children about the death of his favorite son, Joseph. He contrived to fool his blind father with false evidence, and his sons do the same thing, even though their father is sighted." Family system approaches emphasize that families seek to transmit not only genes, but ways of acting, patterns of response. The author of Harriet the Spy had a children's book, Families Never Change. Now after many years, he finds

out that Joseph is still alive, and his heart seems like it stops. Did he then erupt in laughter, this son of a father named Laughter (Isaac)? It recalls the reaction of the disciples to the resurrection. After all, this is like the dead coming back to life, only after decades. What were your family's patterns of dealing with grief? What messages about death and bereavement did they transmit? How did they judge the grief of others? Did the family perhaps have a "designated griever?" Were they helpful or harmful do you think? A recent study in the online magazine Slate found that many of the respondents yearned for recognition of their grief. A surprising number felt as if they had no good way of communicating their loss, so it felt somehow invalidated. Not long before I was working on this section, we had a mercy lunch at church for the family and friends of an elderly woman who had been in a nursing home for some years. Almost immediately the three siblings took on different sections of the room and lost no opportunity in sniping or making little digs at each other. The offer of a lunch is one of the kindest things a church can offer after the service. It creates a safe to reminisce and cry and laugh. The lunch also gives room for people to try to work out their issues before some jet back home. Grief can re-open old wounds, but it also provides opportunity to heal some of them.

37) Gen. 49-50 -I heard a legend that the bones of Jewish dead migrated back home, no matter where they were buried. Some find it painful that a loved one is buried far from their home. We don't like the notion of being a stranger in a strange land in one's resting place. Sometimes the body is returned for many miles to a family plot. Jacob gives precise instructions about his burial place. Family complications do not cease when we die. He does not mention the favored wife, Rachel, of whom we heard earlier (48:7), but he does mention his first wife, Leah. So in death maybe she achieves what she so longed for in life, her husband's love. Maybe that's part of the reason the parade of crosses at Normandy is so heart-rending. In the TV program, the West Wing, Toby, the communications director of the White House, abuses his authority to make sure that a Korean War veteran, a homeless Korean War veteran, gets a military funeral, at

Arlington. Twice the president's secretary told him, he should not have done it. When it is time to go to the funeral, there she is, coat and hat on, asking if she could come to the service. (Watchers of the show know that she has lost 2 sons in Vietnam). Recently, one of our Bible study classes looked at the book of Tobit, a so-called apocryphal book of the Greek version of the Old Testament. There, one of the fundamental obligations of the faith, even at the risk of persecution, is the burial of the dead. Since Genesis 2 speaks of us being earth creatures, we are returned home in a mythic sense. Cemeteries used to be church yards, and in the 1800s they were designed to look like parks. Most of them are oriented on an east-west axis, along the lines of the setting and rising sun. The writer and funeral director Thomas Lynch makes his living preparing and helping families to deal with the corpse. Even though, he can do so a a professional remove, he still wants some degree of personal involvement. He prizes time outside the country where people may make the casket or dig the hole for the grave. The sons of the writer Andre Dubus decided to build the coffin for their father when they were able to get home to discuss funeral details. It makes a lot of sense to hand over difficult tasks to funeral directors, but we sacrifice the reality of the loss to some degree when we absent ourselves so much from the dead body. It takes real courage ot face finality.

38) Zeph. 3:14-20 ends with an upbeat note after much gloom. We can take only so much gloom, or so much celebration for that matter. We need to find a pattern, the drumbeat for dealing with loss; we need someone to show us the steps. Indeed most apocalyptic material has hope tied to portents of doom. One of the reasons for the afterlife could be that God so delights in us that even God cannot bear to lose that life forever. Even intense grief does not have to last forever. I remember a woman whose husband died suddenly and unexpectedly at home said that everything look gray. As the months passed, she started to see some colors again. Verse.17 speaks of God rejoicing over you. Do you tend to think of God in that way? What would you think God would rejoice over you about? How did God rejoice in your loved one? How does God rejoice

in your loved one? We are not sure of the meaning of the next line; it could be to renew you in his love. Certainly that is a spiritual aspiration: to be renewed in the love of God. Maybe it is renewal in the sense of the renewal of a neighborhood gone to seed and doing a lot of fixing up. We can feel as if "nothing new under the sun" could ever appear. Things can look shopworn and stale. It could also be to "quiet you in his love." In grief, I find this a potent image, where God quiets us as a mother quiets a small child who has scraped a knee. "there, there," God says," it will get better." So many things can rage inside us, so many screams. A few deserve such screaming, and some are the result of minor annoyances that we have permitted to fester or to grow. What needs quieted or renewed in your life?

39) Zech. 12:10-13;-uses the power of mourning for an only, or perhaps a beloved, child, or a firstborn child, as a way to get into the depth of mourning. I don't like to compare grief, but the loss of a child is particularly potent. It robs us of an imagined future, of our role as parent to them, of marking milestone events with them. All parents who have lost a child to death dread the question about children. Do you say the number of living, or include the number of all children? If you are young, you then may hear, "well, at least you can have more children." Maybe they have heard: 'well, at least you have other children." In response God will pour out a spirit of compassion. I have heard that some therapists triple the time for the usual year of mourning to three years for those who have lost a child. These are rules of thumb, but they are indicative of the depth of that loss. For such a loss the words of the 13th century Mechthild apply where she asks God to be present "in a soul torn in two, lie therein/you must lay yourself in the wounds of my soul." In another piece, we heard of Joan Didion as she faced the sudden death of her husband as their daughter was very ill. After his death, the daughter died as well. Didion has written a memoir of her daughter as she comes to grips with her relationship with her daughter, just as she is struggling to come to grips with the death of her daughter. Some of the book deals with the regrets any parent has in the mistakes we make in dealing with our

children, that hazy barrier that prevents us from seeing them, and indeed ourselves as parents clearly. Joan Didion (13) in <u>Blue Nights</u> writes" when we talk about mortality, we are talking about our children." Realizing the depth of grief, the prophet in our passage not only mentions four clans that represent the entire nation, but the land itself, among those who grieve.

40) Num.27: 1-11 and 36: Even the most careful plans cannot cover all contingencies. One of the lasting impacts of grief is its permanent alteration in our imagined future, in our best-laid plans. Numbers 36 deals with the distribution of property after death. To face an unanticipated legal issue, Moses has to arrive at a new formulation. A major task in grief work is coming to grips with the new situation we are finding ourselves. Years ago, when our father died, my mother had to learn to drive a car and write out checks. We all find common cause with the daughters of Zelophedad. We all struggle to work with tradition and have tradition live in the face of new, unforeseen exigencies that may push us into some new uncharted paths. Otherwise, tradition becomes the dead hand of the past, instead of a dynamic faith for the living. The ability to start to make plans again is a sign of healing, as it is a sign that we can approach the future again. Instead of facing the uncertain future with rigidity, it is often more healthy to face it with flexibility. After the incident comes Joshua to succeed Moses in resolving disputes and a line about not wanting us to be like sheep without a shepherd. We are incapable of covering every possible contingency. We have to do a new thing instead of trying to squeeze an unanticipated, unforeseen event into a slot where it will not fit. People shook their heads in sadness that the name of Zelophedad's family would not have a male heir. We would say no one to carry on the name. Instead, his brave daughters, with his name, have been carried through the ages in these two Scriptural stories. In a way, we are all their children. If law and plans remain utterly static or grow rigid, they become inhuman forces of control, not attempts at harmony. The dynamism of interpretation allows law and plans to cover new situations, new contingencies. In other words, we read a living Bible.

41) When I was just starting out in ministry, a woman yelled at me after a graveside service because I read words from the book of Revelation, mostly because she did not like it. It has garnered a bad reputation from people using it as a cookbook for the end of the world and for its lurid images. The book Revelation draws from many OT images and often expends them. It is so less mysterious when we realize that it is using an existing set of images, even though they are often drawn from sources that we may well have not touched on in Sunday School or in our own Bible reading. Some folks at church are taken with the root meaning of apocalyptic material, that it takes the lid off to see what is cooking underneath. Rev. 21 draws on Isaiah to give a picture of life with God. I'm drawn to v. 3 that speaks of being united with God in some sense. God has all the time for us in the world. Heaven has all the room we need. The image of the pearly gates and the streets of gold are known to us, but they do not come as immediately to mind as that of a more Biblically soaked culture. The jewels call to mind the decorations of priestly vestments in Ex. 28 and 39. So, it is not an image of wealth, at least as its primary object. The point here would be that we all have access to God. We will indeed be a kingdom of priests, all of us, as we will have access to the divine presence. Our lives will be permeated with divine presence. "In him we live and move and have our being" will acquire a much deeper sense. The sea will be no more, that symbol of death, chaos, uncertainty. In essence, we are getting a picture of an Eden without threat, where the serpent has been excised. It's a picture of the temple sanctuary vastly expanded, to encompass all of life with God.

42) James 1:17 sees God as the source of good, not evil. This is his direct response to those who say that God is a source of evil. It is a direct response to those who see God raining trouble down on people for no apparent reason. It reacts against our tendency to see God as being blamed for evil. The god of James is a good God. It reminds me of Calvin's emphasis on God as a giver of the gifts of creation, care, and redemption, and our response is one of gratitude in the face of sheer grace. As the

hymn says" all good gifts around us are sent from heaven above." In other words, we should resist the common expression that God takes our loved ones. To me that sounds inhuman. It sounds so arbitrary as well, like Zeus hurling thunderbolts. Indeed God is the source of the good gift of life itself. God offers blessings not curses. James sees evil as emerging from human failings and mistakes and sins, not from a divine source. Following that, consider some of the blessings your loved one dispensed in your life and the lives of others. I'm not saying that we idealize someone who as died, as Edward Kennedy said in his eulogy for his brother Robert in 1968. Where did you see the goodness of God touch the life of your loved one? What good did you loved one accomplish? What good what left undone? What good did you bring your loved one, and what good did they bring to you? What good may result from our response to the death? Can you even bring yourself to see some good in the death itself, a cessation of suffering for instance? What good did you bring them?

43) I Peter 5 (see Charles Talbert 1991) is part of several sections in that letter on Christ's suffering and our suffering. Some think the letter to be an extended meditation, even a sermon, on the life of the baptized. (It works with the issue of deserved and undeserved suffering) Verse 7 tells us to cast our anxieties on to Christ. In a crisis, we sometimes load burdens on ourselves. We may blame ourselves for the crisis itself or our response to it. For many of us, it is a salutary relief to be able to cast the burdens outside our sphere of influence on to Christ. When you don't feel as if you have the strength to go another step, oh, how we want to be able to cast the burden on to the shoulders for someone else to carry. Notice it's not asking to share a burden, but to throw them on to Christ's shoulders, so we are free of their weight. Finding help is admitting that we cannot carry it on our own. Instead of harping on this as weakness, Peter also pushes for strength. It is as if in recognizing our weakness, we are opened up to discover strengths we may not even realize that we possess. What strengths have you noticed or found in yourself during your time of grieving? Elvis Costello composed a song with Burt Bachrach, "God Give Me Strength." The title itself is a good short prayer. Where was that

prayer answered for you? How is it being answered right now in your life?

44) Hebrews 11 and journey- It's a good metaphor to see that all of us journey through life. Most of us go as did Abraham (v.8), unsure of the route or the destination as we travel along. That includes our journey to death and beyond. We may try to gather accounts of "after-death experiences," but we do not know our fate after the grave with any clarity. God accompanies us in our journey from birth to death and beyond. We may imagine when and how we would like to leave this life. No departure is without its issues. If we want to die in our sleep, when do we get to say our goodbyes? Christians make the great claim that our journey continues in a new way as this leg of our mortal pilgrimage draws to a close. Think of Bunyan's Pilgrim's Progress toward the celestial city. Recall that he does not make the journey alone and is accompanied by Christian. The road is marked with detours such as Vanity Fair, of special relevance in our time. He makes it through the slough of despond(ency). All people seek to be on the move toward a destination, but grief can make it seem as if we spin in circles. Dan Moseley in Living With Loss likens grief to a meandering car trip with overlooks that we spend time with and can return to if need be. Along the way, we get too enamored of the phases of grief as discrete units that close down when we enter another phase. Instead, his image reminds us that we often return to stops along the way and revisit them, as they become familiar parts of the journey. Grief moves in pulses more than a clear linear pattern, or discrete steps. The pain may loom up like a mountain, but we discover a pass through it in time to make the journey bearable. We may well be encourage to take a trip to get away from it all. That can be an excellent restorative. On the other hand, if we think we can flee from grief, put distance between it and us on a trip, we soon learn that grief packs a suitcase and travels with us. Jonah wanted to flee to Tarshish, Disney world, if you will, but his work was in the place of the enemy, Nineveh. We cannot travel away from the pain on a trip. Nor do we travel alone. Hebrews 11 speaks of a great cloud of witnesses. Who do you like to imagine watching and walking with you?

45) Gen. 24- Isaac was comforted in bringing his new bride to his mother Sarah's tent. Maybe it's a bit of sexual healing as Marvin Gaye would sing. I don't think it means that Sarah's love was being replaced. It is a pointer that Isaac's life is turning a new page. I do think that the hurt of Isaac was being assuaged in finding love with his new bride. Men save a lot of their emotional intimacy in physical intimacy. Finding the right time to resume sexual relations after a loss in the family can be a tricky dance. I find some comfort that an act that can produce life can be a way to heal in grief. My Polish grandmother even expected a birth in a family within a year or so of a death in the family. No parent can be perfect. We all make mistakes and have misunderstandings. We all fall short of our own standards, as offspring or as parents. We rarely reconcile completely. We may have a hard time negotiating the role transition as a child becomes an adult. In using Sarah's tent as a honeymoon suite, Isaac (Laughter) is able to laugh again, locked in a lover's embrace. Sexual intimacy can be more problematic after suffering a loss. It may be hard to get back into sync. Some men may push for its emotional power and release more quickly than some women may deem appropriate. We males pour so much of our relational baggage into sexual intimacy. Guilt may sneak in, asking if this is appropriate time or behavior for the grieving. We may be ashamed that we can feel the urge for relations after a death. Sexual feelings are rich. The solace of intimacy can be most healing. What better to reclaim the pulse of life?

46) Ruth 4- Ruth and Naomi are able to reconstruct their lives. They are able to invest their energies again. Ruth marries again, and in this marriage becomes a mother. Part of me wonders why we did not call the book, Naomi. Naomi no longer insists on being called Marah, bitterness, but accepts her name, meaning joy/pleasantness again. In a beautiful miracle, her angry words about not being young in the first chapter are reversed, as she is able to be the nursemaid to her grandson. She has become young again; even that vitality is restored to her. Death does not have to stop our lives cold forever. Death does not stop light from being visible in our lives again. A lover's embrace starts to heal the hole in the

heart. Ruth went to Israel with Naomi, her mother in law, her only family in Israel. She is widowed and does not appear to have children. Her life with Boaz takes a new turn in that they have a child together. The outsider, Ruth, is now brought into a new family. That child will be an ancestor of David. This is a good example of inner-biblical debate. To try to protect their faith and culture in an empire, Ezra insisted that Jews close ranks and try to marry within their own people, even to the point of divorcing "foreign wives." In our story, a foreign widow becomes the ancestor of the great king of Israel, from whose family the Messiah would spring. For Christians that means that the child is also the ancestor of Jesus Christ. Indeed Ruth is one of the few females mentioned in the genealogy of Jesus. I find it moving that a story of a bereft, isolated family becomes an element in the story of Jesus over one thousand years later, an invaluable thread in the tapestry of God. I don't believe, can't believe, that God somehow pre-ordains these shifting circumstances. I do believe that God is hard at work as God is "weaving the new creation" (Fowler). Longfellow's poem, "Christmas Bells" starts in a bitter vein, as the words of "peace on earth, goodwill to all" ring false. After he works through those feelings the last verse goes: "then pealed the bells more loud and deep/God is not dead, nor doth he sleep/the Wrong shall fail/the right prevail/with peace on earth, goodwill to men."

47) Powers and cultural ideas-I was out of seminary before I started to give any sort of sustained attention to the various ways powers and principalities appeared in scripture. The principalities and powers of the NT can well be examined as ideology. (See Walter Wink's trilogy) We all live in a force field of standard practices and ideas that have a hold on us and prevent us from "thinking outside the box." Indeed they are the box itself. Cultural considerations of what is appropriate come roaring in judgemental fashion right after loss. The power of ideology marks the line between the permissible and impermissible without recourse to stated rules. Perhaps the most powerful American cultural cue in facing death is its widespread denial. In a way, it is maintained in the fairly recent insistence that the life must be celebrated. In other words, we are being

told that it is impolite or inappropriate to express grief at funeral. It is the intrusion of positive thinking imagery into a funeral service. People need permission to grieve in this new cultural moment. One can have tissues available. (If you want to stop them crying, offer them a tissue.) To influence candor, one can say that "I don't have virgin ears," and that may give allowance for vulgar language or to say things about God and faith, or about others, or about themselves that won't be repeated but may well need to be said.

With medical miracles, more and more people have had little experience with death as young people. We live in a time of desperate attempts to appear youthful. Vanity now has social and economic force behind it. We shift some of our religious honor to the technological priesthood. We see it as a personal affront when technology fails us. We try to make a good out of suffering by thinking that it leads to some larger good. If it isn't good for something, isn't it just a waste? We resist being reminded that the road to progress is not smooth, so we treat suffering like a demon that needs to be expelled.

I was an altar boy, so I served a number of funerals. In our little community, it was expected that you paid respects at the funeral home, and that lasted a number of days. I remember vividly how the women of the neighborhood would a just the amount of food they would make it the size of the family that would be coming home. I can see the parade of boys walking down the street to bring over food that their mothers had prepared. Maybe I shouldn't say parade: it was a sacred procession.

48) Judges- Sometimes our perspective gets skewed in loss. Sometimes nothing seems worthwhile. We can fall into the rut of saying that the whole world is going to hell in a hand-basket that everything is going downhill. Anyone led to say that the world is going downhill and has never been worse has not read the book of Judges. After the lightning triumph of Joshua, Judges looks at the instability of early Israel as it continued as a confederation of tribes under threat from other groups in the area. Judges is a bloody book as it descends into national and moral anarchy. Genesis starts the creation with a purpose that is conducive to life. Judges

shows an anti-creation impulse, to make a world conducive to death. At the same time, no century ever saw the buckets of blood as the last one. I've always been struck by the end of what seems to be a taunt about the death of the general, Sisera (5:28). It imagines his family member looking out, waiting for him to return. There we see an imaginative ability to empathize with the enemy. Who does not know the anxiety of waiting for someone to come home, or to call? The heartbreak of knowing that she could peer out forever is palpable. Samson ends his imprisonment by taking down a temple and those within it. The book ends with a crazed call to action by a priest. Recall that a priest is a mediating figure between earth and heaven. Bal in her study of the book <u>Death and Dissymmetry</u> sees a parallel structure in the book. While part of it is about political fragmentation, the treatment of women at an individual level shows a moral fragmentation that centers on violence as well.

49) Bathsheba and David after first child (2 Sam.12:15) -David violates many commandments after he commits adultery with Bathsheba and tries to cover it up. Worse, if that is possible, he misuses his power as king to so and destroys an honorable soldier in his army in the process. Sin has consequences. Nathan resorts to telling a parable to get David to come back to his sense of justice, to return to himself. Nathan then turns the story toward David himself, with the shattering announcement, "you are the man." Nathan tells David that he will not be destroyed for his plot to kill Uriah to cover up his affair with Bathsheba. In a horrifying addition, he learns that the child from his adultery with Bathsheba will not survive. David prayed with all of his considerable might and skill for his newborn, but it is to no avail, for the child dies. His servants were afraid to tell him, out of fear of his reaction, on himself or them. Instead, he begins to move on; he has done what he could. He has prayed his heart out. Not everything is in the power of even the great king of Israel. He moves from outward signs of mourning and faces life again. I do not know if he found peace; maybe it is resignation, but he was moving toward acceptance. I can only imagine the strain of guilt that hovered over his marriage to Bathsheba. After all, David had a military murder engineered to get him

out of the way. Later, the great king Solomon will be born to them, whose very name connotes peace, well-being, and wholeness. Most of us have prayed so hard. Most of us do not move so quickly into resolution and acceptance. I get the sense that David prayed as hard as he could, knowing full well the verdict and sentenced rendered for his sins. Ps. 51's head note places it as a prayer of David's after he comes to grips with his wrongs.

50) Saul and Endor (I Sam.-Saul was the first king of the Israel. He did not seem to be an ideal choice. Most of the OT does not speak of heaven. It usually sees death as the end. So, the very idea of a heaven or hell, an afterlife, seems to be a later development. For instance, Ps. 23 reads as dwelling in the house of the Lord my whole life not, not forever, as we usually know it. In an intriguing and heartbreaking scene in I Samuel, we get a hint of a shadowy world after death. Somehow the witch can summon something of Samuel from the shadow realms. Sheol or Hades seems to be the place much more than the joys of heaven. It shows the desperation of Saul that he would be willing to engage in a behavior he knows to be forbidden because he wants some word from the old prophet. Saul was active against necromancy (I Sam.28:3). In his desperation, he appeals to her. Saul seems to be a portrait in mental illness to me, or at least a mind and heart deranged by power: its acquisition, use, and looming loss. In grief we often will go to extraordinary lengths to try to have some contact with the departed. During the Civil War séances were very popular. Mrs. Lincoln, in her intense grief, brought a medium to the white House. Even the president attended one. When President Reagan was nearly killed early in his term, the First Lady turned to astrology. The movie Hereafter shows a young boy going through listing after listing on the internet of people promising contact with the departed. A new book about a boy's near death experience (NDE), Heaven is Real, has captivated large numbers of people. The boy describes meeting a sibling who was miscarried and relatives he had never met. Different views of an afterlife or lack thereof, seem to percolate through the material from gone in the grave to hints of

resurrection.

51) I Sam. 25 Nabal's wife, Abigail (quick)-In the Old Testament especially, biblical characters live out the meaning of their names. She is quick-witted certainly. After her husband had dishonored David's requests, she makes entreaty with David. In hre oath, she has a wonderful phrase that David life "be bound in the bundle of the living under the care of the Lord" (v. 29). After the death of her well-named husband Nabal (fool) his wife certainly reconstructs her life quickly. She sets her course for David, as soon as he demonstrates interest in her. Sometimes, a death opens new doors. Then, we feel guilty about realizing that. At times, we want to force doors open that are closed to us. Often, quick attempts to replace a loss don't work very well. I knew an elderly WWII veteran who lost his spouse of a lifetime. Immediately, he hooked up with an old girlfriend from grammar school. After a whirlwind fling, and a quicker marriage, they divorced within months. Quite simply, the elixir of falling in love is a lot more enticing than trying to drink down the bitter dregs of grief. If we do not attend to it, it seems like "whack a mole" and it starts popping up again in different times and places. Trying to replace a role instead of a person tries to postpone, even deny, the pangs of grief. It dishonors a love to think that the person can be replaced like an interchangeable part in a machine. Yes, love can come again in time, perhaps its own sweet time. My sense is that the love is built on a firmer foundation when we have permitted ourselves the opportunity to grieve, to clear the emotional decks, to cart away its debris before rushing to erect a new long-standing relationship. Rushing into other decisions doesn't make much sense either. In AA, they try to hold off major decisions for a period as one enter sobriety. I think that could be a good rule in grief as well. Grief definitely hampers critical faculties. We may not be able to remove ourselves from our memories and our decisions forever, but for a while, it may be good advice..

52) Jeremiah's anger of being deceived (20:7-12). I think we have an

implicit bargain in our moral imagination that goes; "if I'm good I will be protected from bad things happening to those I love." That may be one of the reasons we are angry at God. God is falling down on the fundamental duty of protection. Surely divine power should be used to prevent evil? Of course, that assumes that God makes a discrete decision when we die. We rebel against a God whose omnipotence we want to see personally. Accidents bring out this sense of God's power to protect as failing us. By their very nature, accidents don;t fit a rational scheme of things. Consigned to life, east of Eden, where did we get the idea of being in a rose garden? That is what most of us think we deserve. We hope that being pious will render us immune from the vagaries of life. Clements, in his commentary on Jeremiah:124) agrees with Kierkegaard that "the greater the degree of consciousness, the greater the despair." "Jeremiah had become frustrated, stricken with doubt." (123). Clements sees this struggle as the crucible for the forging of a new identity. In Monday Morning Church, Alan Jackson has a character who has slid a loved one's Bible in a drawer and lets dust gather on the piano keys where she played hymns. "I can't seem to talk to God without yellin' anymore." One TV example that came to mind was a powerful episode of the West Wing, Two Cathedrals. (Some think this to be the best single episode of network series television, ever) The president's longtime secretary is killed in a crash on her way to show off her new car to the president. She had lost two sons in Vietnam. Bereft after the funeral, the president has the Secret service close off the cathedral so he can have it out with God, in Latin, no less. Is this the action of a just God? "To the cross (to hell) with your punishments. To the cross (or to hell) with you, he says. "What did I ever do but try to serve you," he yells. The Lord does not seem to work in precise contractual terms. Instead, the Gracious God pours out blessings far beyond what we could imagine or deserve.

53) Ezek. 2:9-3:2-Eating scroll and its taste. Prophecy could be enacted as well as spoken. Physical illustration can be a \most effective learning tool. Grief is bitter. Food can lose some of its allure. Sometimes in grief, nothing tastes good, even when we have some appetite. We almost want our body

to waste away to match the numbness inside. Food has little allure. We may pick at something set before us. Sometimes we may crave comfort food or to gorge on ice cream. We may not feel hungry but then eat too much when we actually start eating. Some people drop weight for no clear reason, and others put on the pounds. Of course, eating the scroll is a symbol for incorporating the words into our very lives. The Word of God is spiritual bread, sustenance. Ingesting it makes it part of our life's blood. The Lord's Supper is an act of incorporating Jesus into our lives, body and soul together. This brings an incarnate sense to the psalmist's call to "taste and see that the Lord is good." In both cases, we incorporate the action. We take it into our physical being, and it elicits a spiritual reaction. We are incorporating a life poured out for many, a life poured out in suffering to bring new life for the many, that is, everyone. Within your tradition or others, explore the depth of meaning behind the Lord's Supper.

54) The Lord's Supper is a memorial and more than a memorial. I've served on our committee on Preparation for Ministry for those seeking a call to the pastorate. We require a look at the sacraments (2 in Reformed tradition) and they usually require some additional study, especially the levels of meaning of Communion. Yes, Jesus did say do this to remember me. My Reformed tradition has poured much thought into how we speak of the 'real presence" of Christ in the Lord's Supper. Indeed Calvin spoke of the Spirit lifting us up into the presence of Christ in heaven, instead of Jesus moving "down" to meet us. It encompasses the communion of saints from the creeds. I always think of the end of the movie Places in the Heart, where the small rural congregation's sanctuary starts to fill up with the living and dead as the communion is passed around the faithful. Communion is Eucharist as it remembers with thanksgiving the work of God through time, and the work of God in our own lives. We speak of the sacrament as a foretaste of heaven. In the song, Betty's Diner, Carrie Newcomer imagines the coffee shop as a secular sanctuary of Communion where people with different roads in life find solace with "eggs and toast, like bread and wine.". One man lets his Earl Grey steep as he can't sleep in the months since his spouse died. The

sacrament was called the medicine of immortality. I would like more of the healing aspect of the sacrament move a bit more to the front of our concerns.

55) Joshua and standing stones- What a burden to be the transitional leader after Moses. That could well be the reason the first chapter starts out with such powerful affirmations of God being with Joshua and the people. I think of the standing stones of Joshua when I am in a cemetery, after I heard one of our elders, George Bayless, speak of them during our annual Memorial Day tribute in the churchyard across the street form the church. I find them heartbreaking when the crosses fill Normandy. When we visited Washington D.C., I warned our daughters that I would get choked up and cry some at the Vietnam memorial, but it did not seem so odd, as others were weeping too. The Bobbi Ann Mason book In Country comes to its climax as a family seeks some solace in a visit to the Vietnam Memorial's stark beauty and homemade memorials strewn in front, as if the entire edifice were an altar. Where we lived for fifteen years, a large number of the stones are small ones that date from the early 1800s. They are stones for infants and children who died too young. Sometimes they are markers without names. In the same cemetery stand ornate stones bearing a family surname. Newer stones may have a photograph within the stone. Personally, I don't get much out of visiting a cemetery, but I certainly appreciate the silent witness of the markers. I am drawn to one of the earliest stones in the cemetery across the street from one of the churches I served; it is the wife of the founding pastor of the church from 1828. In the Indiana countryside, people make markers with wooden crosses and some flowers to mark the site of an accident that took a life on the roadway. Memorials are an aid to the memory of the living. They create a bridge to memory for those who follow them. In a public tragedy, we often create makeshift memorials of flowers and cards and crafts and pile them up At Princess Di's death the makeshift memorials became enormous. What memorials, especially public ones, have you found meaningful or moving?

56) Micah 4:1-5 is an image of shalom-every person would sit under their own fig tree. John Adams and George Washington used it as one of the goals of the revolution. It is another vision of safety, security, satiety, such as green pastures and cups running over. Maybe it includes a bit of what Jefferson called the pursuit of happiness. In my generation, workers used to hope that their children would be able to "make a little something for themselves." Unexpected death shatters our sense of security and safety. Can one return to a sense of shalom after a death? How I craved a sense of inner peace or shalom after the death of my brother, or after divorce for that matter. I don't know if a sense of the self, or finding a quiet center of the self can ever be able to be unmoving in the face of dire circumstance. We look for allies, some aid, some help and helpers. A number of times I have heard a wife say that she never loved her husband more than when he took off work to help out with basic chores when someone's on his wife's side passed away, especially without being asked. It seems to heighten the esteem of the spouse, as she sees herself held in higher regard than the demands of the job. To sit under the fig tree is a vision of not being burdened with the constant ticking off of things to do, people to see, and most of all the nagging reminders of things left yet to be done or already left languishing on the calendar. The book of Micah seems to oscillate between judgment and mercy, a fait accompli and hope. This passage, among others, demonstrates the power of imagination over the merely factual. Constructing a new image of the future may well lead to a different future than a trend line would predict. The seed of hope may well produce growth, when a basketful of computer statistical printouts gather dust.

57) Mark and Gethsemane prayer-Even Jesus did not get every prayer answered. (Sharyn Dowd has this as a centerpiece of her book, Prayer, Power, and the Problem of Suffering.) In spiritual agony, Jesus asks, maybe begs, that the cup of suffering be lifted from him. It is not in all of the old manuscripts of Luke, but many have Jesus in such agony that the sweat falls like drops of blood from him. In one of my few mystical moments, I envisioned Jesus seeing all of the suffering of people into the future as he

struggled there at the garden. Jesus suffered terribly physically, but the suffering was not limited to his body. Calvin saw this as the start of the descent into the hell of God's own facing the full weight of sin and its effects, including alienation form God. Grief certainly has its Gethsemane moments. No dark passage is ever so steep as to deter Jesus, Emmanuel, from being God with us. The final Harry Potter movie has his Gethsemane moment when he learns forma device that can project memories that he will have to face death in order to help defeat the evil Lord Voldemort who has been on a rampage destroying many he knows and loves at his beloved school. In the movie, the freight is carried silently by the young actor, as no dialog is given. John Claypool preached a sermon four weeks after his daughter died of leukemia. He reflected on the story of Abraham and Isaac and the joy of Abraham coming down the mountain with his son alive, but Claypool's child is dead and gone. Oh, how he prayed for her, her pain and her healing. He was so sure that his prayer would be answered that he was shocked when her last breath left her. He rejects the road of silent acceptance and the path of trying to comprehend the loss's rationale and meaning. He does find a fruitful path in recalling that all life is a gift. His child's life, even though terribly foreshortened was a gift (in Long and Plantinga, Chorus of Witnesses, pp.121-130). After years of reflection he can write: God never asks us to feel a certain way, but to trust no matter how we feel (57: God, the Ingenious Alchemist).

58) Ecclesiastes (2:1, 24; 3:12-13. 5:18, 7:14, 9:7) tells us to enjoy life even though it appears to be meaningless, a search in vain for lasting happiness. His advice speaks to all of us, including the bereaved. His solution is to move away from the big themes and big promises and focus instead on the small joys that are available every day in the ordinary. If we think we can discover one key to unlock all of life, then existence will seem meaningless. Efforts toward a "theory of everything" may well be doomed to be in vain. He sounds like Freud that we are here to love and to work. Jesus told a story about a man giving a party (Lk. 14:15-24), but the people gave all sorts of reasons for not being able to make it. Life offers us countless invitations to enter it more fully, but we often decline them. In

grief, we are not sure when to accept life's gracious invitations. Sometimes, nature's beauty draws us back into life. Sometimes, it is a brief respite from pain, and we see something simple as fresh and new. Ecclesiastes has a good sense for this truth. In the vistas of the everyday, small things reach out to him to be able to commend enjoyment. A fresh clean shirt can lift the downcast spirit. A sign of moving through grief is our capacity to start to heed those invitations to renewed life. William Stafford writes of 'any sight, any sound, that music the soul takes and makes its own.' Not long ago, I officiated at a funeral for a lady who loved life. She loved her make-up, her hair done just right, her nail polish, and especially her jewelry. At he assisted living center and later the nursing home, she was called "Miss Hollywood." Different types of music appeal to us as a preference, and some styles touch the heart and mind in different seasons of life. Yo Yo Ma selected a moving piece from Bach to play at a service for the assault at the Boston Marathon. Gustave Mahler lived in a family touched by death too many times. I recall that at least 10 of his brothers and sisters died young. the question of death itself influenced his expressive work. You can read the notes to his second symphony and then pick up easily the sounds of emptiness and the sunny shaft of light in the music that is the hope of resurrection.

59) John 15:1-8- Vine and branches and connections- Mitch Albom's Five People You Meet in Heaven tells us "all is connected." Raised as hardy individuals, this is a difficult message for most Americans. We tend to see each other more as atomistic individuals. Events in life are not isolated but get connected into the pattern of our time here in a mosaic, or the points of a painting that make sense only when seen from a distance. Grief is a sign of our deep connection with each person. At the same time, it will leave us feeling disconnected from oneself, from other people, and our God. Grief affects the entire family system. If family systems tend toward keeping things in a rough equilibrium, then a major change such as a loss upsets that hard-won, well-maintained stasis. Jesus has an organic picture, the vine and the branches, to get at the living characteristics of our relationships. We are all connected. Death affects the whole

organism. When one branch is removed, the whole vine is affected. We are all diminished. Yet when that branch is removed the vine lives on. Jesus continues to provide life-giving energies to the rest of the vine. Jesus is the medium through which the branches to grow and bear fruit. Notice this image is not a leadership pyramid of hierarchy or competition. The vine and the branches is another way of speaking of the communion of saints. The so-called silent, and the greatest generation, were joiners of clubs and organizations. That sense has faded, at least a bit. Robert Putnam captured it in his insight that more people are 'bowling alone" instead of in leagues or scheduled groups. Grief groups are a way of creating community under the sad need to hear others who are undergoing similar experiences of loss. Grief groups create free space to express one's pain and hopes, but it also creates shared space to realize that you are not alone. Some of your experiences and reactions are so similar to others that it is almost like hitting play and viewing and hearing slightly different takes on the same episode. For some, they are invaluable aids in finding solidarity in a community of the suffering.

60) Mourning into dancing Ps. 30:11-We read a passage such as this and wonder if that time will ever come. How can someone even speak of dancing when every bone in the body seems to ache? Where is the proper line to be drawn when mourning could turn into dancing? Sometimes weddings have been scheduled and the celebration is in close proximity to a death in the family. You may get urged "not to ruin Christmas for everybody else" with outward signs of sadness and mourning. It took years and years for my aunt to be able to decorate her house for the Christmas holiday after the death of her son not long before Christmas. There will come a time when you will be able to dance again, when you will want to dance again. The melodies of life will not always remain a dirge. One of our contemporary troubles is that we don't know the steps to move from mourning into dancing. We have lost both the steps to lament and to celebration. I wish moving from mourning to dancing was like a divine light switch. For most of us, it is a process more than a flick of a spiritual switch. (I especially wish for a switch as I have to take dance

lessons to prepare for our daughter's wedding. Having never learned to dance, I dread this process). To stay with the metaphor though, we need to learn the steps to move from mourning into dancing. Part of our arid culture is our utter loss at what to do and how to act in both mourning and marking transitions over time. Even if we know the steps, we may not feel like dancing, barely have the energy to sit in a chair. (See Dancing into Mourning from Clayfire, from Lam. 5:15).

We urge the grieving to be gentle on themselves, easy on themselves, patient with themselves. After all, if we are to love our neighbor as ourselves; it presumes love of self. A generous, open, compassionate heart allows us to be so to others as well. It may not be wise to expect others to be patient with you, as they want you to move quickly from mourning into dancing. Death causes anxiety in all of us, and one way to deal with it is to avoid it and any discussion of it. So one's need to talk and process about a death runs headlong into their discomfort. They may openly wonder how long will you keep bringing up the loss and in that hackneyed phrase, find closure. Consolations are offered but they may not be ready for accepting the offer. Ann Weems in Psalms of Lament(#5) writes of friends leaving "baskets of balm at my feet, but I cannot bend to touch the healing to my heart." Oh, to feel that relief. Oh, to look forward to a day when that relief is felt. To be able to dance again is a mark of healing.

61) Ps. 139 (v. 7)-"where can I flee from your presence, and (v. 12) "even darkness is not dark to you." The God of light is not overcome by the darkness of the natural evil of death. I think of John's prologue as well, "and the darkness did not overcome it" (1:6). While we may be consumed by it so are afraid of it, with the God of light we know that a light at the end of the tunnel beckons. Move to v.16- "ordained for me written in your book." What would you like written or excluded in your book of life, or that of loved ones? Then we encounter: "Lead me to the way everlasting." It makes me think of the children's books, The Runaway Bunny, and the story of the nut brown hare, Guess How Much I Love You. They both deal with the sense of growing autonomy of a child but the need for security

that the parent will be as close as need be. Our youngest daughter is amazed at how many children's books are shared memories of people her age in college. Sight is the primary sense in this psalm. (See Brown on the use of the senses in the psalms). Darkness makes our eyesight fail, but the Psalmist says that God's light banishes darkness. At a spiritual and emotional level, even when we are in deep darkness, God's light can search out the good. To me to have one's name written in the book of life means just that. It is difficult for me to make this image concrete and from it conclude that the days of our lives are pre-determined. Fatalism is not Christian. Celtic Christianity, in its prayers, emphasizes that we live in a constant web of the divine presence. We do not go through this life alone; we are not left solely to our devices. Indeed the breastplate of Patrick: prayer with its "Christ before me, Christ beside, Christ below me, Christ above me" pushes this enveloping sense.

62) Ruth and Boaz (chs.2,3) show that the possibility of love does not end with loss. Mourning does not shut the door to love forever. Sometimes we do move too quickly to try to replace a loss to avoid the pain. At other times, we hide behind our doors. We learn to grow comfortable with the loss on our own. The grieving will hear that they need to get on with their lives. If they do find someone after the death of a spouse, then they may get told that they are moving too fast. Children may feel that their beloved parent is being replaced. I know one gentleman whose son told him to take up drinking instead of considering marriage. In this case, they explore options to help them to go on living. they make plans and seek to implement them. In a desperate situation, Naomi and Ruth concoct a plan that they hope can bring them some security. In the dead of night, Ruth will greet Boaz at the threshing floor. She is taking an enormous risk that she can read him properly as an honorable man. Ruth is at risk in acting on the assumption that she and Naomi can predict his behavior. If the Scripture makes a moral judgment on their plan, I do not see it, unless is very success is its verdict. Making plans is a sign of hope in the future. It is a sign of a renewed trust in one's agency, not passivity. Making plans moves one from being a victim of circumstance to a maker of alternatives.

It is certainly bold and poses great social risk for Ruth. I personally lean toward it being a plan for seduction, but even if it isn't it certainly places immense confidence in the character of Boaz. Sometimes we misplace trust, and other times we find our intuition borne out. To contemplate such a renewed risk is a marker of moving through the valley of the shadow.

63) Stephen is martyred, the first Christian martyr. The word now has an evil connotation the way it seems to be thrown around for suicide bombers seeking their 72 heavenly virgins for murder being termed a religious act. Lives are still taken in the name of a cause that rides over claims of innocence. Stephen was one of the first deacons dedicated to acts of compassion for widows (Acts 7). He has a vision of God's glory, God's sheer presence, as he is dying, and of Jesus at the right hand, the power hand, of God. He dies like Jesus in that he, too, forgives those who killed him. Jesus committed his spirit to the Father's hands, and Stephen asks that Jesus receives his spirit. Before this, Stephen gives a long recitation of salvation milestones in the history of Israel. Stephen is part of a long chain of courageous peoplewho place their lives on the line. In the Roman Catholic tradition, his day is remembered on December 26th. Saul, to become Paul, was there minding the coats of his attackers. Stephen will live out the meaning of his name, crown, garland, as he will be crowned in heaven. It is most important for us to see that a life was not lost in vain. Martyrdom is perhaps the great religious attempt to make a death worthwhile, to find reason for a life being snuffed out. to face grief takes real courage. Where have you found your heart strong? When has your courage faltered? Do you feel a martyr to grief at times?

64) Revenge is desired when a loved one is hurt. It is a normal response, but it does not show human nature at its best. I desire revenge against those who take down so many lives in gunfire, even if I suspect mental illness drives them. It is good that we leave vengeance ot the cooler mind of the state in such situations. A good way to acknowledge but not act on

revenge on a personal level is to read a cursing psalm such as 55, 56, and 109. Many others have small curse elements within them. We learn here that even the feeling for revenge can be made into prayer, communication with our God. Just because revenge rises up within us, it does not mean that we have to act on it, any more than we have to act on any impulse or notion that floats into our hearts or minds. Mystic River showed the paroxysm of grief at the discovery of a daughter's remains. It turns into a story of revenge based on assumptions, not evidence. I recall Mario Cuomo opposing the death penalty because he wanted the law to rise above his own desire for personal revenge, and look to society and the law to take the edge from personal revenge and its escalating nature. Revenge may well satisfy a desire for a justice that seems reciprocal, as in an eye for an eye. In the end, it still feels empty. The ache remains.

65) The writer of Ecclesiastes is pictured as a depressive, but he does love life. He would probably counter that he is a realist (ch.7). He says better a live dog than a dead lion (9:4). He finds small things in life as valuable after the big quests for wealth and fame prove fleeting. If the big answers to big questions seem elusive, then we are urged ot do what we can. He emphasizes the joys of wearing white clothes, of sharing a warm bed, of working hard (9:7-11). A widowed person would respond that one of the hardships of their loss is in no longer sharing the bed with their loved one. One of the simple pleasures that makes life worth living is denied them. A simple invitation can be a great boon to recovery from deep grief. A neighbor can invite you over for coffee and you realize that you have not done a single social thing since the funeral. At times, some of those invitations are set-ups, as another widowed person is invited along, unbeknown to you. We are often clumsy in our attempts to reach and do a neighborly, kind and gracious thing. Joseph Campbell said: "find the place inside where the joy is, and the joy will burn out the pain." That advice may take a while, if you think that the joy has been extinguished from one's life. It may be in the background, like a fire banked for the night, but with renewed openness it will burst forth again, in due time.

66) Zakar means remember in Hebrew. It has a remarkable sense of bringing the past into the present, to make the past live in the present (Mal.3:16). In a sense, that active memory is a shadow of resurrection. Still, memories allow people to exist in our hearts and minds; they are gone in the present and our future, here on earth. Isn't that part of the pull for asking psychics for some sort of connection with them, to close the chasm of absence for a brief, bright moment? As I was writing some of this project, I was called to another position. In moving, I ran across some items of my brother who has been dead for more than twenty years. The pain shot through me as if it was a recent loss. I had stood at his gravesite only months before and did not react like that. We know we are making some progress when we can remember our loved one and not break down. We are making some progress when our memories move from idealizations to something approximating reality. It is a sign of moving through grief when we don't feel the need to only burnish memories of our loved ones, but can look at them whole, both good and bad points mixed together in the reality of human nature. Lately, many people compile pictures on a bulletin board or forge them into a DVD that plays on a continuous loop at the funeral home. In a way, the loop recreates what flashes in our memories, bits and pieces of, fragments of a life as we encountered it. Mostly, they are candid photos and rarely posed, studio ones. We remember them in flashes of real life in real time. In "Leaves Don't Drop," Carrie Newcomer recalls her mother "singing while hanging clothes/though the notes weren't perfect heaven knows." As time passes, we find it easier to remember our loved ones in full, the mixture of traits, good and bad, that we all have and share as human beings.

67) Joseph, who helped raise Jesus, disappears from the gospel narratives, after Jesus is 12, in Luke 2. Perhaps, at some point, he died. With little to go on, we can project all sorts of qualities on to him. The gospels don't even agree on the name of Joseph's father. (Apocryphal gospels add detail to Joseph and the child Jesus).We assume he was a carpenter, or some sort of skilled craftsman (Mt. 13:55). Like his namesake he had dreams and worried like any father when his son didn't return with them after a

religious festival. I am willing to go so far as to wonder if the ease with which Jesus spoke of God as a father emerged, at least in part, due to his relationship with Joseph as a model. That could go a bit in explaining the solicitude of Jesus for widows and his ability to say "blessed are those who mourn." It seems to me inhuman if Jesus did not mourn. It seems less than divinity represented if Jesus did not mourn. The TV special, Jesus shows a scene of the death of Joseph. I commend using it as a spiritual exercise and try to see the response of Jesus to Joseph's death and his response to it. How do you think the two "natures" of Jesus, divine and human would relate to grief? What temptations to power would rise up in Jesus? What do you cherish about your own father? What parts of personality did you reject? What behaviors did you move from? What legacies did he leave you, personal and material? When do you see some of your father in yourself?

68) "Alive or dead, we are the Lord's" (Rom. 14:8). In the final view, our lives are not our own. We cannot claim possession of the life of another, perhaps even our own. So we live on borrowed time. Living or dead, our existence is in the hands of the living, loving God. Put differently, we are God's prized possessions. When we buy a house, we are not merely staking a claim on it, we are seeking secure title. Calvin was fond of calling the sacraments a sign and seal. Uncertainty clouds our thoughts, so we seek some security. The sacraments are physical signs to help us grasp that we are in the caring hands of God. In much of Protestant theology, with two sacraments, instead of seven, both of them center on being life-giving, emblems of the new life in Christ. Alive or dead, we are in the embrace of God. C.B. MacPherson wrote of possessive individualism as part of the movement toward liberal democracy and rights. Instead of thinking that "the earth is the Lord's and the fullness thereof," we consider life itself to be a private possession, not a gift. The Creator God holds title to the life in this world; if you will the earth is god's, not ours. It's an appealing idea to see us under the care of God in this life and the next. Not everything is up to us. The very notion of Sabbath is to give release from constant burdens. Sabbath gives us a constant reminder that

the world is not in our hands. It is not easy to let our grip on our loved ones slip away.

69) Rest and eternal rest-Anyone who has witnessed suffering is grateful for the rest from suffering that death brings. Some fear that the afterlife will be boring. for the restless spirit, for the wandering soul, for the incessant traveler, the image of rest comforts. When my mother passed away, I almost immediately thought that at last her anxiety had been healed. For the many of us who live lives with full calendars, this rest may sound vaguely threatening. Still, for the sleep-deprived busy person, a long period of rest is enticing, maybe especially for someone who works hard physically as well, who is bone-weary, the prospect of rest is alluring. On gravestones and in our thoughts, we say, "rest in peace." Since earliest times, we associate rest with the Sabbath. God rests on the seventh day, after all of the lab or creation. In Hebrew ethics, with the memory of Egyptian enslavement, Sabbath rest was extended to servants and even animals, and the land itself for farmers. With the hectic lives we lead, a good long rest could well be the best healing. Certainly, we need a rest from the burdens we carry, "the things we carry."

70) Sabbath-Dealing with loss requires time, courage, and patience. It requires a zone of space where we can explore life clearly. Sabbath was designed to set apart one day a week to create space to worship and rest. Even grief needs a rest. Is it possible to set aside a day a week and declare it a grief-free zone? OK, would it be possible to set aside 2 hours, or 15 minutes as a grief-free zone? Only slaves work 24 hours a day, seven days a week. We are not made for grieving all of the time either. We speak perhaps a little too easily of grief work. That labor needs a break too. 24/7 grief will consume us. The spiritual adept Mueller wrote: "Sabbath requires surrender. If we only stop when we are finished with all our work, we will never stop, because our work is never completely done. With every accomplishment there arises a new responsibility... Sabbath dissolves the artificial urgency of our days, because it liberates us from the

need to be finished." r -Sabbath can be a time "when I will pamper my soul." Sabbath tells us that the world can go on without our active involvement. As my grandmother would say, "the world continues to turn in a circle without you." Yet, grief time is holy time. So, maybe we could look at grief as a Sabbath time from the usual work of the day. It is a time for recreation/re-creation. If the Master Craftsman took a break after the six long days of creation (Gen.2:4) we can use a rest from the intense labor of grief. For a variety of personal reasons, some of us find it very hard to go to church on our Sabbath day after a loss. What are spiritual practices that you have found restful or restorative?

71) Lk. 8:40-56Mt. 9:18-31-Few things alarm us as a terribly ill child. Jairus must have been frantic when he went to meet Jesus. I would assume his name is from Hebrew, meaning enlightened. That is a good name for a leader of the synagogue. Then his hurrying Jesus along gets interrupted when someone else's need intrudes. . In Matthew's version, one would think a different spirit is at play for the girl has already died. Jesus spends some time with a woman who suffered for 12 years, but this was an emergency, as his 12 year old daughter was in distress. Some report that time goes in slow motion when we are in an accident. I imagine that Jairus must of thought that they would never get to the house in time. Surely, he wanted to hurry Jesus along. Then, upon arriving at the house, when he hears the mourners' cries and songs, he knows that it is too late. Even impending death does not rush Jesus. For the grieving time takes on a menacing quality. I remember a widower saying that he does fine during the day, but he dreads the coming of the night. Jesus seems to take events as they come, it seems. Jesus stops to spend some time with a suffering woman. Instead of seeing prayer with God as a possible intrusion on God's schedule, consider how Jesus took the time to spend with a suffering woman, without letting anxiety overtake him. God has all the time in the world for you. I ran across a social psychology experiment on seminarians asked to go to an important meeting, and then to encounter a person in need of help on their way, an obvious replay of the parable of the Good Samaritan. It is not an easy thing to balance duty and compassion when they collide. We do the best we can. We hope and pray for the calm ability to act beyond our reactions.

72) At Easter, Christians have a definitive answer about God. Life, not death, has the last word with God. "Come on up for the rising" sings Bruce Springsteen. (I played this once for folks at church, and it was not appreciated, save for the few fans in church.) On Easter we go a bit overboard with brave bold statements of death being destroyed. For something destroyed, death sure seems to pack a powerful wallop. The fear of death would be a bit closer to the mark, or perhaps better, death's finality or final victory. Mark's gospel ends without a resurrection appearance. It ends with words of awe and fear and trails off. Where to go with this non-ending? does it mean we go back to the beginning? Does it mean we move into a resurrection world that we cannot fathom, so it is left open? We can't help but wonder about a world beyond and what it is like. As I write some of this, I just viewed the Clint Eastwood movie, Hereafter. Its focus is on near dear or out of body experiences and places a scientific collection of statements along with a psychic ability to enter into another realm, so it is not about heaven per se. It does have some achingly good work of the desire of the bereaved to pierce the veil between life and death. At the end of "The Rising" Springsteen gives a sort of benediction. The polarities are underscored by the refrain: 'dream of life." In the creeds, Christians say, I believe in the resurrection of the body. Notice we do not say that our souls will live on, that our hearts will go on, but a resurrection of the body. It is good that Easter is in the spring in the northern hemisphere, at least. It is the time for new life, plant and animal, to be bursting forth. On the other hand, it is dangerous, as Easter is not part of the natural cycle of winter into spring, of dormancy into blooming. It stands against the natural pattern of death and decay.

73) Mt. 26-7, Mk. 14-15, Lk. 22-3, Jn. 18-19-The death of Jesus slows down the narratives in all four gospels. To be able to come to grips with the horror, they go over the information with care and attention. it reminds me of how often people need to rehearse where they were when they received bad news or what they noticed when present when someone died. An excellent question from a child is: why is this day called good?

Most Christians would agree with Hebrews that Jesus was sinless. So that obviates the possibility of punishment for an innocent. Yet, Jesus died. Jesus died too young. Jesus died a horrific death on a cross. Surely Jesus did not deserve to die. Innocence does get treated cruelly at times. Unfairness is part of our fallen social landscape. Perhaps, the crucifixion should put an end to our easy talk about when we deserve to die or who dies at an appropriate time. Mark's ending (15:34 0 is one of a haunting cry of desolation and anguish. Matthew combines the loud cry with Luke makes the final cry a prayer from pos. 31:5 as Jesus commends his spirit to God. For John, Jesus knows the end is near, says it is finished (or completed) bows his head and gives up his spirit (19:19:30). A cry from nature in apocalyptic reaction (27:5`1-52). 37) has Jesus quote Ps. 22 in the abandonment of being forsaken and ending with a loud cry. I can imagine Death dressing to the nines and having the most elegant soiree imaginable when the good Jesus went to the cross. Could even Death imagine a rising from the sealed tomb? I find it hard to follow the train of thought of Anselm that God's honor required a death to allow honor to be reclaimed, or Calvin's version of a substitute to accept the criminal sentence deserved by humanity. Somehow, as Paul says, God used a terrible crime against justice as a vehicle of reconciliation. God is able to wrest good from evil, while we are more able to work evil from good many times. Our various images of and theories of the atonement all attempt to wring meaning out of the death of Jesus and place it into a meaningful perspective.

74) (See Serene Jones and Rambo books on trauma) Violence enters our awareness anytime we open a newspaper. We accept the loss of life due to violence with eerie calm, or maybe it is numbness. I work on this not long after the massacre in Tuscon. A federal judge was murdered, a member of Congress was in a prolonged rehab facility, but hearts also went out to the family who lost a lovely nine year old daughter. A friend of mine is trying to offer pastoral care to a woman whose estranged husband tried to hammer her to death with their child in the house, as their divorce was being finalized. Certainly violence is a complicating factor in our grief.

I recall the grieving parents for their eldest daughter, killed by her estranged husband. The mother needed a long time to come to grips with her inability to protect her daughter. In this world, how could she have protected her 24 hours a day? Where were the guarantees that her efforts could have deterred a determined killer? Through their trauma, I discovered a support group for parents of murdered children. Others may turn toward organizations that attempt to create more security in this blood splattered land. Violence leaves much trauma in its wake. Left untreated, trauma haunts its victims. We have learned much to serve to help people who are injured to the depths of their being. It is perhaps the deepest healing.

75) Ps. 85 I have always loved the phrase of waiting for a world when justice and peace shall kiss. Earlier we hear that God will speak peace/shalom to his people. For me, it is a political vision of heaven, of the realization of the kingdom/reign/way of God in our midst. Yes grief results from illness and accident. Far too many times, it results from violence and injustice. Keeping an eye out for that distant horizon can move us from the intense focus on emotional processing of early grief. In other words grief can be a private response to crying public needs, or our failure to heed them and place them in a secure structure. (As I write this, I am trying to cope with my cold fury at important budget and economic decisions of an administration). Even if you suspect that your trouble comes directly from the hand of the Giving One, maybe even as a punishment, this psalm reminds us that \God's anger fades, withdraws in response to other divine attributes. it is not a permanent feature in the face of peace, steadfast love, and mercy. Recall, please, that the word translated as peace is shalom, a broader term that encompasses well-being, greeting, and general health. Look at how the poet links the natural world with the virtues. Toward the end, in v. 12, the NRSV has increase, as in agricultural production, but it can be a richer term, abundance, an explosion of diversity and fruitfulness. Your life can point that way. We may not live to see it come to fruition, but activates our desire for a better way for us to live together.

76) John 9- Right away the blame game starts here. The question is not how can this man be helped? Not only do we try to find the reason, the cause of suffering, but we have a nasty habit of wanting to blame the victim for their circumstance. "Who sinned that this man is born blind?" Some punishment must lie behind his affliction. We harbor a retributive mode of justice much more than the dream of a restorative justice. As usual, Jesus will not go along with the assumption here. Many of us harbor a dark suspicion that somehow we are being punished for some transgression with a death. Part of our need to blame comes from the stark fear that not blaming someone put us to blame. It is as if we are built to try to make sense even of the senseless. We seek cause and effect, even when none is to be found. Jesus does find purpose in his healing, to let the light of God shine. Physical issues of blindness often find a spiritual counterpart, and restored sight is often a sign of spiritual insight as well. It is no accident that a physical healing causes us to examine the issue of spiritual insight as we consider physical sight and blindness. Indeed, this comes close to the definition of sin, an inability to see Jesus clearly. Part of the reaction to the blind man's vision is its threat to comfortable, established ways of understanding faith and its results. Susan Pitchford in God in the Dark, says "to induce suffering in anyone, including ourselves, in the name of God is to take than name in vain" (101). That gives impetus to the story as religious leaders hold investigatory hearings for the healed person and his parents instead of rejoicing in this marvelous healing. We resort to inspections, hearings, and procedures when our cramped views of God are taken to task, threatened, especially with expansion of our limited perspectives.

77) John 5 asks a most pregnant question from Jesus," Do you want to be healed?" Jesus asks the question of a man who has spent years and years waiting, hoping, for a miracle. The notions seemed to be that if were near the healing pool, if a healing angel went past, the water would be disturbed, and you could be healed by getting there at the right moment. Sadly, in grief, prolonged grief, the answer may be no. If grief stops, do I

lose my connection to my loved one? What if I have rebuilt my identity around being widowed, or being a survivor? What if I cannot imagine any other way of living any more than to live with this hurt? Death can attack our very identity and warp it into a container of loss. After a while, we may be half afraid of feeling better because it's been so long that we may not recognize it. Jesus speaks to a man who had been paralyzed for years. Grief does immobilize us. In the movie Last Chance Harvey, the Emma Thompson character says something to the effect of having grown comfortable in being alone and expecting to be disappointed. If she fell in love, she would open herself up to hurt, and she would rather be with she has grown comfortable with. In King John Shakespeare wrote: "grief fills the room of my absent child (but place any loved one here)/lies in the bed, walks up and down with me...stuffs out his vacant garments with his form/then I have reason to be fond of grief." At this point, what has kept you immobilized in your walk through grief? Can you isolate some places where you are getting in your own way? What needs to be healed in your life? Avoid the temptation to consider only the physical but look toward the aspects of the spiritual, the emotional, and the mental that immobilize your capacity to be moving forward.

78) Sometimes the word for grave, sheol, means just that, the burial plot, the grave. Death was the end, the finish. At other times, Sheol seems to be a Hebrew version of the Greek underworld, Hades. In other words, the idea of different realms of the dead evolved over time, perhaps due to encountering explicitly dualistic beliefs. The animated movie Hercules has an eerie view of it with spectral wraiths. Look at some of the art work of jesus entering the abode of death in what is called the harrowing of hell. My sense of it could also be merely the grave. In other words, dead is dead. How do you think that notion of living this life then would have an effect on how one would live a life? To some degree belief in the afterlife allows mistakes or unmet dreams to be fulfilled in the world beyond. Resurrection hope started to appear late in the period before Jesus due, in part, to this stark doctrine. Part of the impulse for resurrection is the basic unfairness we encounter in this life. Somewhere the scales should be

balanced out, and the next life becomes that scene to help redress injustices that are untouched and unaddressed here. In the psalms it is used as a motivation to God for healing. Who will praise you like me if I am dead and gone? It's a way of asking God, "wouldn't you miss me when I'm gone?" It assumes that the relational God develops a deepening of that relationship through the person who is praying. Perhaps God even looks forward to interacting with us.

79) (See Alan Segal's books, especially <u>Life After Death</u>)-The "bosom of Abraham: was a locution for heaven in the time of Jesus and was used in the story of the rich man (Dives in Latin) and a poor man named Lazarus (Latinate name for Eleazar, God helps). We also get a terrible vision of life apart from the bosom of Abraham. Some literalize the story and help picture the glory of heaven and the pain of hell. It seems to me to be an illustrative story. Still, the chasm that exists between the two realms is ominous. To get at a sense of the afterlife, many people listen to the Sarah McLachlan song, "In the Arms of the Angels." She sings "in the arms of the angels/ far away from here..."Paul Simon in his new recording, So Beautiful or So What?, has a song, The Afterlife, that re-imagines heaven with lots of bureaucratic paperwork and long lines. I admire the playfulness of it, as it drains some of the terrible seriousness we bring to our speculations of the afterlife. He also has a song, "Questions for the Angels." Instead of a place, the story of Jesus chooses a person, the patriarch of the entire people. So, the beginning is the end. In Bible Study, just this morning, as I write, a gentleman offered his fervent belief in a literal Hell, on the grounds that it is unjust for the evil to co-exist with the good forever. How do you regard the notions of heaven and hell?

80) Mourning music and ritual-for some of us, music can soothe the ache within, but not right away. Over and over, I've heard people say that they are not able to listen to music at first. It seems to touch a chord to deep at the moment. In the myth of Orpheus, his music is so heartbreaking for his lost Eurydice that it melts even the heart of the ruler of the Underworld. I

just heard a woman on NPR speak of a piece she wrote for her brother who played clarinet. He has since died, but she notices that when she conducts the piece, people are moved and shaken to the core , so come cannot speak. A number can say, " I've lost someone too." One push for contemporary sounding music is that many older hymns sound funereal to begin with. Sometimes we can only listen to the blues or a requiem. Two hymns on my funeral instructions are Here I Am, Lord and Be Thou My Vision. Some people have been urged to repress feelings so much that they need to stimulate their appearance. For many, music does just that. Rosanne Cash wrote a song, "September When It Comes." It was suggested to her that her father join her in the recording. It is heartbreaking to hear her father sound resigned to his decline "I can move no mountains now." The last of the American Recordings series by Johnny Cash is replete with facing of mortality, a mortality you can hear in the weakened voice in many of the songs. He even wrote a song inspired by the words of I Corinthians 15:55. One can go do a computer search and find loads of songs compiled by folks to touch on aspects of loss. If you only listen to one genre or period of music, you may well be surprised at the parts touched with differing lyricists and melodic landscapes. If a family is willing to try, it can be a meaningful and even healing experience to consider different hymns and music for a funeral.

81) Song of Solomon -Love is as strong as death (8:6). Is it stronger? Does it not persist past the grave? This is a love song. To lessen its erotic charge, it has been made into an allegory of the love between God and the people. Nonetheless, it is romantic and sensual. As embodied beings, or ensouled bodies, it is a good thing to praise romantic love in the Scripture. Granted, mystics often use erotic language to express their spiritual yearning, but it seems to me to be a profound misreading of this song to try to move away from its embrace of physicality. In chapter four, it goes from head to toe praising the features of the beloved. (That convinces me that these are young lovers-could you imagine a similar song as we move past middle age?) Death brings the loss of an imagined loving future and brings to an end the passionate acts toward a spouse, with a spouse. It

deprives us of sexual love, of the intimate joining of bodies as a vital aspect of love. One of the guilty or frightening thoughts is whether we will feel passion again. Are we betraying our vows, are we betraying them, if we love again, even if the vows say until death do we part? Still, our commitment to our loved ones does not end with death. Gregory of Nyssa struggled with this issue as a theologian and in his personal response to the death of his sister Macrina. They were grieving the death of their brother Basil. On the Soul and the Resurrection is a sophisticated attempt to match philosophy with Christina theology in the midst of personal crisis. Gregory saw that the soul imprinted the body with its identity. Macrina goes further and demonstrates to him that the resurrected body has identity with the deceased, but it has to be different, otherwise we would continue to face illness and death. Love embraces an entire person, and their absence in full, makes the ache so real. Mystics crave a sense of union with the Beyond, for part of love is the desire for union, of seeking to fill the gaps of one life through another. In so doing, we feel whole.

82) (See Donald Capps Biblical Approaches to Pastoral Care). I received a phone call as I was working on this, and my caller wanted to know a bit about post-modern thought. He asked if it could fit within the Bible. After a moment I replied that the book of Proverbs would fit some of its concerns, as it does not show a particular concern for precise order, indeed some of its thoughts seem almost randomly constructed, but its wisdom is not left in the abstract but emerges from reflected experience. In its way, Proverbs is a meditation on the path of life and the path toward death., wisdom 10:16,17-25-12:25-28-11:4, Proverbs reflects a worldly wisdom that sees death as the end (11:4). It also contains practical words on healing:12;25, "an anxious heart weighs a person down, but a kind word cheers them up." Move to 12:18: "reckless words pierce like a sword, but the tongue of the wise brings healing." It knows well the feelings attached to grief: 13:12 "hope deferred makes the heart sick." Regard 14;10 "each heart knows its own bitterness," and then, 14:13 'even in laughter the heart may ache and joy may end in grief." Examine 15:13 heartache cruses the spirit" and 18:14 "a person's spirit sustains

them in sickness, but a crushed spirit how can bear it?" Look to the evocative 25; 25 "cold water to a weary soul,: while 30:16 gives the hard truth that "the grave never says enough" Wisdom was and is practical. It takes the abstract, cold logic and warms it within human need and experience. When I was in seminary, Proverbs was skimmed over as something akin to Polonius giving advice to his son. In part, it was seen as merely practical social learning, not of the bold status of revelation.

83) Aaron's sons were killed in Lev. 10. Somehow, we get the notion that religious work should give us some immunity from the pain of loss. When death occurs as a result of religious activity, we are left in a quagmire of confusion. In the open narrative of Hebrew prose, we are given some facts but we do not often get access to the thoughts of the characters. Surely it would be a complicated grief, as they disobeyed the strict ritual requirements. We don't consider often the impact of loss within a family of a niece or nephew, a cousin. At the end of v. 3, Aaron was silent in seeing his sons consumed for the sake of proper procedures in the face of the holy. I hope that he could find some comfort in his priestly duties, but surely the bitter taste of their death would intrude on his work. Most of us have moved past a belief that God unleashes death for ritual errors. At the same time, we have lost a sense of the holy as being awestruck in the face of divine capacity, given our weakness and vulnerabilities. In one of the Harry Potter movies, Harry brings back the hero, Cedric. When his father realizes that he is a dead hero, he cries out in a burst of grief. While Teddy Roosevelt wanted all of his sons to go to war, he was devastated when his son Quentin was shot down in WWI, and he died not that long after. He may have loved the abstract romantic views of martial glory, but now the pain stifled his romantic view of a glorious end on a battlefield when it was a child of his own, not his own courage. . It continues to be a horror to kill or be killed in the name of God.

84) Esther was orphaned. Orphans at times speak of having no solid sense of home, of belonging. Her own language had been taken from her, and

her name may well have reflected the name of the Goddess Ishtar. She is not bereft of family, as her uncle Mordecai looks after her. In this tale, she wins a beauty contest to replace a queen who embarrassed the king. She gets a year of spa treatments and is installed as queen to be at the king's beck and call. Now she is faced with the threat of a pogrom. To try to prevent it, Esther endangers her own position in the court of the Persian king. The former president of CTS in Indianapolis said "Esther had it good, but her people were in trouble." The king's edict about needing to be invited to approach the king puts her in a seemingly impossible situation. Then irony piles upon irony. Her feast becomes a funeral for the wicked Haman. The gallows he prepared is used on him. I can only imagine the delight of a colonized people in hearing this story of reversal of fortune, of being hoisted on one's own petard. Grief sometimes seems to be placing us into all sorts of no-win, no-exit situations. God's name is not mentioned in Esther. She is thrust into making a dangerous decision. She does ask for a fast, an occasion for prayer, certainly. God does not act in a miraculous fashion here. God works through human decisions and actions. I wonder if one possible reason that this book is not in the Dead Sea Scrolls is that decidedly secular cast. Esther's story is a way to approach God in a time when we don't attribute much directly to the hand of God. This would appall the great forbearer of the Reformed movement, John Calvin. For him, the core of the relationship between us and God was to be grateful recipients of the constant, gracious gifts of God in creation and redemption. How have your experiences and understandings affected your relationship with God?

85)Nahum- This bloodthirsty desire for revenge against powerful enemies is rarely used in church, but it has its place. Who doesn't want revenge against a powerful nation that causes death in war and oppression? This is an oracle that the power of God will be unleashed against an oppressor. For that matter, if a loved one is killed by a drunk driver or a careless driver, who would not want to get back at them. The desire for an eye for an eye wells up in us. Laura Bush wrote of her struggle to deal with the remorse of having a friend killed in an auto accident when she was at the wheel. Even if we can not find a proximate person to be properly angry with, we will invent one in our desire, our thirst for blame and then vengeance. It feels half-finished if can't find some object, some cause for our pain. Jesus moves beyond the ethics of an eye for an eye. As has been said many times, eye for an eye would leave the world blinded. Forgiveness may well start with the decision to forswear revenge as an option, let alone one's right. The book is well aware that few will bemoan the destruction of oppressors. Yet, at 1:7 we are told that the Lord is good, a stronghold in the day of trouble. Indeed punishment will not last. At 1:12 "I have afflicted you and will afflict you no more." Note the lack of restraint in the language in Nahum pushes a consideration of language and grief. We realize it is a touchy subject and use all sorts of circumlocutions and euphemism around it. To a degree, that is all to the good. Some of the direct language about death assumes intimacy of relations. Funeral directors have a good sense of this. While they are performing an intimate service, they are not kin, but professionals. They need a language to deal with the load of emotions surrounding their work without assuming closeness but sharing a sense of the moments. They have work to do, and so they try to drain some of the shock away from more telling words. Euphemism is not only a way to shade the truth; it is an attempt to shield us from the impact of words. Some words are appropriate only for kin, not professionals.

.

86) To weep seems a deeper word than cry. "Weep with those who weep" (Rom. 12:15) has a true sense of community. It is a mixture of empathy and sympathy. It is a sign of solidarity. Notice it does not turn off tears, but it shares them. To weep with those who weep gives permission to cry. It goes beyond saying that it's all right to cry. It even goes beyond telling someone that not crying would be a more alarming state. To weep is an emblem of community. Community accepts the state of a person where they are and stays within that frame, at least for a while. it does not try to impose on that person our sense of how they should be responding. Trevor Hudson said "everyone we know sits beside a pool of tears." In

Shadowlands, among many scenes, an affecting one is where the Hopkins character is in the attic with Debra Winger's character's son. As they talk, their emotions, so bottled up, open through tears. I deeply distrust those who insist that suffering is therapeutic, or that if forms a contrast point for us to appreciate the better days. I have long detested C. S. Lewis's book on suffering, the Problem of Pain, when he calls it God's megaphone. His abstract analysis of trouble certainly changed when he faced it as a personal crisis, instead of an intellectual problem. John Swinton's book Raging with Compassion turns from trying to solve the problem of evil and suffering as an intellectual puzzle, but urges us to in the church to engage in acts of compassion. One of those is hospitality. Think of it as making room for and making people comfortable in sharing their needs and feelings, or offering a safe, shared, free space for them to do so. The current push toward funeral as celebrating life is inhospitable to hospitality toward the expression of grief.

87) Gal. 6:2- bear one another's burdens. President Clinton used this as a theme in his sermonic First Inaugural. I think of the old hymn, Blest Be the Ties That Bind as an explication of this verse. In some ways, this little phrase captures the depth of community. I want to be careful here. We cannot bear the grief for another person. Paul also says that each person bears their own share of a burden (6:5).To try to live within another's experience invites aggressive intrusion into another's life and responsibilities. We do better to tend our own gardens. A great act of community by a church is to offer a mercy lunch for the family after a funeral. It is one task that does not need to be checked off by the grieving family. It gives the opportunity to tell stories and share memories. Anyone who listens to someone go over and over details of a death, their grief is acting in a manner to make a heavy burden bearable by sharing the load a bit. Craig Ferguson, a comedian, hosts a late night talk show. After the death of his father in Scotland, he departed form his usual format and told stories about his father. He wanted to replicate a wake with his audience, where we tell stories, not all of them flattering, but ones that capture the essence of our view of the person. An act of community kindness is to

have a chance for someone to tell those stories, repeat those stories, to have some listening ears. David Rensberger (Weavings, 9/10/02:39-40) writes "suffering has no scale...no one, least of all God, requires that our pain reach a certain magnitude before it is worth noticing. The minimum number of persons who must be affected...in order for it to count is one." As I review some of my material here, Steve Jobs, the co-founder of Apple Computers, died from his long struggle with cancer. A profusion of short statement emerged on Facebook, and people took to the net to make their own memorial sites to honor his passing. Blog posts noted how they felt connected and touched by a man whom they had never met. We are linked in layers of relationship in this new world.

88) Miriam's death- Her name has the sense of bitter tears, yet she could sing a song of triumph at the Sea. The basic name is shared by the mother of Jesus and a number of women who were disciples of him. They too were destined for tears. She watched over her brother on his river trip in his little basket boat. The same woman who sang in triumph over the defeat of the minions of Egypt would not triumph forever. Miriam did not see eye to eye with Moses all of the time. Indeed she was punished for daring to challenge the leadership of Moses. We often have "unfinished business" with those who have died. We accumulate history with them. At one point Miriam and Aaron oppose Moses's leadership. It could have been a most reasonable decision. On the other hand, their opposition could have emerged from envy. Envy resents good fortune and superior positions. It finds itself incapable of cheering someone in a position or in possession of something that we may well believe we are mores deserving, more entitled, more worthy than the holder. It is very easy to slip into envy when we regard those whose families are intact. Envy corrodes our ability to rejoice in the good fortune of others. We wonder why not me and may secretly hope that they too lose what we want. We can't even see the good that we do have as we fixate on what we may want and do not have in the hands of others. We want to pull others down to our level. Grief can reveal our vices as well as our virtues.

89) Ec.3 has a balance worthy of Dickens in the opening of a <u>Tale of Two Cities</u>. It is a powerful demonstration that life has rhythm. I'm of the age group that my first exposure to it was not in church but in the Byrds' song "Turn, Turn, Turn." I find it appropriate to read when someone who has lived a long, full life has their body almost seem to wear out. It also looks at what is fitting. We discern when it is time to sew or to rip up. We learn what is appropriate and inappropriate during a given phase. At the same time, I am a bit reticent about telling someone else when the time to sew and the time rend would be. In seeing the forest of pattern, we often lose sight of the individual tree, even unique ones. To discern patterns may well take more distance and objectivity than we possess in times of crisis and stress. On the other hand, the cadence of the passage lends some stability in a time when so much seems chaos and uncertainty. On the other hand, we realize that we too are part of the patterns of life, a pattern that includes life and death, laughter and mourning. In the midst of that pattern, that oscillation, we do well to love each other and to love our work and the pleasures of food and drink. A number of them do relate directly to loss, at least in some form. "A time to rend and a time to sew; a time to laugh and a time to weep" has obvious linkage to the condition. One of our troubles in our do-it-yourself-build your own model culture is that we lack a sense of when it is appropriate to laugh and weep. .

90) Jer. 29 plans for you-Many people find deep comfort in the thought that God has a hand in events. Some even see God as in control of events. We don't hear people speak much of pre-destined as pre-determined in life, but we do hear of God's plan for our lives. The popular series on the purpose-driven life took this as axiomatic. Here, I don't see it as a specific plan that is kept secret but a desire for our welfare, the general welfare, if you will. The word welfare is the word, shalom, often translated as peace. Even if we see God as punishing, the door is open to welfare and restoration for us all. I do not believe that God has some sort of death timetable, where the exact hour, date, and manner of death are all pre-arranged. Some folks do. It takes the sense of ultimate control of our lives out of their hands, and that can be a comfort. It can also become an

excuse for all sorts of careless behavior, since it is God pulling the strings of our lives. I do believe that plans for welfare and hope are for the afterlife of inexpressible wonders. Consider some of the choices you make, the options you have as invitations to open doors that could result in welfare for your future. Sometimes we rush into decisions to change things in our lives in an attempt to try to erase reminders of our loved ones. A considered act such as Jeremiah's is a declaration of hope, a rediscovery of a future.

91) Rom. 6 has baptism as a ritual act of inclusion in both the death of Jesus and the resurrection. We are gathered into, incorporated into the life, death, and resurrection of Jesus. Paul touches on this theme frequently. He seems to say that we are bound to the entirety of the life, death, and resurrection of Jesus. A funeral prayer says that our baptism has become complete in our death. I don't know if I would put it quite that way. We may well be glad to accept the resurrection part, but the part about united with the cross of Christ, including his death, leaves many of us cold. However, if we share in the death of Christ, it may leave some of its sting out of reaction, especially if it then follows that we are part of the resurrection, of which Christ is the "first fruit., (I Cor. 15:20-23 the pioneer" (Heb.12:2). As Paul said, we are made a new creation. It is as if we drown in the waters of baptism, strip off the old as we would old clothes, and are offered the birth waters of the womb of new life, clothed with the virtues of the spirit. When he was troubled, Luther would write on a blackboard, remember your baptism. Certainly that process continues in the new dimension of life we enjoy in the presence of God. Indeed, he says we are alive in Christ. That will include even death as we are joined into eternal life with Christ. Our loved ones are united with Christ. We are united with Christ. Take some time to examine the sacraments as vehicles for this participation in the life of Christ.

92) Release from this body of death (Rom. 7:24) is a cry that we all share. I have said repeatedly that if I never hear the word cancer again it will be

too soon. Death stalks us all. I hate looking at the newspaper and seeing the headlines of car crashes, the list of war dead, and obituaries. Entropy attacks the order of life and motion. While I support free standing hospices, it is overwhelming to be in the presence of so much death. Our younger daughter has her freshman writing class under the rubric of zombies and the burgeoning literature and shows about them. Paul equates the present age as one addicted to sin and death. Earlier, he shows a deep awareness of our psychology where will power does not seem to be much avail against the power of sin to the extent that we often proceed to do the opposite of what we wish we would do or not do. We crave release from being part of too much loss. I fear when we say closure, we really mean we can go on and push the life that is gone from us to the periphery. Closure does not mean that we can or should expunge someone from out lives. Perhaps by this time your load of projects and distractions has lessened. The thank you cards are written. The paperwork seems more manageable. Instead of feeling some sense of accomplishment and relief, you may start to dread their completion, since now you may have to face this body of death without the shield of tasks to be handled. With Paul, we don't want to face Death anymore. Enjoy the periods, the plateaus, of release you may discover all the way.

93) I Cor. 15 spiritual body- A spiritual body sounds impossible, but it is a good phrase for that very reason. Paul is struggling to suggest a transformation as immense as a seed growing into a great plant. Even in our age, how is it possible that such a small seed has the genetic information to become a huge towering plant and that the little seed has the energy to push the seedling through the soil? Paul is struggling to speak of a transformation that still respects the identity of the person's life. After all, we are embodied souls, physical beings. We do not resurrect into featureless ghosts as much as we will rise into our best selves. I like to imagine that we will enjoy our loves and experiences intact. Don't forget that Paul sees the realm of the spirit as the realm of life, in opposition to the realm of sin and death. So he describes a resurrection body as the body elevated into the realm of God, a spiritual body. A transformed, enhanced body may get at part of its dimension. In his recent book Accompany Them With Singing, Thomas Long makes a case for more

respect for the body itself in the funeral process. We live embodied lives. I do not hold with so many that the body is a mere shell, and the important part of us, the soul, has floated to God. One of the earliest powerful opponents of the orthodox Christian story was the Gnostic element. It was a faith of and for the chosen few, an esoteric brand for the illuminated ones. It saw the body as a prison for the spirit. How do you regard this spiritual conception of the soul?

94) Acts and magic (chs. 8,13, 19) Sometimes we want our prayers to be magic talismans. If only we know the right words, the prayer would be answered. We may even want to turn back the clock, like Superman stopping the rotation of the earth, or Joshua having the sun stand still. Magic hovers around the edge of religion. If only we new the right gesture, we could get what we want when we want it. We like the sense that it is esoteric, so that only those with inside knowledge have access to its secrets and mysteries. If only we could find the perfect prayer, the right guide, the right therapist, the right medicine, and then our troubles would be over, or at least bearable. In the back of our minds, we want God to be a magician, able to make the bad things disappear. Children sometimes are victimized by magical thinking and torture themselves with the thought that their angry thoughts or words led directly to harm of someone else. Even as adults, we see a movie about a superhero and wish that we could turn back the clock, or have the ability to rush to save a loved one, or be a brilliant scientist to come up with a cure. The book of Acts has a search for magic, notably with Simon Magus in Act 8 (singular for magi, by the way). Grief can be a search for magic, a pill, a person, a belief that will rescue us, maybe even transport us to a different place. Truth be told, we want God to be our foremost magic helper.

95) Acts 20:7-11 The sublime and ridiculous often live together, even in the face of tragedy. Eutyches falls asleep during a sermon, but he falls from a height to his death. What were some moments of high or low comedy around the funeral of a loved one? The book of Acts has a theme

of death and resurrection that plays through it. Eutyches lives out his name (good fortune) and is raised. I remember having to direct traffic in my robe when our funeral coach broke down on the way to the cemetery and then the competitor gleefully gave us a helping hand with their funeral coach. I've heard cell phone ring tones come off at the most inopportune time at the funeral. I've seen kids crash into a carefully loaded dessert cart. At one point, I was directing traffic in my preaching robe. Ecclesiastes speaks of a time to laugh and a time to weep, but we are not sure when the appropriate time is to laugh again. I did a service for a man of great good humor who directed that we offer a cold beer to anyone who wished one, as long as they said something nice about him. One guy got up twice. Norman Cousins attributed healing to laughter therapy watching old comedies. In time, maybe laughter therapy in watching a comedy or reading someone funny may be the ticket to help move out of the dark well of sadness that seems so pervasive. To be able to laugh again, without feeling inappropriate or guilty, is a boon to the grieving. Laughter is indeed medicine to the heavy heart. Laughter promotes the healing of a broken heart.

96) Rom 8:38 nothing can separate us from the love of God in Jesus Christ. Recently, I read a piece in Christian Century that noted that ministers favor this passage in funeral services for some time. All manner of horrors stalk and strike human beings. Paul has the courage to name them, to face them. He refuses to see them as curses, however, but part of our course through this life of troubles. They are not signs of divine disfavor. We may well feel abandoned, forsaken, alone. We search for signs that maybe our loss is some sort of punishment. When my brother died, I clung to this passage life a life vest: nothing could separate him from the love of God; nothing could separate me from the love of God in this time of trial. The way we grieve, or don't grieve cannot separate us from the love of God. The manner of a loved one's death cannot separate them or us from the love of God in Jesus Christ. The age of a loved one cannot separate us from the love of God in Jesus Christ. Perhaps this passage is popular in funerals as we may well be abandoned, alone, in the face of loss. It has

the advantage of admitting that bad things happen to good people. Even if we have a laundry list of troubles, we are reminded that these do not have the power to drive a wedge between us and the love of God in Jesus Christ. They are not a sign of disfavor from the hand of God. For me, the passage points away from God's power as controlling, as power over. God's power emerges through a matrix of love.

97) John 14 is often read at funerals. At times, it is an expected reading, and its familiarity brings some comfort. We certainly do crave peace in such a time. In my Father's house are many rooms (mansions). I find it an appealing image that life with God has plenty of room. For that matter, I like the old word, mansion, as it has the allure of some opulence and luxury. I heard a joke where "two ministers and a cab driver all go to the pearly gates at the same time. The two clergy have virtually identical bungalows on a nice but undistinguished street. The cab driver is shown a mansion that would make Trump blush. The next day the ministers cannot contain their disappointment and ask how the cab driver received such an abode. The response: 'you should have seen him drive. He brought more people to prayer in 4 hours than you two did in your entire careers." It has an element of comedy to me when Philip says that they have no idea where Jesus is going, so how can they know the way? Jesus then points to himself as the compass they need, we need. At the funeral, few of us know the way out of pain. What is this peace that Jesus gives, but not as the world gives? It is not the peace of numbness, or a chemical peace of alcohol or drugs to deaden ourselves in the face of death. Dulling the pain is a real temptation-we look for an anodyne, so the threat of alcohol and drug dependency is a real threat in this time. The world doesn't look any clearer through the bottom of a whiskey glass during loss than it does with beer goggles at one in the morning when you're 21. Drowning sorrows cannot wash away the pain for very long. Finding the capacity to laugh again may well be the better road.

98) Rom. 12:4-5, I Cor. 12: The communion of saints is a creedal affirmation, but it certainly emerges form passages such as these. I have

good intentions to use different creeds from the Presbyterian Book of Confessions. Usually, I forget, and we recite the Apostles' Creed and speak of the communion of saints toward the end. Communion of saints emphasizes our connection in baptism, indeed as human beings. Love respects neither time nor space. We are linked to others across the globe and in the world beyond.(Elizabeth Johnson) The Archbishop of Canterbury, Rowan Williams, writes in Tokens of Trust that "just as we can trust God because he has no agenda that is not for our good, so we can trust the Church because it is the sort of community that is, a community of active peacemaking and peacekeeping where no one exists in isolation or grows up in isolation or suffers in isolation. The slogan of the Church's life is 'not without the other'; no I without a you, no I without a we." The communion of saints links the living and the dead. I think of the end of the movie, Places in the Heart, with Sally Field, where people appear in the church at Communion. Communion is a portal of heaven to earth, the communion of saints. For many people the internet offers passage into the communion of saints. A large number of web sites appeal to the grieving in all sorts of ways. Part of their success would lie in normalizing the fact of grief. I am not the only one going through this; look at all of the people who share similar experiences. Human life also blooms with all sorts of different approaches to coping with loss. The sheer abundance gives us pause in thinking that a "one size fits all" approach should be the norm.

99) I Peter descent into hell-John Claypool writes: "God lives at the end of our ropes." Mostly due to my neglect of providing different affirmations of faith, we recited the Apostles' Creed in the two churches I served. Sometimes people express disquiet about the descent into hell; some because it is a vulgar word, others are sincerely confused by the whole notion. I remember one man disliking it as he was afraid that people in hell would now be forgiven, instead of receiving condign punishments for eternity. He took hell to mean the place of eternal punishment, not the place of the dead. Ancient church writers pictured the descent into hell as the "harrowing of hell." The picture would be to go to the very 'gates" of

death, and there to open the gates. Think of the story of Heracles. Our youngest daughter remembers vividly how the Disney movie Hercules had him go into Hades to rescue a loved one. She was upset by the visage of all those lost people swirling about. Some significant time and effort has been exacted on this little phrase. (Barth, von Balthasar, Lauber, Lewis) Reformers made a noteworthy move when they saw the descent into hell beginning at Gethsemane. In other words, they saw hell as separation from God, and that process of suffering began for Jesus in the Garden all the way through his cry from the cross from Ps. 22, "my God, my God, why have you forsaken me.?" Others ask if something happened on Holy Saturday, the time of being buried. For me, it means nothing less than Jesus Christ undergoing the tragedy of the human experience all the way to the grave. Not even death is too big an obstacle for the love of God to face. One can see some interesting change s in artwork with this theme. In some, Jesus is taking Adam by the hand and guiding him, with a train of others, out of the mouth of the abode of death, while devilish figures are crushed by the sight. Death's hold on life will not get the last word. Death is facing its own demise.

100) John 11- Jesus does not hasten to the side of his ill friend, Lazarus. At times, the gospel of John presents Jesus as a mystical figure who seems to ride above the concerns of mere mortals. Then, as we are amazed at the sheer self-possession of Jesus, John then breaks into a description of a Jesus who definitely knows and exhibits his emotional side. Timing may not be everything, but it is important. Few things give us a list for the endless 'what if" litany more than timing, especially with accidents. Then, we even start to blame ourselves as the arbiters of timing. Accidents stand powerfully against the idea that the Gentle God directs every discrete action as if we are puppets. Lately, we seem to want people to move through grief with incredible speed. We schedule funeral time to be shorter and shorter so we don't miss work. I know a man whose spouse was mystified that he grieved the death of his younger brother into a second month. The guilt and "if only" quality of decisions came to Jesus forcefully. Both Martha and Mary use the same phrase, "if

you had been here, my brother would not have died." They say my brother, not your friend. Now there could be no question that Lazarus was dead and gone into the grave for a number of days. I really don't know if we can find the right time to say some things. Could that be part of the reason Jesus seems to be unhurried even when he arrives to not rush to the tomb but to spend time with the sisters? Roberta Bondi in <u>Memories of God</u> (43-4) notes that Jesus values these women and does not criticize them when they share their feelings, their consternation and confusion, with him. In <u>Encounters With Jesus</u>, Frances Taylor Gench says simply (87) "Death...does not break the bond of the believer and God." Granted we have windows of opportunity when someone is ready and capable of hearing and doing certain things. There may well be times when it is never the right time to say something. Timing does pervade this story, for it is an introduction to the death and resurrection of Jesus. Indeed, the very raising of Lazarus is a death warrant (11:53). Given the timing issue, it is good to note that this passage on eternal life of course applies to eternal life in a new dimension. This passage cannot be left to funerals alone, however. John is insistent that eternal life is a present reality for us in the here and now, a gift that places our lives within the very life of the Eternal One. This may be the right time to say that even in grief; we live in the fullness of eternal life at this moment. We do not have to wait for fullness of life to return only when we are reunited with our loved ones after death. When Lazarus emerges as a moving mummy, Jesus tells those who are gathered to "unbind him and let him go" (v.44). In our time we can turn this phrase just a bit. We can be sorely tempted to entomb ourselves and our future with our loved ones. We get wrapped up in their burial cloths. We find ourselves unable to let go. Here the words of Jesus echo in side: let him go.

101) Mary and Pentecost (Acts 2) - Mary bore Jesus, was witness to the crucifixion, and now is present at the birth of church at Pentecost. She goes full circle. The same Spirit who overshadowed her for the conception of Jesus appears again with a fire over her head too, with the unpredictable fresh breeze of

the spirit blowing through another room. Even Mary seemed to need to be with the people with whom Jesus spent the time of his mission. One of the reasons for the disciples being together was their grief at the loss of Jesus. Even with Easter appearances, the ascension signals the end of those appearances. Pentecost is fifty days after Passover (the root of the Greek name, after all). Fifty days was not a lot of time for the disciples, and the mother of Jesus, to come to grips with his death, his resurrection, and then a subsequent ascension. Catholics hold to the article of faith that she was assumed into heaven. We call the Spirit the Comforter, the Advocate, the Helper. All these are versions of the Greek, paraclete. (When I was a kid, I heard this as parakeet and wondered if the dove was a fat version of one). Much, much later, in seminary, would I learn that the Paraclete is straight Greek, meaning one called in along side. We say that God's own self, is called alongside us to stand beside us to help, to console, to pray, to plead, to advocate for our situation. In the midst of troubles, God is on our side, or as Paul says God say Amen, Yes to us. Upon reflection, Pentecost is a festival day that tells us that we can go on with our lives after the terrible wound of death. The Spirit does enliven us to move on, to move forward with our lives, even in the face of loss. Peter's speech flies on the wings of the dove whose gift of understanding binds all the different languages together. this story is Babel's opposite. There language was confused. Here at Pentecost, different people hear one language spoken as their own, a prelude to the UN translators. In some ways, one's grief is unique. In other ways, it does cross cultural boundaries. In the old anti war film "Hearts and Minds" one of the American military says something to the effect that the Vietnamese do not know grief as do Westerners. The next cut is that of a wailing mother, and no one doubted they were a witness to grief. All of us love, so all of us grieve. Cultures may differ on the mechanism, but can we judgethe propriety of the methods of others?

102) John 19 -Many of us know the squeeze of being in the generational sandwich of caring for children and also taking on some responsibility for our parents as they start to decline. In the

prologue to John's gospel, the Word, is the logos, God's plan, vision, divine logic that enters into the human condition. Mary's womb is the dwelling place for that divine descent. Now she sees her adult son lifted up, not in ascension but on a cross. At Cana Jesus spoke to her of his hour, and now that hour comes in awful form. "Woman, behold your son." Let's get one objection over with at the start. Some folks object to the designation, woman, as disrespectful. Maybe in our culture, it sounds so, but not 2,000 years ago. Here it should read as ma'am, or dear woman, as the NIV has it. Jesus lives out the command to honor our parents even in extremis. He knows that Mary's needs won't end after his death. The words though, woman, behold your son could apply to Jesus as well. I always wonder if the words of the angel, the shepherds, and Anna and Simeon in the birth narratives came to her mind in those terrible hours. Death does not stop the everyday matters of carrying on a legacy to provide for those left behind. It could be an insurance policy or a testament of devotion and expectations and hopes for those we leave behind, who survive. Even in the death throes of the cross, Jesus is concerned for his mother. He does not want her to be alone. Even at the cross, Jesus reaches out toward us as well, even with the hands nailed to the beam. Jesus creates a little church for Mary and the beloved disciple. To say that life goes on is more than a mere cliché. Mary and the disciple are made into a new family, as we see from her being cared for into his own home. Beyond death, Jesus wanted his mother to be with others and to be cared for, if need be. As Jesus prepares to exit the stage, he opens the door for a new type of family, an inclusive one. Artistic visions of this scene, not surprisingly place stress on different elements of the basic scene. As a spiritual exercise, examine, with some care, different portrayals of the Pieta and the preparation of the body of Jesus for burial. What captures your attention? What captures your heart?

103)Is. 25:6-10 Spiritual banquets and resurrection-The Bible reaches for banquet imagery to get at a sense of a better future. Babette's Feast is a wonderful evocation of a banquet turning into a feast of reconciliation. In the movie a woman who has worked for sisters in an old pietist sect of their father hits the lottery. She spends it on a feast. As the feast continues, old memories surface and old wounds are healed. One of the nicest things a church can do is to put on what we called a "mercy lunch" for the family and friends after the funeral. Often comfort food, especially great desserts, is featured. Even seeing some green jello salad takes us back to remembering someone when we were young and served the same food. In Mt. 14:13-21, Jesus creates a banquet in the wilderness for hungry people. I find it noteworthy that he offers this feast after trying to get by himself to mourn the death of John the Baptist. So, in its way, the feeding of the multitude was a wake. In our time, we are placing a lot of stress on laughter at memorial services. My preference is not to forbid laughter at a funeral, but I do like the idea of lots of laughter at a wake, maybe lubricated by some drinks. Laughter gets mixed with tears in the wake after the funeral, where loads of food and drink would appear as if by magic at the home of the deceased. I wonder if we could use the slide shows that have become popular in funeral homes and then convert those into ways of telling stories about the deceased, yes even tales that grow with the tellings, in our commemorative dinners. I've been to a few rehearsal dinners before a wedding where baby pictures are used to speak of the bride and groom before their new life together. Maybe we could do something similar for the deceased as a new dimension of their existence has begun. Perhaps we could have a special dinner to honor them on their birthday or the day of their death. Come to think of it, another reason for a banquet was to honor achievements, such at an athletic or scholarship banquet for high school students. The generosity of a banquet, the sense of cups running over, the sheer abundance lends itself rather easily to the spiritual abundance of love, generosity, fellow feeling and other vitalizing virtues. Our passage from Isaiah may draw from the where leaders had a feast on Mt. Sinai, but now everybody is invited to a feast on Mt. Zion. As Patricia Tull notes in her Isaiah commentary (384) God plans the menu, and the party is so good that mourning clothes are forgotten. What do you see as virtues and vices that enable one to journey through grief?

104) communal grief -At times we struggle with communal grief in the face of a local or national tragedy. Some of the psalms provide prayers for national, public loss as well as our individual griefs. When I was little, I remember the TV as a national funeral home after the assassination of JFK. With the proliferation of channels, I don't know if it holds as much power as it once did as a national gathering place. For younger people a locus of grief would be the Challenger disaster or the shooting at Columbine, Colorado. I suppose 9/11 is the equivalent of Pearl Harbor for the WWII generation. I was on my way to teach a class on Psalms for a local school, and the news get getting worse on the radio. So we worked with Psalms of communal concern and lament that morning. After 9/11, I found much of the national events sterile in comparison. No matter one's age, we see too much death on the news: from war, or famine, or pestilence. We have a difficult time trying to absorb the impact of so many losses, so we tend to seize on one or two in order to both personalize the loss and make it comprehensible. To a lesser degree, many of us were saddened to hear of the deaths of two bandmates of Bruce Springsteen, Danny Federici to cancer and Clarence Clemons to a stroke. With the rise of mass media, these people occupy a place in our lives. As i was driving into church this morning, I heard strains of a hymn from the Oslo Cathedral as a nation tries to come to grips with an assault on the city center and then a horrific bloodbath at a youth camp. Years ago, I had the privilege of getting to be present for a presentation by the writer Elie Wiesel. You look at him, and it seems he carries the burden of history on him, as he carries the mantle of being a voice for those millions killed in the Holocaust. His expression and manner of speaking seem so careworn. In his novel Night, the great question is asked, "where is God?" The reply in the novel is "here on the gallows with us." As I was going through this section, I caught glimpses of a huge memorial service for Penn State Football Coach Joe Paterno. Alumni and fans drove for miles in the winter to be able to share their sense of loss and admiration for him and his lifetime of work. That religious sense of being utterly lost is captured in Lamentations (2:9) mourning that they can find no Torah. Torah means law or teaching. The first five books of the bible are also called Torah and read in services. My

sense of the passage is that religion is not present, not being taught, another devastating loss of culture and its transmission.

105) Jer.6:16 the movie Cast Away ends with the Tom Hanks character at a crossroad. A crossroad can be a paralyzing moment if we don't have a good sense of which road to take. No direction beckons us; no path seems appropriate for our travels. We may well feel lost. We can't find our location on the map, as no GPS system can plumb the confusion and fear that may accompany a fateful decision. Even small decisions seem overwhelming. As the Allman Brothers song, Melissa, goes: "crossroads, will you ever let him go?" (Gregg Allman's memoir has some insightful comments on his dealing with death, or not, as a young man). At different points in the grief process we do come to some decision points. we think of the future of the "road not taken." Of course we can turn back from a decision, and grief can even be pictured as a series of detours and switchbacks. Deep inside we know that if continue down a certain path, it will mean some long-term trouble. We may well try to avoid being at crossroad points in order to keep pushing decision points down the road. Sometimes it take a while for us to recover the courage to choose. Finding the ability to make some plans is a sign of health as we move through grief. It may be wise to lower crossroad expectations. Instead of imagining one decision to be perfect and the others bad, we can move to the axiom of President Clinton that we cannot let the "best become the enemy of the good." We can continue to try to turn back, to retrace our steps, to find our way back to the past. We can make a decision to chart a route to a new future. Time does suffer a rupture in loss. Our mental construct of our imagined future is ineradicably changed. Yet, that rupture allows time's flow to move in different channels. Early after a loss, I am uneasy about people making crossroads decisions. As the mind clears, we find more and more avenues for decision. Some of the directions we choose are not easily to make u-turns. Lately, a spate of interest has centered on religious discernment as a tool for decision making. When we come to a crossroads, we can use our normal aids to decisions but integrate them with religious tools and models. In religious

circles, discernment has become a watchword for decision. Please consider employing its methods when you face an important decision.

106) Nehemiah rebuilds (1-6) - He mourned that the ruins of Jerusalem had been left to decay. He is a colonial administrator in ruling Persia. He was personally as secure as one could be, but the old homeland was struggling so, especially its old capital. A major task of grieving is starting to rebuild a life in the face of loss. In time, that could well be the major task in undergoing grief, the reconstruction of a life in the face of loss of a life. I do note that he built the walls, the defenses of the city. He sees the city as needing the basic structure of walls, as we would speak of infrastructure today. I imagine him seeing a desolated, only partially rebuilt city. My mind goes to the devastated rust belt cities of decaying factory sites and streets strewn with broken glass. Loss has a way of battering our best defenses. While need of course to be open to the world, no boundary, no defense leaves us too vulnerable, too subject to attack. Rebuilding takes work and effort. we may have to learn all sorts of new skills within new roles. What will become the "new normal?" Like the people in Haggai, we may be disappointed at what the rebuilding accomplishes. Our old structure of life seemed so good, so right, so impervious. Rebuilding often encounters many obstacles, as in Nehemiah. the obstacles can emerge from within or without. The well-meaning and the malign can both prove problematic in our rebuilding. That is one of the great task of grief work, rebuilding a life. No one has the right to ask us to put our lives on hold forever. Even the marriage vows speak of 'til death parts us." Roger Rosenblatt looks at the difficult work of rebuilding in his memoir, <u>Making Toast.</u> Their daughter, a physician, dies of an undiagnosed heart ailment, and he and his wife move to help their son-in-law raise their three young children. Part of what constitutes family is knowing basics: how do you like your toast and who makes it. Rebuilding a life will include some major decisions. It also is the accretion of small decisions that give life its texture and balance. I often mark the passage of time for those who have suffered a loss when the casseroles stop coming

in, when doughnuts aren't being dropped off for breakfast. It starts to be the time to make one's own toast for breakfast. It's an alarm clock for the time to make one's own toast for breakfast.

107) Ezek.37 -Catch me in a despondent mood, and I may well look at history as a 'vast slaughter bench" a giant bone yard, especially with the seas of blood of the unlamented 20th Century. Ezekiel is given a vision of death. Not a sign of life is given, only a vast array of bones bleaching in the desert sun. Can these bones live? No, they are the very symbol of bleached death, a skeleton of structure without the breath of life. A Christian answers, yes. While it is directed to the nation, we could turn the unit to individual lives without too much damage to the text. Many Christians read this with an Easter set of glasses, anyway. Dry bones are not the sum and substance of human life. The old song, 'Dem Bones isn't in our hymnbook, but I've croaked it out for the children in church more than once. For Christians, resurrection is not resuscitation. It is a new creation. My sense is that the creator from nothing or chaos is certainly capable of bringing out new life from this old world. Can these dry bones live? Yes, only by the power of the Creator of life, the One who seems to be interested primarily in the promulgation of life, new life. In the Bible, the word for spirit is the same as breath or wind. Here, just as the breath or spirit of life enters the craft of constructing Adam and Eve, the spirit of life is necessary to create, or re-create, a living being. As in the stately Gen. 1, the creation is an orderly one, a step by step process of moving from death to life. The Creator of life will not be deterred by the presence of death. Only God could take the very symbol of death, dry bones, and make them the basis for restored life, new life. Death can threaten to dry out our lives too, to make our interior and exterior life a desert. A sense of dry bones in the interior landscape does not have to remain permanent.

108) Is.58:12 and the breach-Loss may crumble our defenses, the walls we erect to protect us. In castles, when the walls are breached, the battle does not go well. A fearsome word is the announcement of a breach in the hull of a ship. I don't know if we can ever say that the hole in our hearts ever fully heals. Scars may well remain, and new defense are erected. Not only do walls defend us from the outside, they also serve to keep things inside. I doubt that grief is ever fully healed. The breach caused by death is a permanent one. It can be repaired brick by brick, I suppose, so maybe it would be better to say that a soft spot remains in our defenses over the years. In some support groups, the members refer to those without a recent loss as civilians, as if they are a corps of battle-weary veterans who cannot hope to communicate with those outside the group. Loss does mark a permanent break in the smooth lines of our life's narrative. It may well require a bridge to "a whole new life" as the late Reynolds Price would say. Frank, in The Wounded Story Teller, speaks of narrative wreckage as the breaks in the clean lines of one's life story and direction and coherence into the future. In its way dealing with grief is throwing a bridge over the chasm that allows us to walk from before to after without being consumed by the chasm. The Judds had a hit song, "Love Will Build a Bridge." One of the most moving Simon and Garfunkel songs is "Bridge Over Troubled Water." We need something to close the gulf.

Nehemiah's story is about fixing the breach in the walls of Jerusalem. James Farwell in "This is the Night," a meditation on the closing of Lent, writes: "God is not absent from suffering, but God works even through suffering We are attentive to suffering as God is at work precisely there" (121). In its way, the church honors grief and anticipatory grief, for that matter, in the entire season of Lent. Note that even here we get a break, as the Sundays do not count as the forty days of Lent. At the same time, it has the sense of preparing a garden, as Lent comes from older English in terms of the springtime. Robert Schuller, the well-known churchman of the Crystal Cathedral, wrote to President Clinton that this could be a passage for his administration. In his next nomination, he spoke often of a bridge to the 21st century, to span the mental chasm separating one century, one pattern of perception, and another. For you, what breaches remain, and where do you see signs of mending the breach?

109) John 14: We can translate the paraclete, the Spirit, as advocate/counsellor/helper. In Greek, it means one who is called alongside someone, standing with someone in trouble. I come at it in the way an attorney is a counsellor, an advocate, a friend, a representative. In particular, I think of how Thomas Shafer of Notre Dame's Law School viewed the vocation of the attorney as friend to the client, the one person who could be counted on to look out for the welfare of the client. It gives a personal dimension to the work of God. I am drawn to the notion of God standing alongside of us as an ally, a friend. Think of the gospel hymn, What a Friend. The work of the paraclete can also come in the form of a family member, a friend, a therapist, clergy or other folks who offer help, who stand with us, who can be counted on for a listening ear over time. One of the fruits of the spirit is gentleness. We do well to be gentle toward ourselves. For me, this is a most attractive image of God. God takes our side; God stands up for us; God looks out for us. I must admit that the idea of God as one's lawyer strikes me as funny. I've seen God is my co-pilot bumper stickers, but I don't I have seen God is my attorney T-shirts. It may be noteworthy that Jesus promises this divine helper only after Jesus leaves the scene. In John's gospel, that means to ascend back to the source. So, as the Counsellor continues the work of Jesus on being on our side, we are given this continuing gift. The Paraclete is another advocate in this gospel, an extension in time and space of the work of Jesus, therefore the work of the Sending One. We need that helper. As Edna St, Vincent Milay told us in Time does Not Bring Relief, we are caught in a vise. We don't want to go to a thousand places since they bring back too many memories but then we resent going to places that hold no memories of the loved one. Throughout the Farewell Speeches of Jon 14-17 we get a sense of time that has become unstable to us, but may give us a glimpse to time as divinely experienced. Time engages past, present, and future fluidly here. When is time a burden to you? When does it

flow smoothly? When do you find it difficult to live in the moment?

110) Is. 11:11 Remnant- God works with the small as well as the large. Eight people were the remnant of the human race in the story of the ark. (By the way, many baptismal fonts are eight-sided to pick up that image). Moses was saved in a basket, a little ark on the Nile. Even when the nation was on its knees, God worked with a remnant, a sapling, a branch, just enough to let a new beginning take root. The Great Builder does not give up easily. Even if it appears that a tree has been cut down and gone, the roots may work to help establish new life in the midst of destruction. God has the patience of eternity. We see it in the parable of giving a fig tree some more time to be fruitful (Lk.13:5-9). The power of the image such as a shoot from a stump is that what appears dead or useless is still a factor for promoting new life. Advent is the time in the church year where we are reminded that new life can emerge, as in Is. 11:1-10. Things may seem dry and barren, but life is resilient and persistent. Even though things may feel empty inside, there is a spark of life that will ignite again. A little is plenty when it comes to life, new life. Even if it seems that part of you died with a loved one, a spark, a glimmer of light and life persists. Given time and care, it will shine again, perhaps in different colors, perhaps not so brightly, but it will shine again. Resilience is such a vital virtue. To me, it is the ability to bounce back, so it requires some flexibility, not the rigidity than can snap. We place some flex in long bridges, otherwise they could not stand the strain. Years ago, E.F. Schumacher had a popular book, Small Is Beautiful. God respects scale. The Great Gardener patiently works with the materials at hand. Bit by bit, day by day, renewal can and does occur. In a similar way, God is not deterred if you feel as if your life is but a remnant of its former grace in the face of death. God can work with the mustard seed, the acorn and watch them grow and flourish. The kingdom of heaven (Mt. 13:3) is compared to a small seed growing up to be a shrub, not a redwood, a shrub.

111) Jesus wept. (John 11:35 could also be Jesus began to weep). When our youngest daughter felt burdened by having to memorize a Bible verse, I mentioned this one, and she was delighted by a two-word verse.(If I recall correctly, she discovered some verses in Chronicles that had but a few names). This is such a striking sentence, so I am glad that it is set off in a two word verse. What elicited those tears? Was it grief for Lazarus? Was it being cut to the quick by the identical charges by Martha and Mary, "if you had been here, my brother would not have died?" Were his tears in concert with their tears? Did the sight of all those mourning his friend move him to tears? Some say those tears are a sign of the humanity of Jesus, indeed I just heard this in a discussion on Christology and the Presbyterian confessions in an evening workshop. I agree, but I wonder if they are more a sign of the divine "nature" of Jesus Christ as well. We read that Jesus was greatly disturbed in spirit and deeply moved." (embrimaomai and tarasso). One could also say angered, agitated, indignant (Gench, Encounters:88). She goes further to wonder if this is John's version of the struggle at Gethsemane. At what would Jesus be so disturbed? Perhaps it could be the sheer toll of death on the lives its cold hand touches. The sheer amount of human suffering may have stirred up Jesus. It could be an effort at self-control in the face of the death of his friend and the grief of the sisters. Maybe he reflected on previous losses in his own young life. He may be afflicted with many of the "if only" times in life. He had so much healing left to do, so many gifts of life to offer, but now death was threatening to swallow that all up for him. Jesus wept, so why are we bound and determined to forbid it at funerals? Jesus wept, so why is someone doing well if they don't cry. Jesus wept, so why can't males cry more easily in our culture, even as it has changed noticeably already? In our time, I can just hear people saying how hard Jesus was taking the loss of his friend, since he shed tears. I can hear the advice pouring in that he shouldn't cry, as Lazarus was released from illness, that he should celebrate the life of Lazarus, that he was upsetting the other people there.

112) Mark and Matthew have Jesus "moved by compassion or pity." The verb is a strong one that could mean that Jesus is torn up inside (splagchnizomai). I prefer the term gut wrenching. The opposite would be to be unmoved. Brian Blount, now the president of Union Seminary in Virginia, sees it as being moved toward action, not mere sympathy, so moved to compassion could be a better version. In Mark 1:41 Jesus is moved by the plight of a single leper. In Matthew, he is moved by the felt needs of a large crowd. When Jesus saw pain, he reacted with healing. He did not blame the victim; he did not bewail large social forces, he was moved to work on the illness. Jesus used the moment as a call to action, not emphasizing the presence of the feeling and meditating on it. That charged a feeling, that impetus to help is evoked by the presence of suffering, whether it is an individual issue or it is heightened by social indifference or social activity that harms people. In my view, Jesus continues to be moved by compassion. What we go through continues to tear Jesus up, I think. That includes compassion for the grieving. Jesus experienced human turmoil. Jesus was not above emotionally charged responses to human need, human pain. Again, I am unwilling to consign this reaction or response to the realm of human solidarity alone. How is this not a divine reaction as well? For here we see a divine response to suffering as well. Jesus continues to reach out to the hurting with healing. Of course, they could be tears of joy as he was anticipating the great gift of life for Lazarus and his family. Some would say that being so affected highlights the human in Jesus. I would agree, but could it not just as well highlight the divine within him? It is difficult for me to grasp divinity somehow above or removed from us. Patrick Miller (Interpreting the Psalms:110) writes that "God is at cross purposes with suffering."

113) still small voice-I Kings 19- In Ps. 29 God's voice thunders over the heavenly court and all of nature. Sometimes we look for internal miracles, a great epiphany that will sweep our doubts away. Instead, Elijah found God not in theophany but in a sound of sheer silence, or what other translations term a still, small voice. Elijah here is on the run from a regal death sentence. He

has been on the road for days and days. Now he reaches the place of revelation, the mountain of divine presence, the mountain of the Ten Commandments, the very place where the traditions associated with the awesome presence of God seem to originate in Scripture. He receives a panoply of divine power, but after this comes a "fine silence," a still small voice as it has been termed. I picture Elijah at the end of his rope. With all of the noise we cover ourselves in, we may well drown out that voice. Silence can be uncomfortable. We may prefer to hear noise than the still, small voice. Still, it is insistent. Sometimes it is in the quiet moments that we most clearly hear the gentle leadings of God, the Speaker even in silence. Sometimes we fear the quiet moments for what we may hear or find illumined. Sometimes that still small voice pushes us where we do not wish to go. Sometimes it illumines a dark portion of our self that had become lost to us. we live surrounded by sound and noise. We can't sleep if it is too quiet. All of that input may well be "multi-taskng" but I wonder if it is a way of keeping thoughts at bay, of not permitting space for them to form and grow. When we played our music too loudly, our mother would yell, "I can't hear myself think." When I was a boy we were taught "prayer is talking and listening to God." It takes practice and some effort to quiet oneself enough to hear the often faint stirrings of the divine whisper. Part of our resistance may well lie in what we do not wish to hear but suspect that we may hear those very things. With all of our defenses up, maybe we are afraid of having some secret part of ourselves exposed. It strikes me that a defense against some untoward feelings toward God could be an inability or unwillingness to pray. I am confident that the gracious God in Jesus Christ would not begrudge us a desert period, a cooling off period without prayer. The door is always open in heaven to our communications. Like a good friend, God is happy to pick up just where we left off.

114) I Kings 18 We are proud of our children. We may even live vicariously through their accomplishments. No matter what, they are family, even or especially when they disappoint us. No matter how much Absalom attacked David, no matter that he led a

rebellion and publicly shamed him, David still loves him. The private needs of the father outran the public needs of the king. Part of David surely realizes that his refusal to discipline his adult children lay at the root of some of the trouble. Our relations with our children have complications always. We go through chapters with them, but are responsible for them. Each stage of development calls us to renegotiate our relationship. That process does not stop when they become adults. Our college-aged daughter is more sensitive to perceived boundary violations than is her college graduate sister. Grief does become more complicated when we had a complicated relationship, even a broken relationship with a family member. A parent feels the failure of an offspring gone wrong. I think of James Cagney talking to his mother in The Public Enemy. It takes an extraordinary compassion to be like Sister Helen Prejean accompanying people on death row, as portrayed in Dead Man Walking. "If only" questions rise up as accusers against us. In part, David could not bear the guilt of his own parenting. in part, he truly would rather die than to see his son die. Parents will say that as they have had a chance to live a full life, compared to the age of their children, at any age of their children, infant through adulthood. I hear God repeating the words, "my son, my son" at the crucifixion. What a terribly foreshortened life to die so cruelly on top of it. To grasp at meaning for that death we conclude that Jesus was some sort of atonement offering for all of us rebellious Absaloms against God the parent, his own a Davidic messiah. Guilt haunts many of us. Gordon Kaufman (Systematic Theology:241) wrote on forgiveness as the antidote to guilt: "guilt clings like the bloody spots on lady Macbeth's hands. No rationalization can destroy it...A barrier is set up which cannot be overcome-except by the offended one's forgiveness.

115) David and Amnon-complicated grief (II Samuel 13-16). I have seen figures that grief processes can get stuck and do not have much improvement for a long, long time in perhaps 10-20% of cases. A 2008 article in Psychology Today brought out evidence that the neural circuitry in complicated grief shows that their reward centers flash on, as if they are still expecting to see

the loved one appear before them again. They have been unable to integrate the loss. Family relations are often strained beyond the breaking point. Faulkner used the Biblical story of David and his family as a base for <u>Absalom, Absalom</u>. Amnon rapes his half-sister Tamar. Absalom takes her, his sister, in. Her brother Absalom murders Amnon in plotted revenge and David does little to punish either terrible act. Absalom acts out in revenge as he see the complicated grief of his sister. David may be a great public figure, but he is a poor father. Absalom took on the role of the avenging angel of justice. When we feel justice is denied, it increases the desire for private vengeance. That is probably where the germ of the idea to then take over the kingdom of his father began to sprout. Sometimes our grief is complicated by difficult relations or the lack of relationship. The long parade if only...starts up and the number continues to climb.Then death takes away a chance at restoration of them. Complicated grief takes long to process and may never be fully integrated into one's memories and life. At this point, you may start to wonder if you are enduring complicated grieving, as all grief has its complications. Check with a counsellor, but intense grief that lasts for years could well be an indicator of it.

116) Lamech in the early, primeval Genesis (4:23-4) accounts is hurt and angry. Lamech wants revenge. Notice he is not proportionate in his rage, as he seems to be bragging about taking life. God had protected his ancestor Cain by promising a sign of protection and a promise that the divine hand would avenge his death sevenfold (Gen. 4:15-16).In the end, even an eye for an eye does not seem suitable for our rage. We want more. If we follow Lamech's goal, we soon realize that it still doesn't seem to be enough. No matter how much revenge, the scales still don't seem balanced. The injunction of Jesus is to forgive seventy seven times (or 70 times 7 times). I have a sense that Jesus is using the number involved in Lamech as the base to answer his students question if they could possibly be expected to forgive more than the religious standard of up to three times by drawing on Amos 1. Notice also that the primeval history connects technology and the arts with the children of Cain, that

they are somehow involved with violence perhaps. While Abel was a victim and Cain tries to hide from crime as did his parents, Lamech seems to be an extension of Cain's violence. The issue of letting go is at the heart of the Greek word for forgiving, to not hold on to something. Forgiveness is an issue in grief. In some instances we are motivated by revenge in the face of death. It is better to acknowledge the feeling. It is then wise not to act on it. When we start to shout for justice to be done, we usually mean punishment. It is not good to put the plan into motion. As with cursing psalms, we do well to place those feelings into the protective cocoon of prayer. Sometimes we are told to rush to forgiveness. That is a worthy aspiration at times. Forgiveness may well take some time. It may well be discovered within, pure gift, more than making a determination for it. Lamech sought revenge sevenfold. The truth is that revenge feeds on more. Nothing seems enough. No amount of revenge seems to get at the gnawing sense of injustice and pain. Mario Cuomo was angered by questions about the death penalty that made it personal instead of social. His response was that of course he would want revenge. As a public official he was called ot a higher standard than his personal desire for revenge. Even if revenge is achieved, it still feels cold, and the same gnawing ache returns without surcease. Indeed, revenge adds weight to our loss and may make it harder to bring into our more fruitful way of dealing with loss and pain. Revenge may well not bring the sense of finality we seek, but instead it can leave our wound fresh and open. Even if we can make someone suffer the way we have suffered, what have we done but add to the pain of the world? We may ask ourselves if our loved one would want us to act this way. It seems to me that we give voice to our conscience, to the best part of ourselves, through them. "Be angry but do not sin" says Ps. 4:4. That may take a lifetime to learn.

117) Is.43:19, 42:9,48:6- I have long been intrigued by these passages. "Behold I do a new thing/now it springs forth/do you not perceive it?" This is related to the words of Revelation,

"behold I make all things new." When we get down, we look and see the same old things, or as Ecclesiastes said, "nothing new under the sun." In grief, one day often blends into another murky day too easily. In the midst of that terrible sameness, God is at work. Remember not the former things (43:18) is an imperative that directly precedes our first citation in this long prophetic book. Perhaps, we need to be able to forget, to let some of the past go in order to be able to spot the new in our midst. Life does combine opposites. Maybe we could interpret it as what to hold on to and where and when we need to let go. Indeed that is one of the major tasks of grief: to learn which to do. I do want to be careful not to merely celebrate the new. New ideas, new methods are not better just because they are new. Perhaps one of the great examples of automatic, unreflective thoughts would be the notion that new means better, or that old means outmoded or somehow worse or less. When I was a child, it seemed every advertisement blared "new and improved." It may take some time to adjust to the "shock of the new." Alvin Toffler made a career as a futurist on the basis of his work, Future Shock. In my lifetime, I have seen so many management fads capture attention, only to be discarded with next month's trash. When should we embrace the new? Recently, the rush of change is examin in Present Shock. Sometimes the new has a bitter taste, because it is in the absence of a loved one. Even in the old pain of grief, God is at work on a new thing. God is not chained to the past. Already, your revised self is emerging from the ashes. We crave a time when the new thing will be the old pattern of death being put down. We do not have to be in a rut. We do not have to remain caught in a vise or a trap. Have you yet perceived any stirrings of the new? Where would you like to see evidence of the new? Where and when is the new making you fearful?

118) Ps.116 has many touchpoints with the bereaved. The prayer is written in the aftermath of facing death. It faces the pangs of Sheol, the abode of the dead. I would think that the psalmist is grateful for being delivered from a near-fatal illness. We can extend it with its notion of death pangs to the bereaved fairly easily. Verse 3 has such vivid words: snares and pangs, distress

and anguish. It is a miracle that the psalmist can look back on it and can do so only as the prayers have been heard. In v. 8 we get three acts of kindness from the hand of God, perhaps separate, perhaps overlapping. To "deliver eyes from tears" gets at a plea for help as well as any Scriptural plea. Unable to stop the tears, the psalmist needs to be rescued from them. At some point we want to, need to stop crying. By and large, that is an internal monitor to be followed, not the advice of others made anxious and hurting for you in your tears. We move to "precious in the sight of the Lord is the death of his saints." This should not be read as a precious death, as if God prizes the death of his holy ones. Instead, God watches over the saints, that they are held close, precious. (The expression is found at Ps. 72: as well). As I am reviewing this piece, we just had a choral All Saints Day service at church. I love the idea that we can wrap our losses up in song and prayer in church. I love to see a knot of people be able to share their losses together through liturgy's words and movement when we are at a loss for words and what step to next take. James Limburg has pointed out that while this is an individual claim of praise within a communal context of the set of Psalms from 113-118, not everyone was "supportive" of the needs of the one praying. In that sense perhaps, "I shall walk before the Lord in the land of the living" is a declaration of defiance, as well as amazed awareness of where one could be in movement from the past.

119) Jer. 4:23-31 and the shaking of the foundations- I taught Bible classes to Commissioned Lay Pastor candidates in our denomination. Walter Breuggemann alerted me to this passage in an old VHS tape I used for them. A common apocalyptic image is the breaking up of the order of creation. In its way, nature reflects the inner turmoil of suffering ones. T.S. Eliot wrote of Webster who was haunted by death to the extent that he could notice the skull beneath the skin Few things shake our foundations, leave us in chaos, as does grief. Pick your image: upset the apple cart, turn everything upside down or topsy-turvy. Things that we just assumed would be just so, things we take for granted, vanish. What seemed so secure, so stable, so certain,

does not remain so. We take for granted that our loved ones will be with us. We can scarcely contemplate a future without them. They are part of the scene of our lives, as expected as the figures in a well known play or the Nativity scenes we set up every year. We may then realize that some of our belief system may well rest on shaky foundations. Even if we think we have the strength of our convictions, "all that is solid melts into air" as Marx said. It seems as if Jeremiah sees a retreat into the primordial chaos, or maybe the triumph of entropy. Moral chaos is met with natural chaos, so the form of creation itself disappears back to the ancient darkness, the void, where life does not exist, where all could be seen as desert waste. Sometimes the most we can do today is go through another minute. a number of people have mentioned the Anna Znalick song that advises us to "breathe, just breathe." (It is also what the Cinderella character tells herself in Ever After.) I think of the prayer by Teresa of Liseux (BCW:828) "just for today/what does it matter, O Lord, if the future is dark?/ to pray now for tomorrow /I am not able/keep my heart only for today/grant me your light/just for today." The little prayer of the Little Flower has great merit. Prayers can be formal and large-scale, or they can be small and intimate.

120) human/humic/humus-Gen.2- In the second creation account, we are decisively of the earth, well more than the earth, good soil. Adam's name is a place on soil, just as the human is related to the word humic. We are part of the natural order, and mortality is part of that order. Some see our souls as trapped within this mortal frame. I see us more as embodied souls. The life we know is experienced in this world, with our senses to a large degree. Part of that would be our reliance on the sense. We can use them to help find some measure of calm and serenity. We can use them to evoke memories, if we care to, as did Proust famously smelling the madeleines. Sometimes our senses will take us to another place in memory. Humility comes from the same root. Death humbles us, but it need not humiliate us. Humility is the virtue traditionally to counter pride, but so could the virtue of care. What I mean is that we have limits, none more so than death. Learning to accept that is part of wisdom, I think.

Humility has the sense to know that if we try to fly to the sun, we will fall like Icarus. When our reach exceeds our grasp, we set ourselves up for disappointment. The threat of the primeval chapters of Gen.1-11 often touch on this theme of transgressing the limits of the human, the Fall or the tower reaching God at its end. Part of divinity's scope is immortality, and that is the boundary we resent in our limitations. We may dream of being ungrounded, of somehow rising above the cycle of nature. Even if we consider ourselves the apex of evolution's production, we are not disengaged from nature. We can still be felled by a microbe. So then, we "farmers" return to the farmland, return to our origins. Ash Wednesday is an excellent reminder of our mortality. Its ashes are a mark of humility. No one escapes mortality.

121) John 11- I always like the KJV of Martha's response when Jesus wants the tomb opened, "it stinketh." Lazarus is dead and buried and decaying. Part of me sees cremation as merely accelerating the natural process of decay, but it is a less repulsive sense of decay than the grave, certainly. I have heard people use words such as "cleaner," more antiseptic. I'm of two minds on cremation. Part of me sees it as trying to shield ourselves from the painful reality that the body does decay. The same goes for our concern about placing the casket in a watertight vault. I asked a funeral director recently if they provide an opportunity for the family to attend the body on its way to being cremated and he looked at me as if I were crazy. Thomas Lynch, the poet and funeral director, thinks otherwise, about attending a cremation if not my mental state. I've noticed that cremation usually is tied with a shorter period of visiting at the funeral home or church. Cremation often does not have a service connected to it at all. Learning to say goodbye is a basic component of grief.

I am so impressed with the ritual flair people devise when they consider placing the ashes: from skiing downhill in the Rockies to diving in the ocean to skydiving with them. The Presbyterian book of Common Worship has prayers designed to notice cremated remains instead of a body. Some worry that cremation could get in the way of the full or complete resurrection of the body. It seems to me that the Creator of the universe would not be deterred from a speedier return of a body to its natural elements. I have not heard similar fears about people blown to bit in accidents or in war. Even when someone is gone, they seem alive in the machine world of data files. Jean Nordhaus in Posthumous tells of how invitations for tropical vacations still seek us after we gone, at least through junk mail. The resurrection of the body may well assert that continuation of our bodily selves, much more than a body itself.

122) good death- A part of me immediately replies-no such thing as a good death. To some degree, we see a good death as sudden or quick. Others want a chance to say goodbye. Others see it as a release form pain or debility. Some of us would like to die suddenly in our sleep, but what about all of the things left undone or unsaid? Shakespeare in Measure for Measure writes: "'tis too horrible/the weariest and most loathed worldly life...is a paradise/to what we fear of death. "I have come to see some basic planning as part of a good death. Obviously, the pre-planning of the funeral takes immense burden from the family if they want to honor the wishes of their member. We certainly consider an extended period of physical suffering to be a most difficult one. Some of the struggles of the dying haunt us for quite some time. It is a holy opportunity to stand with the dying. In the end, I don't see the manner of death as some sort of sign from god judging the manner of a how a life was lived or reaching out to punish the living either. Have you thought about where you would like to die? Would you like to be by yourself or have people with you? Who would you like or not like with you? (I am now thinking of Tyrion's reply to the question in Game of Thrones).

123) Hosea 13:14 is a most difficult text to translate and interpret. It is hard to see if it is a threat or promise. Is compassion or revenge hidden from the eyes of God? Realizing this, I will choose to give positive spin to the material. Our passage could be looking toward the death of Death. In other

words, a question can be answered if God will rescue from the power of Death, and the answer is yes. Indeed God could be claiming that God's own self will plague the plague of death and destroy the place of destruction. It at least is imagining the death of death itself. It is one thing to portray death as the Grim Reaper, but this reminds us that death is triumphant in this world, with the exception of Easter. Easter hymns boldly sing of death being entombed but that is for the new age, the not yet of Christian hope and aspiration. Here and now, Death is a gleeful thief of life. In the last century Death's celebrations must have reached a maniacal intensity in the face of all of the blood spilled. Dread continues to be a real and potent force in life, and it rises up especially when we feel insignificant, confused, and somewhat powerless. In a hymn, God of Grace and God of Glory, we sing of "death of death and hell's destruction" Christians hold that the resurrection demonstrates that death is not and will not be ultimate. The final victory is in the future. We are engaged in hand to hand, street to street combat with death every day, and it is not acting like a defeated warrior signing surrender terms. Perhaps, it already knows that its power is limited, and one day, one fine day; it will no longer have a hold on God's world. At Easter we sing of "death of death and Hell's destruction." We sing of a brighter future

124) Ps. 25:17- Death does not respect holidays. We want the holiday season to be immune from trouble, but trouble comes. So Death stands at the ready to ruin the holidays. The pain of loss does seem heightened as we so want the holidays to be a reprieve from the troubles that come to all of us at one time or another. it seems to violate our sense of rightness for the holidays to have death intrude on them. It may be wise not to overdo for the holidays. If you have a meal together, put the loss into the prayer before the meal, but do not make it the sole part of the prayer. Bringing it out in the open can drain some of its potent threat from the gathering. It may be wise to admit openly that you miss someone and even have a brief ceremony or ritual to mark it. It could be as simple as a new ornament on a tree, a dish that they liked served at Thanksgiving, an Easter egg with

their name on it. Some folks make an empty place setting at the table. A toast to the absent strikes me as a good idea. At some point telling some stories or recalling stories they told is a good way to stay connected. To help deal with it, please consider doing something at which you excel to bolster your self-esteem. As I review this, we are approaching my, our, first Christmas since my mother's death. I've had a nagging suspicion that I am forgetting something, and then I realize that I am thinking that I have neglected to get her a present before Christmas. I am unusually late getting Christmas cards out this year, and I wonder if her loss has more than a bit behind it. For years, I planned when to visit for the holidays, and the need for that is gone. The girls and I made our last trip back to Pennsylvania for her funeral, during the Christmas holidays. So far, Christmas has an extra tinge of sadness served with the celebrations.

125) Gen. 6:3 cites violence as the critical problem with nature. It is the proof that creation has gone wrong. It drives God in the primeval story to want to wash over creation and start anew with a remnant of the old creation in the ark. Nature is "red in tooth and claw." It often lacks that calm of the falling leaf being integrated into the natural cycle of life. Some of us like the nature shows that show the color and pageantry of nature, and others like the gritty realism of the struggle for survival that does include death. As part of nature, we are also part of that constant struggle between survival and death. We have made enormous strides in creating the ark of medical science and public health measures. It allows us to ride atop the waves of illness that constantly assail us, the threat of internal violence to the order and harmony of our bodily processes. Surely illness does great violence to the workings of our bodies. Certainly accidents do violence to the integrity of a body. Most terribly, the violence of human beings, hand to hand or the mechanical processes of drones continue to afflict us. Violent death attacks our hopes and prayers for safety and security. Violence indeed violates the integrity of the body and the self. Violence and trauma are so intimately connected. By Gen.9:8-17 God has made a decision to make covenant with humanity, even though we are afflicted with

evil in our hearts. Despite our deep flaws, God will stick with us. God announces that the rainbow is a sign of peace, shalom, well-being not only with us but all flesh. Amy Plantinga Pauw, the theologian, wrote a piece for <u>Practicing the Faith</u> on dying well. She tells a remarkable story of a Latin American church where the names of those who died at the hands of violence and injustice are read aloud. With the roll call, people call out, present. for me, it was like reading a contemporary account of the book of revelation, where the congregants look past physical reality to connect with an unseen world beyond. It is a shout of opposition to violence, that violence does not erase the meaning of lives, or even their continuing presence in our lives.

126) Ec. 3:1-15   Henry Ward Beecher, the great 19th century preacher, wrote: "no grief has the right to immortality." T.S. Eliot in Murder in the Cathedral wrote: "in life there is not time to grieve long." Grief certainly alters our perspective on time itself. We figure that we have plenty of time in our banks, but now it has sprung a leak, and all of those precious sands pour from the hourglass. Suffering punctures our pretenses toward being self-sufficient, tough, and invulnerable. In part, our intense grief has a component of losing that teenaged sense of being invulnerable. We mourn the loss of an important illusion. In the faith death does not have the last word, but life does. So, unending, intense grief cannot be the goal for the living. It is a real, potent temptation to live one's life in unending grief. Perhaps we think it is a demonstration of the depth of our love. Perhaps prolonged grief is a way to try to relieve feelings of regrets that our relationship was not what it could of been, should have been. Perhaps we may inwardly surmise that our grief holds them alive for a while longer. I do agree that the hole in our heart never fully heals, does not disappear. It will always be triggered, at unexpected times, by a sight or memory. If mourning becomes a way of life, extended over years, then grief has our whole world in its hands, not God's. At the gym, the man next to me spoke about making a decision to start to go out a bit more after a year. The very impulse to do that is a sign of putting grief in its place as we go on living. It is no accident that we use the hourglass or a clock as a sign of the transient nature of life and of time itself.

Life is too short to be spent only grieving. We live in an instant culture, with an emphasis on quick decisions, quick results, even if we have minor resistance in things such as slow food v. fast food. In "Stones in the River" Carrie Newcomer wrote a song as a result of seeing a beloved ravine area clear cut, along with what she and her daughter termed the mother tree. In the immediacy of pain she demonstrates the maturity that we do what we can in our time here, but we may not see the fruits of our labor, even in our lifetime. That is a profound tension. We may be haunted by all of the incomplete, unfinished segments of life. On the other hand, we carry on, hand over, a legacy to others to enjoy. Newcomer spoke of planting lilac bushes everywhere she lived, even if she did not remain in the area for long. She likes to imagine someone opening a window one fine spring morning and being hit with the scent of lilac.

127) Heb. 5:7 Jesus offered up prayers with loud cries and tears. I usually associate this with Gethsemane but it certainly could be at other times as well. It could well be a sign of deep and sincere piety, of pouring out oneself to God in prayer. I would guess that many of those prayers issued from frustration at the sheer tragedy of the human condition itself, the sheer volume and weight of it pressing down around him. He would not heal everyone. Few things demonstrate the humanity of Jesus in a religious sense so much as this little line from Scripture. If Jesus could approach God with loud cries and tears, then we have religious authorization and permission to do so. Especially in Luke, Jesus goes off to a deserted place to pray, and that usually signals a turn in the narrative. Those times of prayer could be offered up with loud cries and tears as well. I have the Salman picture of Jesus in so many church rooms and halls in my mind of utter placidity. I also have the mental sense of Jesus in movies as being possessed of a Buddhist calm and serenity, so the citation from Hebrews captures attention. (That is one of the reasons the theologian Douglas John Hall mentions the movie, Jesus of Montreal, at times). A frustrated Jesus may well be worth some consideration. Frustration results when our goals are not being met in the time and manner we may wish. We often

place unrealistic expectations on ourselves about the duration and intensity of our grief. Jesus had so much to do in his life, his sojourn here, and that was taken from him with a fierce suddenness. I think of the final temptation scene in Scorcese's movie Last Temptation of Christ, where Jesus gets a vision of a normal life, where he would live well and long to be surrounded with children and grandchildren. So much of life was slipping through his fingers. What haunts you about the missed chances for your loved ones? Death stalks us, as life is a precious gift, and we feel hunted.

128) Col 1:18, Rev. 1:5-firstborn of the dead is an arresting phrase to get across the resurrection making the tomb into a womb. One's firstborn has special significance, as a new generation arises. Few moments are as holy as to hold one's first newborn for the very first time. What seems to be the end is a spiritual beginning. Abraham is tested by being asked to sacrifice his firstborn with Sarah. Death that destroyer of life becomes a womb for new life, in a sense. Jesus Christ was "born anew" at Easter. The only begotten son of the Father, the firstborn son of Mary and Joseph is recipient of a second birth as the hymn, O Little Child of Bethlehem, reminds us for our destiny as well. In a way, our lives turn a page after loss. We sometimes mark the passage of the years as before or after a loved one died. When we were kids, those of us who were the oldest got a kick out of hearing that most of the stuff in the house seemed to have been purchased "around the year you were born," as in "that stove is as old as you." We put symbols of fertility and young life in Easter celebrations. Death is sterile, so to call Jesus the firstborn of the dead utterly reverses its power. Only God can make a tomb turn into a womb. Only God can turn death into the occasion of new life. Only God can make a new beginning of what looks to be a full stop. I now wonder if then we could be called thrice born in heaven.

129) Ezek. 18 stands against the notion that we somehow are to

pay for the sins of generations before. The Torah does mention this even in the basic attributes of God (at Ex. 34:46-7). It marks a note that we are responsible for ourselves in our own time. It also shows a line of development in Scripture. In other words, Scripture is not necessarily static. I am very partial to the notion that in reading Scripture we are less hearing a monologue but are hearing a symphony. Different voices and genres speak to us through the centuries. They are in conversation with each other. Not only do we get to hear those ancient conversations, we get to join in with them, inter-religious dialogue through the centuries. This is certainly true on the issue of God and human suffering, as different themes crash into each other. Perhaps, at different points in our lives some models fit better than others. We make a mistake if we try to raise one understanding above all others and then try to impose that one viewpoint on to others. When hurting, we get a sneaking suspicion that we somehow, someway deserve to pay for some wrong, so that loss and grief become some sort of atonement. (See book and movie of the same name). One of our issues becomes that no amount of payment ever seems to be sufficient. I don't know if the more difficult balance would be the unrelenting call for more from others, or the unremitting call for more from within. We are not called to atone for another's wrongs. In an early sermon it was said that "God has more light yet to shine." This Scriptural passage stands against Biblical rigidity. Here we see a movement from the terrors of the announcement of divine character in Exodus to a much more individual accounting. The Bible has timeless truths, of course, but it also charts a development in our relationship with God and each other.

130)- In seminary, we tend to learn to divide a text up with little devices to mark division or shifts. One notes that Jeremiah has seven confessional sections of deep prayer recorded in the book with his name. In Jer. (15:18) the prophet asks "why is my pain unceasing, my wound incurable, refusing to be healed." These confessional portraits of prayers are stunning in their eloquence and their sheer boldness. Pain can make us stammer out barely intelligible statements, but it can also be the seedbed for eloquent prayer. In my view, we are right to admire off the cuff prayers. At the same time the spirit works through preparation and care as well. Cranmer's Book of Common Prayer is a testament to the literary aspirations of prayer for the faithful. This gloom and doom prophet reveals himself in these secret moments to be a person of anguish over both his words and the reaction to them. Many know the quote from the late second century church leader Irenaeus. "the glory of God is humanity fully alive." Jeremiah has recalled better days, when his relationship with God seemed lithe and fresh. Now, when he needs God's presence as an oasis, all he finds is dry creek bed.I love that when things are going well, but it almost feels like a cruel taunt when I am low or sad. Yes, at times, we do feel that our wound is incurable, but that does not make its so. It is good to admit it to oneself, and it may be especially good to admit in prayer to God. It does seem, especially in the days and weeks of grief's start that we wonder if the pain, the constant ache, the gnawing of loss will ever stop, or even give us a chance to breathe. No matter what we seem to try, what advice we take, the wound seems to stay wide open, impervious to healing. It almost seems to be able to taunt any attempted medicine, therapy, advice, action that offers a chanced of "being better." In the eyes of God, is any wound incurable? Applied to the wound of grief, how does it refuse to be healed? Are there some self-imposed obstacles that place in the path of our own healing?

131) Eph. 3-height, depth-Life is too complex, too rich to be limited to one dimension or aspect. I notice the angles of vision in this passage as it seems to me to give real dimension to our faith, but it also gives us some markers for a life. Use these points to describe a life. What were the high points for your loved one? If you are reticent to name some, that is fine, for we never fully peer into the inmost recesses of people's experience. What have been high points for you? We often say that someone is deep or has unplumbed depths. Where do you know or suspect of some depths in them? It can also be a way to try to chart our love. Where would these markers apply to your relationships? When Jacob was on the run, he stopped to rest and had a dream

of blessing. When he awoke, he named the place Bethel, house of God, for he said that "surely God is in this place, but I knew it not." That is an excellent affirmation when we do not feel or sense the presence of God, when we feel we are out on a limb alone. Surely God is in this place too. Surely God is with us in the place of grief and loss. "Surely God is in this place as I struggle with these feelings and thoughts that keep welling up at odd moments, but I knew it not." Only with hindsight do we realize the presence of God, as the struggle itself may keep us from seeing, from having insight at the moment. Go through the length of you loved one's life. Maybe you could mark milestone moments on a graph. Perhaps you would choose to chart the graphs of your lives together. What heights did you share? What valley moments? What depths within each other and with yourselves did you discover together? I do realize that it is a task that may seem to be at odds with the glorious narrative we are tempted to create after loss, but it can be one rooted in experience and serve to burnish memories. Go through the length of you loved one's life. Maybe you could mark milestone moments on a graph. Perhaps you would choose to chart the graphs of your lives together. What heights did you share? What valley moments? What depths within each other and with yourselves did you discover together?

132) Lament psalms, including Ps.13- How does one pray in grief? It may seem formless, but prayer can give some structure, some form, to it. A good way to start is to use lament psalms as frameworks for our prayers. They make up a plurality of the different types of psalms. Sometimes we are so upset that we cannot find the words to even start a prayer. Then, we get worried that the format may be improper. Here, we are assured of a proper basis, as they are in our prayer book, the Psalms. The lament form opens us to a different dimension of prayer within the different types of prayers it contains. The lament form puts an emphasis on feeling but also struggles to get things in order. The form recognizes that grief is a spiritual issue. Our conception

of God and how God fits into one's life is a component of its complexities. I heard someone say once that in prayer there are some things we need to get off our chests; otherwise they will fester. Pay careful attention to each verse, both for content and for the feeling tone. In time, we can use them as models, but starting with them, repeating them, re-reading them, is a good move. One can try rewriting them in more contemporary language and be quite specific about the troubles we face. Douglas John Hall writes in God and Human Suffering (46) nothing is more needful in our culture than a forum for the open expression of the experience of negation that we as a people darkly suspect but do not, seemingly cannot, allow ourselves to admit, to voice, to feel." In a recent Christian Century, (1/25/12:11-13) Frederick Niedner notes a sermon by Luther after the suicide of a bishop who had been criticized by the church. "In Jesus Christ, the true God breaks into even the most utter despair...God joins those whom darkness has swallowed...there is no place...no depth to which we even might sink, but even there he is Lord for us. Even there he says, "come with me."

My spiritual life has been enriched by the Psalms. Years ago, I was frustrated with the style and content of my prayers. Why not use a biblical prayer book more frequently and more deeply? Where does the arrogance come from that I should expect freestyle prayer to be the preferred method, as if the prayers of the bible itself are less meaningful? I realized years ago that prayers of thanksgiving and adoration did not come easily to me. So, I used the psalms as models to learn how to pray them. Then, I rewrote them in my own style, or I used them as a framework for my own prayers. for some of us, writing prayers can be a very effective way to communicate to God, perhaps especially so in the maelstrom of grief. I was encouraged in my efforts not only by the writings of Eugene Peterson on the Psalms, but his translation and paraphrase of them and other biblical works that eventually became The Message. He really tries to capture the often earthy, direct, conversational feel of the Psalms from Hebrew into English. I've done some presentations on the King James Version of the Bible. While it is a testament to the grandeur of English, the translators erred in making all of

Scripture sound the same, when it does not. So it seemed permissible for me to put them into language that fit me and my moods.

133) Job's friends do the right thing. They engage the ritual practice of sitting in silence with their friend (2:11-13). It is when Job starts to touch some theological nerves that they get nervous. It is not an easy thing to sit and comfort an old friend. Our presence is vitally important, but our words cannot be expected to be adequate to the task at hand. They start to defend the orthodox view of God against attack. They try to provide some rational explanation for the cause of Job's multiple tragedies. When threatened, they then go after the messenger, poor suffering Job. They fail as friends by not being on Job's side. They become more rigid and more strident as Job continues on the offensive. Job is going after their religious construction, and it frightens them. We know that the Divine Voice speaks against the friends in the epilogue, but we still persist in acting like them. I just saw a woman at a visitation insist that everyone in the family should grieve as she did and share precisely her beliefs. We do get anxious when someone's feelings or thoughts unnerve us. For that matter, we often fail to even be present for our friends in grief and find ways and excuses to avoid being present in that cocoon of struggle.

One could do well to be forbearing with those who do not grieve as you do. Many women have a desire to process the loss by talking about it and talking through it by analyzing memories and people's reactions. This is hard for many men who want to do something, fix the problem, and cannot see a reason for rehashing the same material constantly and at length. Maybe being judgmental creeps in more easily when we are under stress, and we get more rigid about using ourselves as the proper model for others. We hear anxiety talking more than a considered opinion. It freezes our ability to think and speak clearly. At fortuitous moments, our friends step up and do what we need at exactly the right time. Being confused human beings, our friends may be unable to know what to do or say. We may get disappointed in our friends and their responses, or lack of them. We say it so easily: "there for me." We often do not have a clue what that means, or have to discover it, step by step, good points entwined with mistakes.

134) Job 19- Job seeks a kinsman/redeemer, someone similar to an attorney who is on our side, who can deliver us from trouble. "I know my redeemer lives." A redeemer was someone who could be on our side, to lend a hand, to help get us out of a difficult circumstance. Ruth and Naomi find one. Janzen in Scent of Water (114) opines that we seek to deal with a calamity "to restore order in those whose lives have been so grievously diminished." In a simple, but heartfelt and expressive way, many people come to a visitation to share memories, sympathy, and a sense of empathy as they recall their own losses. We rely on sympathy cards as a sign of respect and a way of trying to touch the heartstrings and the spirit, to show that we are thinking of people in a hard time with a promise of redemption. . Sympathy cards brought tears to my eyes when I started going through a batch of them after the death of my mother. They are a good way to try to express what we are unable to say openly. Some may be quite sentimental, even sappy; some are poetic, and some even touch the rough edges of grief. It's obvious that people take real time and effort in selecting them. I was surprised how I teared up after going through just a couple of them. At the last, at the end, Job is confident of seeing

God. The future bears a redeemer and redemption, no matter the pain of the present. Job may feel as if he is mere dust, or a mere mortal creature, but a redeemer will arise. The redeemer will act as a reconciler, or a counsellor, bringing god and Job back together out of this period of estrangement and alienation. Christians have taken the phrase, "my redeemer lives" as a prophetic oracle of the resurrected Jesus. When we feel as if we are not capable of doing something all by ourselves, when we are captured, imprisoned, we seek rescue; we seek redemption; we seek someone outside ourselves to bring help, even in the nick of time.

135) The fiery furnace of Daniel 3 is certainly a good image for grief. It does threaten to consume us at times. Still, we can be protected from its ravages just as the story in Daniel allows. It does threaten to consume us. (Here look to Is. 43:2 as well). I noticed that the men were bound when they entered the fiery furnace. I don't know if we can emerge from grief unscathed, but we certainly do survive it. Wolfelt (<u>Understanding Your Grief</u>:145) makes a distinction between resolution and reconciliation. The men did not face the fiery furnace alone. The king spots a fourth godlike being walking amid the three young men. The lion's den is a powerful image as well. Rather than conform to the standards of the empire, Daniel keeps kosher. Even if his life is threatened, he will not budge. Thrown in the lion's den, he emerges unscathed. Scattered throughout Scripture, passages refer to the fires as burning off impurities, the dross. I do not think it is going too far to see all of these stories of threat in the first 6 chapters of Daniel as symbols for the experience of exile, Diaspora, and colonial existence under the thumb of other powers. Those public troubles are the cause of countless private griefs. Still, they are literature of opposition. They admit how hard it is to live under the thumb of others, especially foreign powers. It is so damaging to one's sense of honor and respect to have to bend the knee. It is oppositional literature in that no matter what the powers that be throw at them, they will not be cowed, and they will end up on the right side after all. Even when the worst get hurled at us, we will not only survive but flourish right here.

136) Numbers 21:4-9 Moses is told to fashion a bronze serpent, when the people are being afflicted. by looking up at the serpent, they find healing. In a way, it reminds me of the advice to lean into the pain instead of avoiding it. It reminds me of using snake venom as an antidote to snakebite or even the notions behind homeopathy, or the hangover cure of the 'hair of the dog who bit me." I like that the downtrodden people have to look up at the snake. Their eyes are not downcast; their eyes do not focus on their own ailment. They look up and away. They receive a new focus to promise change, to promise healing. Grief can poison our systems in time. It may require an antidote. Many of us are

award of John 3:16 from being paraded at football games as much as from church. Many of us don't recognize the reference two verses before the one on so many bedsheet advertisements. John 3:14 understands the cross as drawing out the venom that afflicts us all. The serpent has the interesting backstory of being an incarnation of chaos, of temptation to the fall, and of healing in different cultural masks. It is later kept but then destroyed as an idol during the reforming regime of King Hezekiah. J. Christiaan Beker called death a "poisonous evil" when he taught us in seminary. My mind goes back to a sermon the excellent preacher and teacher James Kay offered on John 3's reference to this passage. There he speaks of Christ drawing all of the venom out of our lives. Looking up at the bronze serpent, the people could find healing. By extension, Kay argued that looking up to the cross draws us to healing and draws the poison from us.

137) Num. 11 Hos. 2:14-For Israel, the wilderness came to be seen as both threat and promise. It is being 'lost in a lost world" and a stage for expelling all but the basics, so it permits renewed contact with god without all of the normal distractions. We are in the world yet not of the world. We live in this world, but we are poised to enter the Promised Land that is presaged by the Second Advent and the Promised Land of heaven. So we can use some of the wilderness elements to our own condition and place. Grief can be a wilderness experiences certainly, its chaos and confusion, its sense of being on a journey but being lost much of the time. It has the feel of a desert, where we feel the winds sweep over us, drying out our spirits, baked into submission to forces larger than ourselves. The wilderness is clearly a place of threat: of privation, of direction, of dangers unknown and unforeseen. In Hosea, God shows desperation with Israel, pictured as a disaffected spouse. God wants to go back to their youth together, to the old days, in the wilderness when they had each other. It reminds me of married couples going back in their memories when they had no money and played board games; as they could not afford to go out, but they recall those days in a sparse apartment as happy. Oasis experience takes on not only a poignant surcease but saves our lives. For Christians, it is a small step from manna to

Communion's bread of life. It is a small jump from water from the rock to the cup of salvation. Ambrose called the cup the medicine of immortality. It gets at the depth of the experience. Mortality itself is the illness. Its medicine, a bit like snakebite antidote, comes through death. When Jesus lifted one of the cups of blessing at this last Passover meal, it referred to blood. Earlier and in Gethsemane he referred to the cup as one difficult to swallow. It seems to me that the wilderness is a metaphor for the experience of grieving. It certainly is a place of threat and dislocation. It has the sense of being lost, as all of the familiar markers are missing. it may well be that we feel as if we are wandering in the wilderness as we have no idea of a destination, and if we do, no idea of how to reach it. On the other hand, trouble drives us to our knees. This may well be a time of fairly constant contact with the Listening One in prayer. This may well be a time of real spiritual growth. Just as Israel learned to become a free people in the wilderness, a wilderness experience could have them and us notice a real movement from a more innocent, unreflective faith, to a much more mature, developed, and deep faith as it has been honed through crisis and moved across the Jordan.

138) Is.26:19-27 is a mythic presentation of the reality of chaos and evil in the natural world, "that twisting serpent." Mythic presentations place issues on to a large canvas. As stories, they invite us into the narrative and permit safe space to wonder aloud about the ways of the world. They allow us to keep deep and troubling thoughts at a safe remove as well. So, avoid making accuracy the only goal of religious speech, as in something is "just a myth." The ancient Near East pictured evil and chaos as a serpent such as Lotan or Leviathan, or a dragon. Recall that Israel lived in a cultural environment that included Baal, a mighty youthful storm god who did face the abyss of death. Tolkien called it Sauron, and Voldemort is Rowling's personification of it. Jon Levenson in <u>Creation and the Persistence of Evil</u> sees the threat of the chaos of a world before the boundary markers of creation as a continuing threat and menace to the natural order. When Reformed Christians speak of God's

governance, they mean something similar, that God's hand holds back entropy and allows the world to cohere, even if it is full of tragedy. Even an arbitrary action by something identifiable may be easier to handle than the threat of a random occurrence. Gillian Welch sings of a 'dark turn of the mind." Yes, the Bible has the sense of an Edenic park, but it also maintains that creation is affected always by trouble being kept at bay, not destroyed. That's why the book of Revelation goes to such lengths to have the threat of death in its death throes but still envisions it as enormously hard to contain until the new heavens and the new earth will appear. It would also lead one to think that God remains locked in combat with forces that the good creation needs to keep under control. So, the evil that befalls us can be placed at the feet of the continuing threats to the order and harmony of creation and not at the feet of a God who is actively sending harms as a signal or punishment. Apocalyptic material presents us with insight into the dim future. Here, we are ensconced at the boundary markers of life and death. This visionary material begins to envision something beyond death. 26:19 flatly states that the dead shall live. In v. 14 we are just told that the dead do not live, nor shades rise. Dan.12:2 seems to most of us a fairly explicit imagination of resurrection, a good reason why it is often dated closer to the time of Jesus. While the first half of Daniel deals with the issues of human governance, we are now brought into a divine frame, into the realm of divine time and governance, of the eventual victory of life itself.

139) Death is the last enemy 1 Cor. 15:25-26. (Also see Phil. 1:12-14). I worry sometimes when our brave words at Easter speak a bit much about death being defeated, about death being entombed. Not quite yet. This passage introduces a section of really being aliens here and waiting to be home with God. It almost touches on the sense of "only the good die young." Whose last enemy is death, ours or God's? Nothing points out the already/not yet character of Christian belief than those brave words. Paul is better: 'the last enemy to be destroyed is death." Granted, Easter may allay some of our fears about death, but death's power is all around us. I am often a bit uncomfortable

with all of the easy words sermons and hymns use about the victory of Easter, as if the great enemy is still not prowling around our doors. Such a fearsome enemy requires a powerful opponent of death, indeed the very author of life stands against it. Craig Koester, in his study of John's gospel, The Word of Life, argues that while God is always involved in life, it is the realm of evil and its personification, the devil, that seek to work their will through death (75). A good sign of this is Lazarus as a proleptic description of new life. Yes, he is raised, but he comes out with his grave wrappings. With Jesus, the grave wrappings are set aside. Lazarus will taste death again; indeed, the opponents of Jesus plot his death almost immediately after the raising of lazarus. At Easter, Jesus has set aside the grave clothes. Death will not encumber him again. The hymn, Thine Is the Glory sings that the grave clothes are set aside in where his body lay. It is a hymn to the deep claims of life.

140) Lam. 1 could read like a disquisition on not finding comfort (verses7, 16,17,21). So many aspects of grief are captured in this chapter. Kathleen O'Connor calls it a "topography of pain" in her book on the poems (28). The stomach churns (v.20); tears flow (2, 16); a sense of isolation (12) and feeling worthless (11), shame (7-8) and weakness are obvious (verses 14,3,6,22). The cavalcade of symptoms fit well the acrostic form that appears in guises throughout this poem. The words of Dame Zion are challenging prayers written in a baffled religious heart and mind. Commentators often emphasize the great chapter 3, and rightly, but we make a serious mistake to neglect the deep lament form here as a continuing resource for us when we face real, overwhelming sorrows. Language about the pain suffered is varied and expressive, again another reason to prize this neglected Biblical treasure. 1:16's "my, my eyes," pick up the sting of tears and the horrors witnessed. The laments are trying to alert God, rouse God to action. Maybe the Holy One is tempted to react like the narrator and shield the divine eyes. What we manage to do to each other, what we suffer, could tempt God to avert divine sight. It may well seem to the one praying that God is averting the divine eyes from the horrors all over Jerusalem. It

is a difficult thing to witness anyone in pain but it is a distinct terror to see a loved one in trouble. Dame Zion seems to me to be a symbolic consort, to get at the intimacy of the relationship of Jerusalem and God. God knows well the pain of loss.

141) Praise and kaddish- In Jewish ritual, the bereaved are asked to pray kaddish every day for a year for a parent. In some traditions, one would refer to a child as 'my kaddish prayer of the future." The prayer itself is a bit of a surprise as a prayer for the grieving. It is not a bereavement prayer, but it is a prayer not dissimilar to the Lord's Prayer that praises God. It does not address grief directly. In spite of our pain, we praise God. I suppose it puts all of our lives, even the worst part, before the Maker of all. It certainly alters one's perspective in prayer during grief. Leon Wieseltier of the New Republic magazine wrote of his experience with it. A vast array of thoughts and connections about the faith and its practices crop up during his work with this single, singular prayer. Perspective does create new vantage points. Recently, for the first time I felt as if I made some headway in the parable of the talents in Mt. 25:14-30. Usually, I fell into seeing the difference between the five and the one. I can be blind as a reader too many times. Depending on how one make talent into a modern equivalent, we are totaling the one talent to be a minimum of 300,000 dollars or to keep it easy read it as a million or a billion dollars. This is more than the half-empty, half-full distinction. We may well be pre-disposed to find the negative, to find the lack as we examine experience, and in so doing miss the abundance, even the point itself. Kaddish is done by males in a group for a father. I assume that a daughter can pray these words at home or wok, but the tradition links male to male. That seems to me to be an example of ritual becoming ritualistic and exclusionary, but it is not my tradition. Note this prayer shares grief with a group, so that even prayer of grief does not seem to be borne alone. When we pray in our grief, we share our lives, fully, with God.

142) Ex.12 -Passover is not only about the passage from slavery to freedom. It is about the Destroyer passing over the children of Israel. The sign of blood could be a sign that here is life. Maybe it was a sign that blood had already been spilled. At any rate, the sign of blood on the doorposts was a sign that the lifeblood of Israel would be spared this time. For a people who have lost so much, no wonder it is such a powerful symbol of deliverance. I sense some ancient thought world at the root of this passage, with spilled blood becoming an emblem for rescue from the hand of the Destroyer. Ritual makes even foreboding bearable. A good ritual creates both distance and connection. Ritual often includes a physical element for our senses. Good ritual takes real care with the words selected for an event. Salon (8/7/11) had a piece about two people who could not bear to answer the phone, as it may hold more devastating news. Can it be mere coincidence that the synoptic gospels have Jesus inaugurating the Lord's Supper at his final Passover supper? Here, the Way, the Truth, and the Life is soon to be present on the cross. Indeed John explicitly links Jesus to the Passover lamb at both the start and the close of the ministry of Jesus. After all of these years, the Destroyer still enters our homes. In his commentary on Exodus Gerald Janzen writes (81) "when Pharaoh is in charge of time, one's days become an endless repetition of wearisome toil...past and future are just limitless extensions of an intolerable present...memory and hope are turned into a growing mountain of pain and a shadow of despair,...Passover...turns the past into a fountain of celebration...and turns the future into an open prospect that one can anticipate in hope." In both cases, we eat "road food." Lifeblood moves us from death to the path of new life. It is quite the ironic gesture that the spilled blood becomes a talisman of protection against the Destroyer. In the story, the Destroyer appears only as a counter-curse against the Egyptian regime that sought to kill the males of Israel. In resurrection hope, the destroyer has but a temporary victory. We apss voer from death into life.

143) Prov. 10:7 'the memory of the righteous is a blessing." Isn't that part of the notion of the eulogy? It is a blessing to think of

how someone blessed the lives of others, how they embodied blessings, to say good words about their character and actions over a lifetime. Billy Joel, however, sang the old saw, "only the good die young." We don't have to worry about speaking ill of the righteous dead; the issue is when to stop constantly speaking of their virtues and attributes. To remember, Abraham mourns and finds a suitable burial spot for his Sarah. It is a good idea to have a ritual at the placing of the tombstone. Getting a tombstone is a difficult decision, as again we are torn in honoring a loved one and wanting to be a good consumer. I recall a Jewish custom asks for a ritual at the placing of the marker at the first anniversary of the death. Alan Wolfelt in Understanding Your Grief quotes Nancy Halle (41) "After her death, I began to see her as she really had been. It was less like losing someone than discovering someone." Sometimes, memory can haunt us. Some people report hearing a scold from their parents well into adulthood, well after their parents have died. for others, it is too painful to think of the good times and virtues of the person who died. In Blue Nights, when told repeatedly that at least she can prize wonderful memories, Joan Didion writes that "memories are what you no longer want to remember." We are sorely tempted to numb memory into submission with alcohol or drugs. At the same time, as Didion says (130), "Time passes. Memory fades; memory adjusts; memory conforms to what we think we remember." It may be a salutary experience to do a writing exercise and write out some of the private and public good your loved one was able to do during their lifetime. At some points, that could in fact deepen the pain of losing such a good person. It could heighten the manifest sense of unfairness.

144) Mr. 16, Lk. 24-Messiah means anointed one. In the reformed tradition, we emphasize that the priest, prophet, and king in the Old Testament were anointed. I seriously doubt that those who acclaimed Jesus as messiah imagined that they would be anointing his young adult corpse so early in his public life. Anointing the body of Jesus was a wonderful ritual as part of the process of saying goodbye. It honors the body itself. The sweet smell masked the start of decay, but it also cemented the reality

that the body was dead and buried, not missing, not to return. Now most of us leave preparation of the body to the funeral home, or move to cremation as soon as possible. In some communities, women took on the sacred task of washing the body one last time and preparing the body for burial. It is one of the last acts of kindness. In the time of Jesus anointing the body was an act of time, care, and expense. On Easter, they were worried that no one could help them roll away the stone to anoint the body, as the entrance was sealed away. We still tend graves, place flowers, and keep them manicured. Some go to the lengths of personalizing the stark stone with a picture or symbol, along with the name and dates of birth and death. We are increasingly placing things in the coffin, favored objects, a bit like the Egyptians leaving items to prepare for the next life, but ours are reminders of this one. Synagogues often have sacred teams of men and women who wash the body in warm water and then wrap it in a simple shroud so no distinction is made between rich and poor. In death, no distinction is made for our status. Yet, respect should be paid to everyone who departs this life.

145) Jn.12-Can there be such a thing as holy waste? When a woman pours a lot of expensive ointment on Jesus, the reaction was true. Think of how that money could be used for the poor. Jesus disagrees and sees it as an act of devotion, an act of love. Further, it had a prophetic dimension of showing that the Messiah (anointed one) would soon have his lifeless body anointed at burial and women would come to try to anoint his body in the tomb as the ritual custom dictated. This is one of the few actions that all four gospels report. Here, Mary is the sister of the raised Lazarus. Her action is not only extravagant but of a deeply intimate nature. John makes sure we know the aroma filled the house, and I go to how a large funeral has the smell of flower arrangements, and it can be pleasant or it may be overpowering. At the level of brute efficiency, ritual does not "make sense." At the level of spiritual insight, it is a signifier that point beyond the act to something or someone beyond the concrete. Thomas Lynch, the undertaker and poet, is annoyed at our concern about the cost of funerals. Of course, it isn't useful, but it does feel as a

proper way to say goodbye. Maybe sending a loved one off with a bang is a good way to honor them. Part of our reticence is our continuing uncertainty about honoring the body. Those who see the body as "mere shell" are likely to resist elaborate rituals for honoring the corpse as opposed to the spirit that is in heaven. Stephanie Paulsell wrote on honoring the body as a spiritual practice. It seems that part of funeral practice is honoring a life by being respectful of honoring their body and giving them a proper send-off. It's part of the idea behind the Irish wake, isn't it? On the other hand, one can be dignified and respectful without only having choices at the upper end of the economic ladder, either. I'm on the frugal side, well the cheap side. It is hard for me to see people who are just scraping by putting a fortune into an elaborate funeral set-up. Sometimes, it seems to be atonement money for hurts given over the years. If one does not pre-plan a funeral, it certainly is hard being a good consumer, when one is almost consumed by grief. Then the industry reminds me of a car dealership where you can see one subcompact , but then you jump to your choice of top of the line Mercedes-Benz. Choice is there, but it is a slanted one. Of course we have hidden social messages in the funeral's expense. We are trying to hide wealth or flaunt it. We are trying to make up for a poor relationship with a big send-off. We may be trying to signal trouble with a frugal funeral. We fall into easy judgments about wasteful funeral expenses; they are attempts at a final honoring of a soul and body.

146) 2 Cor. 12:7-10- Paul reveals a thorn in the flesh and I move quickly to a thorn in the soul. (In Greek skolops could also be stake, a reference to the cross?) In Galatians, he mentions an illness. Something relatively small can surely cause a lot of discomfort. Loss works on us, with its sharp pain, as relentlessly as any physical thorn or illness. We may try to ignore it, but it gnaws at us. "Why" is a relentless, nagging question, a thorn in the side. Some wonder if it is an improper question, but I'm no so sure. I think it is a perfectly proper and understandable question, because we try to make some sense of events. One can fear the answer from death would be: "I shall spill your soul."(See

Pilgrim's Progress, Apollyon against Christian). The problem is more directed toward the frame we use to answer the why question: cause and effect, logic, purpose. The method does not seem to do well in answering the question. In the theophany at the end of Job (38-41), God does not grant Job an explanation. Indeed, God is angry that the friends insist on using a calculus of reward and punishment for the sufferings of Job. Janzen (Scent:106) wonders if our desire for an explanation is a strategy to avoid feeling. The search for explanation displaces feeling for cognition. In other words, what displaces those feelings is a sophisticated form of denial, at least of the emotional side of the ledger. I now think of Androcles and the Lion where even a lion limps due to a thorn embedded in its paw. We do well to be careful to try to intuit the pain of another.

147) Job 3,7 and innocent, radical suffering -We say too easily things such as "when the going gets tough, the tough get going," or what doesn't kill us makes us stronger, or even Hemingway's thought that we can grow stronger in the broken places. In Tragic Vision and Divine Compassion Wendy Farley reminds us that suffering can threaten to destroy anyone, especially in terms of radical, senseless evil. In a episode of Criminal Minds, a woman named Hope says in a group, "time wears us down." Granted that finding purpose or meaning in suffering can make it a bit more bearable, but what happens when we cannot find any purpose or meaning in it? Farley is clear that our response to it is to try to fight it, or at least lessen it. While no rubber band is as resilient as the human spirit, they both can break down in time. Sometimes resilience is a delayed reaction, and it takes some time and more energy to be able to bounce back. If you look back over the months, chances are that you can see results of resilience in your life in many places. On the other hand, sometimes the pain seems unbearable. Radical suffering threatens to make us victims and exclude other dimensions of life. Radical suffering resists easy blame that suffering is a consequence of individual action. It tends to implicate a system, or maybe better put, systemic, complex flaws in our milieu. Lamentations with poetry reaches depths that prose cannot. Even

the narrator is moved to tell the fallen Lady Zion that her grief and troubles are "as vast as the sea." In this condition, there is no one to comfort her (1:16-17), no one to help her (1:7). Blame is an attempt to relieve ourselves of a feeling of responsibility, even the feeling that there must be something we can say or do to relieve the suffering of another person. In our anxiety over that powerless feeling, we may make matters worse by blaming the victim. Hear Serene Jones, now president of Union Seminary in New York: "suffering itself is not the source of redemption...it is the persistence of love in the midst of suffering" (Modern Theology, 4/2001)

148)I Pet. 1:6-7, Heb. 12:4-11- Learning from suffering-I'm very, very leery of this notion, as I keep thinking that we need a better lesson plan than suffering. It is difficult to grasp what lessons suffering can teach that could not be taught through different mechanisms. It may just as well impede learning and insight and take years to unlearn some of its bad lessons. I get the idea that as we mature we handle suffering in a more mature way. I guess I notice people are much quicker to apply this learning model to others than themselves. At best, it is a product of hindsight, but in my experience, I do not claim suffering as a gift when I am in the midst of it. Perhaps that is a sign of my spiritual immaturity, but I do think pain tends to drive out noble thoughts in the quest for relief. John Hick speaks of suffering as part of a process of 'soul-making.' Suffering is said to strengthen us, to build up adult virtues such as patience, to steel us for the hard times that always may lie ahead. In other words, suffering offers a chance for growth. For some folks, this is a most encouraging word. It reminds me a bit of a halftime speech by a coach. At times, we do grow through suffering. At most times, people who are not suffering are too quick to offer it as a bromide for our pain. When I hear people say that they would not change anything about the course of their lives, I think that either they haven't learned through suffering at all, or perhaps they mean that they would not have developed into the person they have become with both the triumph and the pain. Suffering certainly moves us from a hypothetical guess about what we would be capable of when facing cold reality. Scripture uses an image of burning off impurities in metal to expose the value beneath. We learn about our capacity to suffer, as well as growing through it. for many of us, the breaking point is further down the road than we would imagine it to be. We do discover reservoirs of strength and resilience. Those who move through grief do report that they have more patience, or they appreciate life more, or even that death has lost its sting for them, even as they continue to miss their loved ones so.

149) Purgative suffering- The idea of purgative suffering uses metallurgy as its image. Impurities can be burned away, melted away, vaporized. It's related to the saying:" when the going gets tough, the tough get going," so that tough times act as a spiritual boot camp and help eliminate some weakness and build inner strength. Santayana wrote "if pain could cure us, we would long ago have been saved." Learning to cope with some levels of pain does toughen us up. Recently, I was reading that the push about antioxidant pills and foods is more facile hope than empirical demonstration. A German team argued that cells need to toughen up to small troubles to be able to withstand more serious assaults. In my view, those who gravitate toward the notion of purgative suffering will tend to see pride, or arrogance at the core of the human predicament. I wonder if earlier coping skills help us when we face bigger issues over time. Erik Erikson always held that his schedule of virtues built upon each other. Indeed they may well interact (Capps in Deadly Sins and Saving Virtues) Our presbytery resource room received a new book by Kalas on the will of God. The author, a professor of preaching, finds the use of the term a powerful statement of religious people, but he finds the notion wanting. I cannot wrap my head or heart around the notion that God actively wills discrete evils to teach us a lesson. Granted, the ideology in parts of Scripture does seem to attribute especially corporate evils to God as a punishment, especially in the Deuteronomistic History sections. Still, other than the mythic account of Noah's flood and the "mighty hand of God" accounts in the Exodus and conquest narratives, we see more God working through intermediary causes, natural forces or political forces.

Artists may use their talents to work through suffering. I think of the old image of the pearl appearing through the irritation of sand. The gifted singer/songwriter Rosanne Cash did just that in the aftermath of the deaths of her father, mother, and stepmother within a short period of time in her album, Black Cadillac. In the song, "World without Sound," she openly craves for the religious comfort her father found, but that seems to elude her. Purgative suffering may burn away the dross, the easy cliché, the bumper stickers that we embrace around our conceptions of the faith. It may burn off some of our arrogance and leave room for humility. We find ourselves in a community of those who suffer.

150) Heb. 1:10 Can suffering ever be redemptive, or as Talbert called it, a boon to others, in his book, Learning Through Suffering. Martin Luther King would speak of it in this way at times. What does it redeem; what does it save us from? How would it work? I am very leery of people telling us that suffering strengthens us, that it is for some unseen greater good, that it helps the aesthetic sense of the world by giving us points of comparison. In its basic sense, redemption meant a relative stepping in and saving you from oppression, saving you or some property from being lost. Isaiah 40-66 seems to be more interested in the word being oriented to divine intervention, perhaps when human redemption fails. For some of us suffering saves us from the illusion of being somehow above the rest of humanity, somehow immune, deservedly immune, from the trial that afflict all of us lesser mortals. For some the experience of suffering moves us out of a self-centered, selfish existence, and to look beyond the self. In the book of Maccabees we start to see evidence of a notion that the suffering of the righteous can work in a vicarious and communal fashion for others. Suffering allows some of us to discover the virtue of compassion. Surely, compassion flows from other sources. So far, in your experience, has suffering contributed to virtues such as humility, compassion, a desire to heal? Parker Palmer speaks of a "heart broken wide open." As Lincoln wrestled with the slaughters of the Civil War, the religious background of the nation influenced his thoughts. He wondered if the slaughter would purge the nation of the sins of

slavery. In part, Lincoln suffered so for all of the families who lost children to the Civil War, as he lost two sons to illness, and another son would die of illness at 18 not many years after the assassination. For someone how struggled with depression, who saw his wife nearly undone by grief, it must have been an enormous struggle to continue the tasks handed him as president. On one of his last days on earth, he remarked to his wife that they had to become determined to be more cheerful, as the war and the death of their son in the White House had made them both miserable. Our minds can be a tool to at least manage our emotions a bit. He found life bearable as he found some meaning and learning in his struggles and those of a nation.

151) Lord's Prayer- Matthew's version is longer than Luke's. We are just going to work with this fundamental prayer during Lent this year at church. To me the prayer's beginning reflects the Jewish faith of Jesus. Indeed its has a similar ring to the kaddish, said during a period of loss. First, I appreciate the relational basis to be able to call God as Father. We see it used in Isaiah. We should stress the our pronoun, as it moves us into community and away from a sense that prayer is but individual personalized communication with the Holy and Blessed One. How we wish it to be "on earth as it is in heaven," as heaven is a place where we no longer face death as a direct, personal threat again. In a short phrase, Jesus puts body and soul, heaven and earth together under the aegis of God's realm, or way, God's vision, God's kingdom. The issue of God's will is a difficult one in prayer. It takes immense trust to align one's will with the will of God, especially when that means to turn our backs on our preferences or desires. In grief, it may be particularity difficult when people have been saying that the death of a loved one is God's will. Personally, I have too much static on the line to ever be certain that I perceive god's will clearly. Indeed, i am frankly frightened of people who so blithely know, without a smidgen of uncertainty, that they know God's will precisely. To pray for one's daily bread shows the audience for the prayer was poor. It also is an entry point to be able to pray for the physical necessities that make life possible. It is a quick antidote to the idea that prayer need be

"spiritual" apart from the needs of the body. This day and daily keep us locked in the present, not the past for which we may yearn or the murky future, but the current situation of our prayer. The time of temptation/trial/testing is the same word in NT Greek. Why would God lead us into temptation? For that matter, why would God test or try us? I wonder if it leans more in the direction of us testing God, as in the experience of the wilderness. If it is time of trial it could be pointing to sufferings connected to some versions of the end times. We cannot afford to lose the end of the section, but deliver us from evil. That is how it concludes in Matthew's gospel. Deliver is a powerful word, more than presence or companionship, or even comfort. The verbs are in the imperative, a mood that always surprises me in prayer and one that I admire from the Hebraic tradition. Would not occur to me to pray in the commanding form of the imperative mood? To me humility would require a more pleading posture. As you recite this great prayer, experiment with saying it in the posture of grief.

152) Blessed are those who mourn (Mt. 5:4)- The reversals of the Beatitudes are striking. Mourners certainly don't see or feel blessing. Jesus could be saying that the least happy/blessed people in the world are to be considered happy or blessed. It could be that the reversals of the new age will hit them first. They will surely receive some recompense, some help at the hand of the Blessing One. "They shall be comforted." When? How? Another way to approach this passage is to see it as a reversal of expectation. No, God does not abandon mourners. No, God is not punishing mourners. No, God is not trying to teach mourners a lesson. Instead, God is with them. God is on their side. Given their condition, they will be comforted. That comfort itself is a blessing, not the previous condition. Our current religious prattle speaks in such a thoughtless fashion about blessings, but not bane. I detect an undercurrent in it that blames the victim for suffering, due to moral failure or insufficient faith. That is one way I can make some sense of something that seems the opposite of a blessing. It is true that hardship does drive us to our knees to communicate with God. When things go well, we

may well claim credit for it and not give God much thought. I do not know if the comfort promised would be for the near future, or if it has a more eschatological, distant future dimension to it. I suppose that one could read will with an emphasis of certainty. At times, I wonder if we see the bereaved as cursed in some sense, especially those dealing with difficult deaths. Is grief starting to be attached with stigma?

153) Is. 59:1 God's hand is not too short to save, nor his ear dull. This is the opposite of the old saying, 'your arm's too short to box with God." In football, we say that a receiver short-arms a pass when they don't reach out for it when they are expecting a hit in the middle of the field by a fearsome linebacker. God is not indifferent to us. God does hear us. God continues to work for the good of creation, all creation. Yes, terrible limits inhere in creation cycles. Luther could be so despairing that he felt as if God were dead to him. The prophet moves to say that we separate from God far more than the opposite. It certainly does feel at times that God is deaf to our prayers. It is a point everyone reaches and wonders what good does it do to pray, as I don't see a change or help? For a long time I have been struck by Fowler's image that God is at work, repairing this world, and at the same time, re-weaving the new creation. Recall that this section of Isaiah deals with people who have returned from exile and were expecting life to be much easier than it was turning out to be. It may be a salutary spiritual exercise to keep a sharp eye peeled for signs of God's working to turn evil or tragic situations into doorways for some good to emerge. Can you recall times when that has been your experience?

154) Is.61:1-11 speaks openly about some direct aspects of grief. It speaks of binding up the brokenhearted. This passage is picked up by Jesus in his sermon back at home in the gospel of Luke (4:16-20). It is sort of a mission statement. The Scripture that was read as the Sabbath reading outside the Torah, the first five books, that was either the one to be read or Jesus selects it.

It was not the 10 Commandments, not something about violence, not something about doctrinal disputes, but this passage written for a disappointed people straggling home from exile. I like the image as it does sometimes feel as if grief is an open wound, a gaping wound needing battlefield care. This passage gives us a wealth of fine images to consider and adopt. I picture God tending the wound like Clara Barton on the front lines. A broken heart comes from many sources, but surely grief does break a heart. The phrase in Hebrew is strong for a broken heart, as it means shattered, torn up, and broken apart from an event or person that oppresses and harms. To keep the lifeblood from leaking out, it needs to be bandaged. The mission of Jesus continues, of course. The Great Physician not only heals sin-sick souls but broken hearts. The Great Physician gives first aid to the downcast spirit as well. In binding the wound, we give it a chance to heal. That takes time. Shakespeare asked "what wound did ever heal but by degrees?" What ointments help heal a broken heart? Notice that the passage imagines healing oil, an oil of gladness to replace the ashes of mourning. What bandages help it heal? Linda Ronstadt sang: "some say the heart is just like a wheel/when you bend it you can't mend it." Oh that we could change attitudes and conditions as easily we change clothes, to replace a mourning outfit with a cloak of praise and gladness. Almost as a response to that thought, we get an image of a garden, with God as a gardener. Alan Wolfelt calls himself a grief gardener and notes the attributes of care, attention and patience required by gardening. It respects the materials at hand. It goes through the cycles of nature and its limitations. Such attributes apply to God as well. Recently, I witnessed the writer Parker Palmer in a performance with Carrie Newcomer and pianist Gary Walters. He spoke of two options for the brokenhearted. A rigid heart breaks into pieces, its shards flying everywhere. A supple heart breaks wide open, able to receive more as time passes.

155) Is. 62:4- The words speak to Jerusalem but could apply to us as well: no more shall forsaken or desolate. The future can be brighter and will be brighter. Desolation can be turned into delight, with time and care. A loss can leave us feeling utterly

forsaken. We don't know what to expect of friends and family, but we know we are not getting what we need at the moment. Instead the marvelous intimacy of a good marriage is promised. As George Clooney said in Up in the Air, when his decidedly single character is asked to help persuade a groom with cold feet to get to the altar: "we do better with someone; the best times of our lives are with someone." Feeling forsaken and desolate can lead to feelings of despair. I like the idea of receiving a new name when the situation undergoes a change. The patriarchs Abram and Jacob received new names, and Jesus gave new names to Simon and Saul. What name would fit your coming through the other side of grief? One of the many things I admire about Biblical prayer is its sheer boldness. In imagining a future, the prayer alerts God to a new reality. in imagining a new future, the prayer calls on God to enact it in reality. In its way, it is a play on "if you build it, he will come.' If you imagine it in prayer, you call on God to make the future a reality. Donald Capps writes on hope: its allies are trust, patience, and modesty, and its enemies are despair, apathy, and shame. Again, hope goes beyond mere optimism. Surely we know things do not somehow go on an upward curve without any effort, on some sort of magical automatic pilot. When some event comes crashing down, then its false promise is exposed, like the idol it is.

156) Is. 64:1-9 Here is a remarkable Biblical complaint. I love the boldness of Biblical prayer. It says that people are not praying due to God hiding from us. In other words, if we had a better listener, if our prayers received more clear responses to their felt needs, then we would pray more. It places a sense of God's absence at God's feet, not our own. This relates, as often happens, to an earlier section (45:14-15). That hiding then relates to aural shrouding: silence. Silence can speak at times, but at other times it becomes almost physically burdensome, like a dead weight. Silence can be deafening. Whitman in Whispers of Heavenly Silence, speaks of the "gossamer thread you fling; catch somewhere, o my soul." Patricia Tull in her Advent 2011 study for Thoughtful Christian writes of v. 1- "God should not merely "look down" on them as in 63:25 but to come down, to

save them, to change things" (p.3). The verbs are in the imperative, issuing commands to God. Prayers such as this imagine a new future and have confidence that the prayer will see that new imagined future come into being. We may learn to talk a good game about prayer being a dialogue, but clear responses are often few and far between. It may feel as if prayer is talking to a wall, or maybe oneself. A spiritual adept whom I know writes out huge swaths of dialogue in prayer journals between himself and God. He calls it his God channel, but when he undergoes a siege of doubt wonders if it is all projection in the end. That intimacy, that closeness is touched by two images in this passage. God is pictured doing craft work; God is an artisan. By extension, God cares deeply for the end product of all that labor: us. In a fairly rare image, Isaiah employs a familial image, God as a father. The ties that bind are one of deep kinship with the Creator. No matter our own paternal experience, we are given the picture of a father suited to our needs.

157) Is. 65:19 is a great picture of hope that no more weeping will be heard. The cause of weeping will not be with us forever. In certain moods, it strikes me as too good to be true. In other moods, it sounds so inviting, just the ticket. God's advent of a new way will change the conditions for those tears. That would be similar to the difference between charity and justice. Charity gives needed help on a case by case basis, but justice seeks to deal with social conditions that give rise to crying human need. This is more than drying tears; the spigot of tears can remain closed. The reason for tears will finally be gone. Blessing will overwhelm even the possibility of an accursed life. Miroslav Volf thinks that some things are so terrible that they will have to be forgotten. Others think that painful memories will somehow be integrated in our new life in a new way. (See Theology Today1/11) This strikes me as just the sort of movement for apocalyptic hopes. When we cannot imagine that they can occur in our life and time without divine intervention, we are in that horizon of far-off hopes. Their very distance renders them safe. Their far-off quality makes it all the more alluring.

158) Is. 66:12-13- Sometimes I require some different divine images. Fortunately, Scripture presents us with a multitude of divine attributes and images. We are not left stranded with only one way to picture God in our thoughts and prayers. Especially when we need some variation due to our emotional state, I am so grateful that we have a panoply of divine images. If pushed, a central part of my image of God is one of anger or disappointment in me. Somehow, the image of God as a bearded figure on a throne in heaven has persisted. I get a different, maternal image here (see also 49:13-15). Even as adults we need parental comforts. It's even a playful image. Playing with the child on the knee could also be translated as delighting in. In part this is a decisive response to the promise (Ch. 40:1). Comfort is now more than an imperative, it is an actuality. As children we rush to our mothers to comfort us when hurt or even upset. What maternal attributes can you apply to God? When I was raised as a boy in the Roman Catholic tradition, Mary was a focal point for spiritual concentration. She served to fulfill the desire for a maternal image in religion, but Protestants relegated her to the back of the train as we thought the Marian devotion was perhaps excessive and detracted form God as the focal point of devotion. Maybe it is easier for you to use the image of Jesus to accomplish this. In her book on Incarnation, <u>Gathering Those Who Are Driven Away,</u> Wendy Farley seamlessly uses female/maternal images for the Holy One, an image favored by Isaiah. It seems almost effortless, as she will flip Mother for Father or the Good for God in Eph.1:3 (p. 151). With many she notes that Wisdom is a female figure (chs.5-6). Different images for God not only fit different circumstances but may fit different spiritual needs or virtues we possess. Recently, in confirmation class, a young man was stunned that Hosea 13:2 would select the image of a mother bear to speak of God, as he was quite open in saying that he pictured God as an old guy with a beard who was seated. Where do you think your images of the Beyond are helpful or unhelpful?

159) Jer. 9:1 first brings up the question, is it God or the prophet speaking? At any rate, it is an evocative image, a spring of water, a fountain of tears. Can any amount of tears reflect the brute force of a loss? We can come to a point when we feel cried out. It is instructive about our own image of God to ask if God can cry. is that a purely human response? Does it indicate more divine vulnerability than we are comfortable with? (See the late William Placher's Narratives of a Vulnerable God). Why would he choose that word, vulnerable? Well, invulnerability would describe the usual Reformed notion of God. If we first assume, though, God is love, then does not love include vulnerability, even for the divine? Later Jeremiah wants to run away from the corruption that causes him so much grief, as well as coming doom. His tears are for his nation, for the suffering of others, as well as for himself. Eventually, we may well be "all cried out" and our tears are spent (Lam. 2:11). How do you regard Jeremiah's tears? How would you regard the tears of God? Does that make God sound too weak for you? Does it make God seem somehow more approachable, even more involving in prayer? How do you regard your own tears? Kathleen O'Connor directs our attention to a story told by the theologian C.S. Song of the tears of a woman whose husband was taken in forced labor to build the Great Wall. Her tears were sufficient to cause the great edifice to collapse and reveal the bones of those who died in building the Great Wall. When do tears seem to have power to you?

160) Jer. 9:21 has death entering a window. Most of us would indeed see death as an unwelcome visitor whom we would not permit entry through the front door as an invited guest. It may be from an ancient story in cultural memory that a god did not want windows in a house as he feared death would enter there. It has the sense of a thief breaking and entering, of slipping in uninvited. Philippe Aries in The Hour of our Death writes that we have tried to make death an obscenity, something not mentioned or seen in polite company. so we try to hide it away, to usher it of our normal lives. Yet, he says that if usher it out the front door, it will surely slip back in through a window. We all would like to close the window to death, at least until we would it consider it

the proper time and place to enter. Some people I know in nursing homes are ready to have the window wide open to death. A woman I know just asked me if I thought God would punish her for wondering why she has lived so long and to what purpose? This is a pertinent image especially for unexpected death, accidental death. Without time to prepare, this type of loss seems to pose some real additional problems for us. It pushes us into trying to find some reason for it, something to help us make sense of it all. Healing can enter by a window as well. Not long ago, I came across a memory by the daughter of the writer Rod Serling, of Twilight Zone fame. She had a terrible time dealing with his death when she was around 20. One summer she gathered up the courage to visit his grave. Then she watched some of his old shows and narration. "I was cognizant of all of the summer sounds in those moments and of this life that moved forward absent my father. I was still haunted by the void, by the reality of this empty space, and yet, those past 30 minutes spent watching his show brought a reconnection with him in a most unexpected way. In the episode's closing narration, I watched my Dad saying, "The ties of flesh are deep and strong, the capacity to love is a vital, rich and all-consuming function of the human animal, and you can find nobility and sacrifice and love wherever you might seek it out — down the block, in the heart, or in 'The Twilight Zone.'" You see, healing came in the surprising breeze that enters an open window, too. The ties that bind are "ties of flesh that are deep and strong." To shut the window is to try to shut down the "vital, rich" human heart.

161) Ps. 23 is so well known that I am hesitant to even work with it. In this area, it is often read at graveside. Even though most of us don't live in rural areas, we gravitate to the image of shepherd. Usually, when we see the Lord as shepherd in Scripture, it is a sign that God will take some things into the divine hand, as the human shepherds/leaders have failed. In other words, we are sheep at times and called to be shepherds for each other at others. I must admit that I don't cotton much to the idea of being a sheep in the flock. The KJV language, I shall not want would now be clearer as I lack nothing, or I will not be

in want, not want as desire but along the lines of being in want. Who doesn't need their inmost self, the soul, restored, especially in grief? Lost in confusion, we need someone whom we can trust to follow. I would think that its most direct words are the translation "though I walk in the midst of the valley of the shadow of death." I think of it as a trail through a dark and forbidding wood. Recently, I saw the movie War Horse. There I saw the valley of the shadow in a different way. The horse get in no-man's land between the trenches in a denuded, lunar landscape of blasted holes, barbed wire, blasted planks and smoke. Think of the walk to Mordor in Lord of the Rings or the hellish construction by the dark wizard that threatens the Ents. So, the green pastures are islands of plenty, safety, and security. Instead of being objects of fear, the road and staff can give comfort. When I see a table prepared by a church or a caterer for a funeral mercy meal, the passage of "preparing at able before me in the presence of the enemies of illness and death, I think of this passage. We may dwell in the house of the Lord forever, or our whole life long, and so may create a view of heaven. Resurrection implies that we indeed are given a banquet in face the old implacable enemy, death. Indeed that can be savored our whole life long, not just after death. It seems to me that to dwell in the house of the Lord forever has a heavenly ring to it, but to dwell in the house of the Lord my whole life long heightens the sense of divine presence. Melodie Beatty, author of Codependent No More, in The Grief Club has a nice exercise she calls the life pact (101), a series of statements to commit to life in its fullness, including our life with God. Part of our pact with life is a script, one in the back of our mind or one plotted and planned about its projected course. Grief often sunders that story's coherence, plot, and direction. The story seems to fall apart. In the turmoil of grief, we are set the task of editing our own life narrative, even as one has slipped from us. Presbyterians like to use the ancient biblical term for a mutual pledge, covenant, a life pact if you will.

162) Ps.102 faces pain directly. It faces the fragility and brevity of life, the one who is praying and who may be thinking of those who have on before us. It uses the familiar image of the fragility

of a shoot under the hot desert sun. I lack the space for a garden in a new place, so I tried some container gardening near the church. i was gone for just three days, and a heat wave withered each plant to kindling. The best and hardest advice I heard about grief was to lean into the pain. That may not be global advice, but it did fit me. Everything in me screamed to avoid the pain, to get distance, distraction, anything. In due course I learned a lesson. To avoid it only makes it loom larger. Trying to avoid it only increases our fear of it. It makes us smaller in relation to its looming presence. In the end, most of our attempts to avoid the pain are extensions of the temptation to denial. Leaning into the pain starts to remove grief's fearsome aspect. I am not saying that one makes it a sadistic habit, that one keeps re-opening a wound that is healing. Lament forms, such as Ps. 13, as a baseline one, help us to lean into the pain in prayer, just as songs of praise or thanksgiving help us to lean into the fullness of those states. Some of us are afraid to even admit to the conflicting and manifold feelings welling up inside of us. We may well be afraid that once the faucet is turned, we will be unable to shut off the flow. The overflow will cause damage, we think. Trying to avoid pain by whatever means necessary, may well make it loom larger and larger and only increase the difficulty in facing up to it. So many millions have faced grief, and you can too. God has probably heard more anger or bitterness or confusion over the years than you can ever approach in a torrent. God has heard honest and candid accusations hurled against the gates of heaven. Recall that laments rarely end in pain. In what seems like a catharsis, they usually end on an upbeat note. Pushing into the pain may well allow room for more positive feelings to enter. A number of analysts of our liturgy in church note the relative absence of the lament form (see Brueggemann, Migliore and Billman, O'Connor). This "tragic loss of lament" teaches a lessened range of proper prayer. It faces a solid wall of cultural resistance, especially when church growth advocates insist on praise choruses and motivational talks as core liturgical values.

163) Mt.12:38, and the sign of Jonah- it is a sign of resurrection.

Jonah gets a second life after being in the belly of the beast, an organic tomb, a place of death. Recall he prays from the belly of the beast. The three days would be part of the symbol structure, I would surmise, so it would fall in with the third day words of Jesus. Jesus would lie in the belly of the beast of death in the stone cold, stone carved tomb, and on the third enter into the Easter life of resurrection. So, the sign of Jonah is new life, resurrection. We don't want to go too far with the comparison. After all, Jonah gets spewed out from the great fish. Jonah was asked to go to where he did not want to go, Nineveh, the seat of empire. Who wants to face the empire of death? Who wants to face the valley of grief? I never thought of this before, but did Jesus want to go to see those who had abandoned him? Perhaps, even here, the mission of healing, especially the emotional healing of guilt and betrayal were necessary. Perhaps the 40 days of resurrection here were, in part, therapy sessions for the disciples. Jesus told Peter that he would go where he did not want to go as well. In Lk.11: 29 the image turns on the repentance of the Ninehvites to the words of Jonah. Repentance does not necessarily refer always to a move from sin, as it means turning around, turning back. In your loss, is it time to turn around, to turn back to help you to move into the future?

164)Rev. 21:10-22:-Some folks find solace in heaven as portrayed in old movies or perhaps more to the point in sympathy cards. I read poems at funeral services that are on the treacly side for me, but are obviously of solace and import for those who ask them to be read or offer them to us. More Biblical folks may fire their imaginations with the images given in Scripture. Some look for a different angle on it. For Christopher Morse, Jesus's image, the kingdom of God/kingdom of heaven, is his anchor. He sees heaven as already here at time, always moving toward us, God's future, as God's Advent. God's way, God's reality, God's unfolding vision is on the move, beckoning us this side of the grave. In The Difference Heaven Makes (36): heaven is: "God's coming forth into the world, remaking, reshaping, renewing all that is dying..." Diane Keaton directed a movie some years ago called Heaven, where different people speak of their views about heaven, and the differences are striking. Morse's fluid conception of the kingdom of heaven, but its concentration on this life did not prevent some sketches of the world to come. Hymns approach it. "Will the Circle Be Unbroken" awaits a better place "in the sky, Lord, in the sky." The rock group U2 has an anthem, Where the Streets Have No Name." In his <u>Reversed Thunder</u>, a book on Revelation, Eugene Peterson calls this section of Revelation, the "last word on heaven" (ch.12). For him, heaven holds together the poles of our material and spiritual existence together. The images are drawn from Ezekiel and Isaiah, from Exodus, among others. The great city of heaven is the antitype of Babylon a few chapters before. Still, it rests on very human foundations, with the names of the fallible apostles on the foundation stones, and the fallible tribes of Israel emblazoned on the gates. Our lives are the raw material of heaven. So, 'there is ...nothing so obscure in my life that it is not, even now, being fashioned into the foundation stones and entrance gates of heaven" (177)

165) 2 Cor. 4:7-12. We are vessels that contain the precious gift of love. Every body is fragile; everybody is fragile.   Indeed, elsewhere Paul calls us temples of the Holy Spirit. Still, we are all fragile vessels, easily broken or chipped. The clay jars are containers for life. Our image of the soul is of some indestructible spiritual power, so some feel free to call the body a mere shell. Even if we are unimpressive physical specimens, we present the image of the living God. We contain the precious gift of grace. That does not have to exist within perfection, but in us. God is remarkably generous. God does not grant grace only to an elite. God does not grant grace to those who seem deserving. Admitting that we are not perfect emblems of stoic resolve and strength is important. A fierce pride in independence can prevent us from getting the help we may well need at times at any level, physical, emotional, spiritual. Our loved ones were, and are, clay jars as well. Full of imperfections, they too contained the soul of life within them. We mark off days on the calendar and are able to face birthdays and anniversaries, changes to beloved places or hearing old songs. For a time, it will be less celebration than the

accomplishment of somehow someway making it through them. I would assume that stone jars of some sort held the wine at the wedding at Cana, just as they held purification water. In the midst of the vulture of death, the reign of death even, we find life in Christ and in the Christian community. That community is described as a cruciform one, living with all sorts of troubles. Verses 8 and 9 describe part of the experience of grief, do they not? "Perplexed, but not beyond measure" (or not driven to despair, or lose heart or grow weary or fainthearted) describes and maybe even prescribes our reactions and responses. If I grasp Paul's thread here, he goes on to say that we do face death's marks all of the time. In so doing we are joined to the death of Christ, but that means we are always tied to resurrection hope and resurrection life.

166) 2 Cor. 6:16 tells us that we are the temple of the living God. I take this to be a communal sense that the faithful form the temple. I am touched by its incarnational sense that God is not distant but is a companion. Many people love the image of footprints from the famous inspirational poem where we get carried for a while. I prefer the image of the footprints walking on the sand together, but I do appreciate that sense of needing to be carried sometimes. More than that, we are temples of the living God. The temple of Jerusalem could be destroyed, our building of flesh and blood may die, but God's dwelling in us will not meet destruction or oblivion. Our lives are already infused with divine presence. God is as close as every breath, every beat of the heart. Maybe at times, the sets of footprints get indistinguishable. I am attracted to the image that we have company in this life. Our passage moves to combine pieces of Lev. 26:12, Jer.32:38, and Ezek. 37:27 to form a composite saying of God's continuing engagement and presence with us. Some are disturbed that Paul's seeming quotation is inexact. On the other hand, his memory is so keen, so replete with biblical images that he is able to weave the passages as if they are quotes from God's own mouth. We are not set out alone. We are made for relationship. The central spiritual relationship is having God as a companion. It's interesting that it is success and

happiness that threatens a relationship with God perhaps more than failure or sadness. When we have a string of mountaintop experiences God may be displaced. Trouble drives us to our knees in prayer. Prayer lessens in importance to the degree we think we are doing well and don't need any help. Prayer is derided as a crutch by some. Do you consider your loved one's life as holding the presence of God? do you consider your body, your life, a temple for God to dwell? If you do, what rooms require special attention? God dwells within the temple of our lives, and even grief includes the sacred precincts.

167) I John 4:7-8- When I get confused or all twisted in knots, I go back to this passage. For all my wanting to blame God for trouble, I am reminded that life is from God and that God is love. God is not power; God is not control; God is love. When I depart from that principle of love, I am on the wrong track. When I place other attributes as a priority in the life of God, I deceive myself. Part of our trouble in dealing with God and human suffering is an insistence that power over the world is the fundamental attribute of God, not love. It is difficult for me to conceive of love as always exercising power over another, over the beloved. Love involves a caring for another, perhaps more than for oneself. It can well involve taking care of someone. Barth (Church Dogmatics IV/1:215-16) writes that Jesus went into a "far country." "We can find no reservation in his solidarity with us...with us in the "stream which hurries downward into the abyss...God has not abandoned the world ..in the unlimited need of our situation...God does not float over the human situation like a being of a completely different kind." What explains such action but love? Our marriage vows say until death do us part, but even that is easier said than done. Virtues such as fidelity and loyalty remain and have to be rethought, renegotiated in widowhood. God's love is faithful, loyal and enduring. Katherine Sakenfeld even translates steadfast love (hesed) as God's loyalty. Mechthild of Magdeburg speaks of Lady Love that seems to open the flood gates for the power of God to flow (see Farley's Gathering Those

Who have Been Driven Away:83-7). Going back to high school physics (the course that kept me from pursuing astronomy) I would consider love in her system to be the attribute that has God's power turn kinetic instead of being potential energies. The letter of John is not content to speak of love as a feeling. No, he wants to see love in action. He demands that love be shown in action, in help, in physical signs and comforts, tangible aid. I think of the response of Eliza where she tells the man enamored with her to "show me" in My Fair Lady.

168) 2 paths life and death Choose life-(Dt. 30:15-20)-This passage speaks to more than pro-birth bumper stickers. In a sense many religious traditions would affirm this word. Pope John Paul II spoke of a culture of death and a culture of life. To choose life means to continue to work on life-affirming patterns of behavior. We can and do choose death-affirming ways of behavior all of the time. Wisdom material in Scripture can be seen as a commentary on this verse. To follow the way of wisdom is to follow the way of life, and to follow the path of folly is to follow the path of death. To get swallowed up in grief for a long period of time is to succumb to a culture of death. To seek paths to enhance life, for oneself and others, is to walk a path that realizes that we are mortal, so life is all the more precious. I remember being astonished when Jimmy Carter quoted Bob Dylan in a 1976 Convention speech about "busy being born, not busy dying." Every day, we choose life and death. Yes, we make choices to live or not, to be or not to be, a la Hamlet. More specifically, our decisions can lead us to affirm the path of life or death. This can be a decision point, as President George W. Bush would say, every single day. Part of me goes along with that, but surely we have moments when this stark moment of decision arrives with special force. Does something feed or starve the soul? Do we look merely to affirm a previous opinion or do we weigh different viewpoints?

169) Numbers 1,26-Death of the old birth of the new- The best of

my Bible teachers, Dennis Olson of Princeton Seminary, used one of the most boring points in Scripture, the census lists in Numbers, to note that it marked the transition of the slave generation into a people who were born into freedom. We are all part of a grand succession of names. It seemed that the old generation was so socialized into seeing themselves as slaves that it was exceedingly diffident for them to adjust to new burdens of freedom, even with the wilderness experience and its mixture of promise and punishment, provision and privation. Sadly, the birth of the new is often accompanied by the death of the old.the people had to adjust to and mourn the death of Aaron (20:29). I get alarmed when I see the number of the WWII generation who are not expected to live out another year. As Kurt Vonnegut said, that leads to the terror of realizing that a high school classmate could be running the government. (Fortunately, the oldest of my generation is now reaching retirement age.) Does anything prove so decisively that we are all in the same boat than death? It touched JFK's family in the White House when Camelot saw a baby die, and stars such as John Travolta and Kelly Preston. As we move through grief, we can begin to see the birth of the new in our own lives. It could well be that a new self emerges out of the trials of grief.

170) Mt 22:13 weeping and gnashing of teeth- I came across a recent book, <u>Razing Hell</u>. (Christopher Morse says hell will close due to lack of patronage) Morse refuses to say that hell is given equal weight with heaven in the Scripture. That is a product of our dualistic desire to keep the scales balanced. When we see cruel injustice not rectified in our time, we project into God's time. Rob Bell of Mars Hill church in Michigan has encountered a a flurry of comments, and a Time magazine cover, on his new work, <u>Love Wins</u>. Calvin linked the image of Gehenna, a refuse site outside the city of Jerusalem, to hell in his gospel commentary. I recall laughing at a Woody Allen line about hell being eternity with a life insurance salesman. I play with that theme at times, such as when I am in the new phone menu hell of a business and think of hell having a phone menu dreamed up by Satan himself. When I am in an endless presbytery meeting, I

consider hell as moderated by the devil who knows the Presbyterian Book of Order. In recent theology, we usually see that fires or darkness of hell as images to get at its central point: separation from God. If sin is a temporary separation from God act by act, intent by intent, hell is the structure of sin for eternity, not knowing God, not knowing love, a life with perhaps others who lives are all consumed by self. Augustine spoke of sin as one's life curving in on itself, and I could picture hell as a constant curving in on the self, so that relationship disintegrates. Grief is a living hell as it pushes us into consistent self-regard. When we see ourselves opening up to others again, we know we are on the right track.

171) Haggai speaks of rebuilding but then being disappointed in the process and result so far. We can get in a frightful rut of always comparing things and even people unfavorably to our memories of the past. We can make such an idol out of the memory of a loved one that no one seems good enough when compared to them. It is a powerful thing to push people into seeing themselves as a constant disappointment who are doomed to never measure up to an old vision. He points to greater things in the future. The future does not have to be a replay of the past. We can act in new ways, not merely behave. Even if we feel disappointed and dispirited, God revivifying spirit is with us. When things seem as nothing, the advice is to be strong, to work, to not fear. It is a reminder to be gentle on ourselves when our progress through grief doesn't match our expectations. We should not beat ourselves up for having some steps backward, even one step forward, two steps back. We should have a forgiving measuring stick to chart our progress through grief. Should we really expect much more of the process of rebuilding than we do of the process it took to build a life before a loss threatened it all? The temptation to push through rebuilding quickly can be countered by being as gentle on ourselves as possible. Inevitably, we will have bad days. We can expect that some days will have made one step forward and two steps back. We can be careful not to set ourselves for failure if we create a vision of recovery from loss that cannot exist in this world. When we start to

idealize the past, it is easy to fall into a trap that nothing in the present or future can ever compare to what once was. Emily Dickinson notes how she analyzed and compared herself to others in "I Measured Every Grief." In speaking with widowed people who have remarried later, they often seem cognizant of not comparing their current spouse to their former spouse, especially after years of idealizing them. No period of time is a halcyon time; no person is perfect, but reality does seem to not match memory or dreams.

172) Hab. 3:17-19 -This is an evocation of faith in spite of all appearances to the contrary. Wendell Berry has said; "be joyful, even though you have considered all the facts." The book has questioned the justice of God. It wonders how long, how long before we see some good, some light. How can a good, just God permit all of the wrongs we see so often? Even in the worst of times, we can give voice to praise, at least for memories. Words seem so weak, but they are what we have to offer. In no place is this more obvious than in a sermon. Author Sue Becker in While I Was Gone relates a sermon her husband Daniel offers in a service. He worries that the old words, Scriptural words and images, no longer console, no longer bear the weight for us. So, he moves to memory. "Pain is memory's first imprinting step." He wonders if we should pity a child who loses someone but has not memory to fall back on. "Memory is a kind of new birth within us...that resurrection-in memory- that, to our surprise, may comfort us." In that is "tender power" (in Listening for God vol. 4,64-66). The mouth goes dry in getting up on Christmas and Easter, but the force of the event always weighs heavily at a funeral service for many ministers. In a thoughtful piece in Interpretation, "The Costly Loss of Praise" we see that a life without praise is a shrunken life. Praise moves our focus from a seemingly independent, autonomous self toward the Praised One. It moves us into a world within divine life itself. It moves us to see that God is not bound by the predictable patterns of life. God has made a new future before, and God can make a new future again (see also Ballentine on prayer in Princeton Sem.Bulletin).

173) Wisdom material in the Bible has a secular slant. In a way, it anticipates the Incarnation, with its attendant interest in living this life, fully and well in the sight of God, our neighbors, and of course, our own selves. Wisdom material in Scripture faces reality with a clear eye. This ancient material has a keen psychological eye for the emotions. Just like life, ti comes at us in unpredictable, often radmom spurts. Prov. 12:25 gives us: "Anxiety weighs down the human heart". In grief we almost forget what it is to have a light and happy time, or a light and happy heart. Later (14:10) 'the heart knows its own bitterness." Some events do lend themselves to sharing, but others remain hard to put into words easily communicated. We are reminded that it is hard for us to fully empathize with anyone, no matter our best intentions. We chafe at the very notion that someone in a similar circumstance can grasp what we go through. We may well fly into a rage when someone who has not gone through remotely the same experience as we have would dare to try to give us advice on how to feel and act, with the assumption that they understand us, and they know where we are coming from. 14:13, "even in laughter, the heart is sad." I remember feeling guilty when I laughed after my brother died. At the same time, our eldest was still a baby, and my laughter with her at being delighted at something helped me out of a trough. We don't have clear areas of demarcation when we can or should feel or act a certain way after loss. Without those markers, it may well seem that our decisions and feelings don't measure up to some vague and shifting standard that we may only possess in the most inchoate forms ourselves.

174) Jonah 4- God acts like a therapist in this chapter. The question is insightful: "does it do you good to be angry, or is it good for you to be angry?" In my hearing, God does ask questions, but this is a more gentle form of the God who hurled storms upon the sea. I don't get the sense that God is angry with Jonah here. God does not punish Jonah for being angry. Jonah responds, to God's gentle question: "angry enough to die." God

does not react harshly to that pouty remark, but God keeps working with Jonah and even tries to explain the divine perspective a bit. For Jonah, everthing conspires against him. Jonah pouts that he lost his shade tree. Plus, his preaching seems successful and now God, the good God, slow to anger, full of steadfast love is giving Nineveh another chance. In other words, Jonah ran because he knew that it was in God's character to forgive even a hated enemy of Israel. (When you think Nineveh think Berlin or Tokyo during WWII or Moscow during the Cold War). That is a familiar feeling to the bereaved. We don't want God to be impartial in love; we want special favors. We may even pout like a child. Of course, anger is a response to loss. Anger has a tendency to isolate us, just when we may well most need sturdy relationships. Anger is a deep-seated emotion as it seems connected with our first moves into autonomy. It has many triggers: frustration, powerlessness. It is part of our character: having a short or long use. Pain may push us into flying off the handle, so it is little surprise that the pain of grief leaves us open to anger attacks. Another is whether we tend its flame carefully. I think of the passage: "be angry but do not sin; don't let the sun go down on your anger." That applies to our relationship with God as well. One issue in grief is to whom anger is directed. Yes, we can have lover's quarrels with Divine Love. God tries to show Jonah that while he loved his shade tree, why wouldn't God love all of creation, including the enemy Nineveh and yes even the animals there. God says that they are ignorant in that they don't know their right from their left. God is leading Jonah into a generosity of spirit. What sort of questions do you think the God of Jonah 4 would ask you to probe your spiritual health? Indeed, when we are in sorrow, we are in ignorance of where to go and what to do. We get so confused it is as if we don't know left from right. God is remarkably forgiving toward hate toward Nineveh. He sees their evil as emerging from ignorance. It sounds like Jesus from the cross in Luke: "they know not what they do." God forgives us in our ignorant groping for answers. God, as we all know, forgives us for the mistakes, the misperceptions and misconceptions, the "missing the mark" that is at the root of some Biblical terms for sin, even our anger.

175) Jonah 2- I think Jonah is praying from the place of the dead, Sheol, in the belly of the beast. It is Ps 139 in the place of deep darkness. Like many, I read <u>Moby Dick</u> in as a junior in high school. Like many, it holds a vague place in my memory. Trible, in her NIB commentary on the book, reminded me that Father Mapple refers to Jonah (508). Even there, God hears the one who has fled to death itself to escape God's call. Even there, in the face of death, Jonah can pray. Even the abode of death can be an arena of prayer. Jonah has been trying to run away, to the edge of the earth, to escape the call of God. Jonah is even willing to be tossed into the sea, not only to save the ship, but may well think that running toward death will keep him from honoring God's call to preach to the hated city of Nineveh. Nothing can escape the reach of God. Now he calls to God. In distress, maybe even death, Jonah longs for the temple, the place of the presence of God, the place of prayer. I rather doubt that would be my first impulse. It is all the more remarkable that Jonah prays when he wanted to escape God's call in the first place. Would not death be the ultimate hiding place from God? After all, he was willing to be sacrificed by the crew to try to appease the deity that they surmised had hurled a storm that threatened them all in the first place. In this remarkable prayer Jonah now sees the hand of the Creator behind the sailors for he says God hurled him into the sea. Who would think that being in the silence of death could become a sanctuary of praise for life and the presence of God in the temple? Notice that the belly of the beast could just as well be the womb of the beast). Perhaps we are getting some glimmers of hope for an afterlife here in the OT. Jonah will emerge from the beast to continue his mission. It's not pretty. (Our daughters, at a certain, age found it hilarious that their Bible had the beast vomit Jonah on to the beach). Recently, our elder daughter was preparing a bible presentation for her dorm assignment and wrote to ask me of vulgar things in the Bible, and I now quote, "'cause you know where so many of them are, Dad." (She recalled her childhood delight in how I told her that part of the story.) Jonah is unceremoniously deposited on the beach, but that unceremonious ejection is the start of a new life. Prayer may indeed by evoked when we are on our knees in trouble. Even if we can't pray as we would like, others are praying for us. Prayer

is a cradle for revived spiritual life.

176) 2 Chr. 6- We call sanctuaries holy places as we invoke, plead for, and assume, the presence of God there most fully. For some, grief has God feel absent, and for others, the presence of God is never more palpable. In our time, we are so captivated with being a "church of one," solitary Christians with a personal relationship, that we have lost sight of Wesley's notion that Christianity is a "social religion." We were just invited to consider this prayer as a model in a recent Bible study. Either Solomon's wisdom extended to prophecy or the final editors of the chapter placed in his prayers some crucial issues for the future of Israel. I would like to focus on the sense of God's presence in that newly constructed temple. My sense is that Israel saw this new temple as a portal into the gates of heaven. This place was at the center of the world. Here one could establish a richer connection to God in this holy place. Mechthild writes of a mystical conversation with God and God responds to her grievous hurt this way: 'I will take this burden first and clasp it to myself/and that way you can more easily bear it." Consider the architecture and feeling evoked by the sanctuary where you worship. Some of us see Scripture as a cathedral of the heart. John Calvin saw the whole of Scripture as spiritual spectacles, glasses to correct our weak and failing spiritual sight. The base for this entire exercise of devotions contends that using a breadth of Scripture helps us to encounter the breadth of God within the wide expanse of responses to grief. Where are your holy places? Have you ever gone on a pilgrimage, sacred or secular? Are there holy things you prize? Are there holy people you wish to emulate? Have you experienced holy moments? Have any of them been connected to dying or death? Has it been difficult for you to go to church?

177) 2 Kings 23:28 -Josiah is portrayed as a good, reforming king who tries to follow the old ways. Instead of glory coming toward him, he dies in battle. One would think that he would be given victory, but he is defeated like any apostate ruler. I could

see people putting such confidence in him, but now it is ashes. He did what he was supposed to do, so should he not be rewarded? Should not the enemy be the one destroyed? Were the gods of the enemy now superior to the God of Israel? Was this some sort of continuing punishment for sins known and unknown? It is infuriating to place hope in someone and have them snatched from you. It is like the dreaded visit of the men with the sad duty of having to inform a family that their brave young one has died in war. The Woody Harrelson movie, The Messenger, takes an unblinking look at the effect of the news on the family but also the toll its takes on those brave souls who have to deliver the news to them. My mother said that when FDR died, people felt lost, as he had been the leader for so long, it was hard to see how the country could continue in the crisis of WWII without him. I was just talking to an old friend recently, and he made the stellar observation that we tend to project our deep personal longings on to the screen of certain public figures. Harold Laswell thought that successful politicians were able to place both inner and social issues on the public stage. Our disappointment and defensiveness arise because it is really ourselves, or at least part of ourselves, that we invest so many hopes. People my age are pulled up short every November 22nd and think of JFK. Vice president biden spoke eloquently of having our heroes murdered in the sixties. We have folded in Lincoln's birthday and recall his murder at the same time we recall the public service of Washington. As I was reviewing this, we recall the 50th anniversary of John Glenn's heroic, risky mission to orbit the earth when we were not quite ready to try this. On the other hand we remember anniversary dates of great heroes who have lived out a rich and full life well. Who are some of your heroes?

178) Acts 17-At Easter, the angel asks the question: "Why seek the living among the dead?" If we live in the past, its dead hand holds us in the world of death. The past can be a blindfold on the light, on a new future. Guilt and regrets from the past can be a very heavy load to carry through our lives. When Faulkner said that the past isn't even past, that catches some of the continuing hold and framing of the past on our present and future. Mike and

the Mechanics capture the sense of regret at things unsaid in the song, The Living Years. Years ago, in getting evaluated for entrance into the ministry, the psychiatrist had me do the old trick of speaking to an empty chair to my father who was killed in a ship tanker explosion before I was three.(My mother was carrying my brother at that time). Please consider writing out a letter or making a tape of regrets with your loved one. List out all of the "if only" statements you can think of.

When we engage the past, we help make it come alive. Indeed the Hebrew word for remember has a sense of bringing the past into the present, having it live again, not being a far off mark on a timeline. Some of us continue to talk with the departed. Some take on an interest of theirs, and we seek to continue it. A child who loved ballet then has her parents fund a ballet scholarship, so that her missed future could be attained by another. Should we who hold to resurrection visit the cemetery often? Most cemeteries are oriented in a baptismal direction, west and east. The idea would be that we face the rising sun, the coming of a new day. Resurrection tells us that things do not have to be a replay of the past. Still, they are the resting place of the dead, not the living. In his missionary journey, Paul goes to speak with philosophers in Athens. With some success, he tries to integrate their beliefs with his own doctrine of resurrection, not an easy sell there. When I was in seminary, we were taught that the Greeks believed in an immortal soul but could not accept the resurrection of the body, so Paul was derided with laughter. James Barr in <u>The Garden of Eden and the Hope of Immortality</u> doubts that easy distinction of body and soul in favor of an integrated viewpoint. Where do you lean?

179) I Kings 3:16 Solomon's fabled wisdom is brought to bear in dealing with grieving women. Grief can make us fear that we are going crazy, and it can, in some instances, lead to crazy behavior as well. Unable to face the death of an infant, maybe not the first child lost to death, a mother takes another infant as her own. Solomon's little experiment uncovers the true mother and the one deranged by grief very easily. The woman who stole a

baby is now willing to see another child die, better to share half a corpse than to be forced to face the death of her own stillborn child. The woman who is the victim of the kidnapping cannot face the death of her beloved, so she could give it up instead of losing it to death. Both women must be in tatters. To lose a child to death, or to lose a child to kidnapping, and be given a corpse is a terror. Every so often, we hear stories of infants switched at birth. Think of the book and film, Sophie's Choice, where a mother is given the horrible choice by an officer to choose which child the Nazi holocaust machine will take. We all may know a lot about death and bereavement, but it does take wisdom to know how and when to apply that knowledge. I have a shelf of books on grief, but I fumble for words just like anyone else when I visit the bereaved. I would like to think that Solomon's wisdom extended to getting some help for the poor deluded woman who could not bear to face life after the death of her child.

180) "Mrs. Job" makes a brief and cruel appearance in chapter 2 (and see 19:17). It is a commonplace to remark that grief puts enormous strain on a marriage, as William Stafford wrote: "lest the parade of our mutual life gets lost in the dark." After all, she has lost everything and her children too. She is at her breaking point, maybe past it, as her spouse is now ill on top of everything else. It is a commonplace that grief does put a strain on a marriage, especially when we lose an offspring to death. Any crisis can threaten to pull us apart as much as bring us to together. In the book and movie The Accidental Tourist, Sarah, a grieving mother says that 'she was murdered too." Maybe Job's wife has heard enough of his struggle with God's justice. Maybe she has felt ignored in her sorrow. Like some spouses, maybe she assumes that Job should grieve just as she does. Often men and women approach grief differently. Women tend to process with words. Earl Grollman (Mourning newsletter) wonders if males speak more readily of their reactions to an event more than being told to speak of their feelings. Over time, I've noticed that men will clam up if they're facing you when speaking of something difficult. That's why men speak more openly at bars as they are

parallel instead of facing each other. I've noticed farmers speaking along a fence where they are both facing outward or speak at an angle from each other when they are across a fence. A man is more likely to say something important at a coffee gathering when staring into a coffee cup than looking at everyone, trying to catch their eye. Given that grief groups are often mostly composed of women, some men may be uncomfortable about becoming participants, so men's bereavement groups are on the rise. This is especially good for older males who have to cross a cultural divide about expressing their feelings, especially in front of women. While women will speak of feeling abandoned, males may speak of the organizing of their lives being torn out, of a part of their life missing. When women take the bulk of the load domestically, this can really leave a widower out in the cold. Carol Lansing's recent book, Power and Order examined 13th century Italian statutes that dealt with the expression of grief by men. Before the ordinances, men would loudly lament a loss in some numbers. The council saw this as unmanly behavior, suitable for women, so fined males who openly grieved. At the end of the book of Job, his wealth, health, and family are restored. I hope it was with Mrs. Job.

181) Hab. 1 and 2 have the flavor of Job to them, as we engage an argument about theodicy. The prophet questions the justice of God. Here, the prophet takes in a big picture of the state of the world, instead of an isolated family calamity as the starting point. With the laments, he too wonders how long? He looks around and sees nothing but trouble. As in Ps. 13, he asks, how long can this possibly last, and how long can we sustain its onslaught? For the life of him, he cannot understand how a pure God can look upon and tolerate all of the evil around us (v.13). Both books find that a traditional view that God merely rewards the righteous and punishes the wicked does not bear up to empirical scrutiny. Indeed, the opposite is too often the case. Sometimes we look at life through a dark filter; nothing seems to be going right. Troubles large and small pile up on one another. We Protestants love to cite Paul's use of the famous quote on living by faith at

2:4. We neglect the verse that precedes it. The prophet wants to see change, and none is in the offing. He admits that God's revelation seems to tarry and linger in a n indefinite future. He is able to say wait for it; it will certainly come. For years I've heard that we should avoid questions about the issue of God and human suffering who are in intense grief. It is said that they would be unable to handle the intellectual issues in such emotional distress. Some say that theodicy questions are in reality pleas for compassion. I'm not entirely sure. They may well be honest questions. The church rarely, if ever, seems to get around to having serious discussions on theodicy. Further, influenced by some trends in cognitive psychology, I wonder: if a book like Feeling Good can help people think their way out of depressive episodes, why cannot the mind be an aid to the grieving? If one presents it as fuel for conversation and not an edict, I don't see the harm done. Indeed, I fear that we make it an edict to only pay attention to emotional processes. At our best, our mind, spirit, and emotions play a role in our struggle and our coping.

182) Haggai 2- We tend to idealize the departed. My father was killed when I was a toddler, while my mother was carrying my brother. It's an odd thing to be raised with an image and a memory that is portrayed as so perfect that one feels doomed never to measure up. That can pose problems as we invest ourselves into the future. No one can compare with them. Nothing seems as good in their absence. It is hard to continue to build bridges of relationship with the perfect, or with the embodiment of its opposite. As time passes, as we come to see someone sharing our human graces and foibles, we can build a relationship with someone who more closely resembles them, not the mental image that has been constructed for us or by us. Still (1:13) "I am with you, says the Lord. Take courage and work" (2:4). Grief work is hard, grueling work. The future is rarely what we imagined it to be, and even if it is, we still get disappointed with it. Expectations sometimes cause the horizon to keep receding away from us. Sometimes we set expectations so high that nothing on earth can match them. I used to tease my mother that when she would get to heaven, she would proclaim it

a disappointment and set to work nagging God about what needed to be improved. Maybe your time with a loved one will be the high point of life. We can castigate our present as "seeming as if it is nothing in our eyes" (2:3). If we keep comparing everything to "glory days," real or imagined, we are consigning ourselves to disappointment. It will sap our energies as we will bombard our efforts with questions such as "what is the use?" That does not mean that the future has to be its opposite in the pit of despair. Even if the good is not the best, it can still be very good indeed. In Hopkins" poem that starts: "Margaret are you grieving" ends with what may be a note of clinical cruelty: "it is Margaret that you are grieving." Perhaps, it means that she is grieving the loss of her future, of her expectations, of her hopes. Perhaps, it is directed to the reader, and we are grieving not the person for whom she grieves, we are grieving with her, for her pain, and in part, to our own.

183) Lk. 12:13-21- We resist transience. We want stability and security. If I understand this sequence correctly, Jesus tells a story that suggests that we try to plan for a future over which we have no control. Things happen out of the blue at times. Perhaps it may indicate that our best plans are done in blithe ignorance of the divine design. It must be Luke's intention to then continue this line with the words of Jesus about the futility of worry. At the same time, Jesus refers to the transience of the grass of the field. God clothes that grass with gorgeous flowers and color, how much more so does God lavish us with love? Even though our loved ones are but transient beings in this life, even though we ourselves are mortal, we are loved, respected, cared for. In the movie Field of Dreams, an Iowa farmer builds a baseball diamond where players of the past, such as Shoeless Joe Jackson, play ball again. For the farmer, the crucial one who gets to visit is his father. He plays catch again, when the father is young and vital, not yet beaten down by hardship and disappointments. One of the characters knew that other days would come, but now knows there was but one day, today, where we do truly live. It is an elegy for missed chances, untaken risks, and lifelong regrets. In its way then its field of dreams is where

heaven gives us a second chance at life, when we are at our seeming peak.

184) Mt. 6:25-34- As Jesus said, worry does not add a foot to the measure of our life span. Grief is a thief of energy, but so is worry. When we need to husband our energies, it is foolish to watch them fly off in the midst of worry. Worry usually becomes an avalanche of extra concerns and burdens, so it robs us our capacity to start to make choices and distinguish between critical issues and annoyances. Many of us confuse worry for caring. We are anxious so much of the time that we regard its absence a suspicious. Worry saps our ability to respond when needed.
 Losing a loved often has real cause for all sorts of worry, economic and social. Death causes all sorts of changes and all sorts of struggles. We may worry about their place in heaven. In part, that comes from our thirst for a sense of control over that which we cannot control. We may worry that we are repeating ourselves. Repetition is not a rut, at least at first. I went to a grief seminar recently and Ken Haugk takes a cue from the line about forgiving 70 X 7 and jokingly says we can hear the same story 70x7 minus 290, before we say we've heard the story before. Inviting people, inviting oneself, to go over what the day the loved one died was like opens floodgates of memory and locked away thoughts and feelings. It helps us to lean into the pain. It is a way of processing the welter of feelings and thoughts and even physical symptoms of the grieving. We replay the events to help dull some of the sting of death. Some play a macabre sort of game of what's the worst that can happen. You may think, "Well, it's already happened to me." As you peer into the future, the little game may well take some of the sting of fear away. In the face of anxiety, we often make mistakes, often overreact, often let the anxiety rule our heads and take over our emotional responses as well. Anxiety and worry can become contagious, so it may be a good move to find some clam and stable people in an anxious time.The great coach Dean Smith said that "if you treat many situations as life and death, you will die many times over."

185) Transfiguration- Mt. 17 is a glimpse into the resurrected life. Jesus has clothes that appear dazzling white, just as the resurrection stories or Dan. 10. Jesus is speaking with Moses who by this time was thought to have been assumed in heaven and Elijah who ascended in a fiery chariot. So, part of the intrigue is that they did not die as we would call it. That is why they would be part of apocalyptic speculation. Yet, Jesus, as the creed says, was crucified, dead, and buried. It is a way for us to enter into Biblically-based speculation of heaven. These people are recognizable, and they have communication with one another. They clearly are not in this plane of existence. The word we call transfiguration is metamorphosis, a change in form, in Greek. Remember in earth science some rocks change over time, as shale changes into slate. Peter wants to hold on to that moment, but life is not lived in mountaintop experiences alone. They live out the vision down in the valley, down in real life. Peter, it seems to me, wants to try to stabilize the image by offering to build booths/tabernacles, perhaps, for the three figures. That is not to be, for their life cannot be lived on the mountaintop alone, but down in everyday life. The disciples get to carry the vision with them. I forgot that Matthew does not have an ascension scene. At the close of the gospel, the disciples are directed to a mountain in Galilee Mt. 28:16). Could tha t place have been the mount of the transfiguration, or perhaps the Sermon on the Mount, or the mount of healings (15:29)? We are not given enough information to go beyond a mere conjecture. I like to claim the transfiguration for our perspectives here on earth, maybe especially in "valley" moments. Our angle of vision has to change in mountaintop moments. Visions of a better future affect our sight now, in this world. Most of all, transfigured sight affects the way we see own self and others. Part of the Christian experience is starting to see through the eyes of Christ, the yes of love. In three songs, at least, on Black Cadillac, Rosanne Cash uses images of impaired sight in her explorations of loss on that album. In "Like a Wave" she sees our veiled, imperfect minds as a relief: "my memory is filing with smoke/it's such a relief not to know." In "The Good Intent": "my brother sold my mother's house/I never shed a tear/I could watch the world in

smoke/there' nothing for me here/I've seen behind the darkened veil/and it's all I want to know." "Burn Down This Town" wants to see smoke to be rid of memories and perhaps all of those living happily without the pain of loss: "the sprinkled lawn and the mirrored hall/the Christmas tree/just burn it all the sky is falling with ash and mud" Perhaps our eyes may see death in a transfigured way. May we know that our loved one's will change in appearance but their core of the self will remain, even as they change more and more into their true self. Alive or dead, God sees us through the transfigured eyes of love. May we all come to see those whom we know through those eyes of transfiguration. The eyes of grief are the eyes of chastened love.

186) Lk. 22:39-53 Jesus knew full well the agonies of facing death. Jesus had the survival instinct, the life instinct, just as we do. Even in John's gospel, where Jesus seems like a Zen master to me in his responses to question, 12:27 has Jesus say "now is my soul troubled." Plus, Jesus had so much to live for, so much good needing to be done. In Luke's gospel the anxiety is intense some versions of it include that the anxiety was so steep that his sweat was like drops of blood. (Is that where the phrase sweated blood developed?) Here the agony, the struggle is so intense it is like that of an athlete, spent at the end of the contest. The early Reformers saw this as the start of the descent into hell, the sense of being separated from God. John's gospel has Jesus facing death like a superhero, but in the synoptic gospels that precede it, Jesus is shaken to the core. Jesus then experienced the fear, the anxiety we know in facing death. I am convinced that the representative function of Jesus in the priestly work included and includes identification with what we all go through in facing death. In an essay on anxiety Lauren Winner in the Christian Century (2/8/12: 32-3) writes of anxiety driving her with constant worries and fears. Shelly Rambo in Spirit and Trauma examines our redemption narrative of innocence, a fall, and restoration through insights of trauma studies. She fears we may be a little too quick in proclaiming triumph in a world filled with trauma. Liturgically, we can get a sense of her looking from the middle of trauma through Holy Saturday vigils. Trauma studies do not fit every loss of course, but they do cast new light

on some of our terrible situations and their consequences.

187) LK. 15 far country and the prodigal- Biblical images can be stretched, sometimes beyond the breaking point. It is such a good story and good image. Karl Barth used it as the image for a whole volume of the Incarnation as the journey of the Son into the far country. One of the remarkable features of this story is that we think we know each character, even though we have been given just a few brushstrokes. We can see others in them, and we are certainly pushed to recognize ourselves in them. I like to think that we contain elements of all three characters within our own lives. Our loved ones are in a far country. Grief places us in an unfamiliar far country too. I like the idea of God running to meet us, as the father runs to meet the Prodigal in the story. Still we are left here like a father scanning the horizon for their return, like David for Absalom or the Prodigal's father here. When the father tries to explain the celebration to the elder brother, the words, "your brother was dead and has come to life" (v.32). When the father throws a party, that celebration is a wedge into revealing heaven. We go far and wide seeking something, but our heart's true home is with home, toward God, not away from God. If you can go with the image, imagine God as the prodigal's father rushing out to greet us, without any regard for formalities. In grief, the younger brother inside of us may flee, and blame God for the distance. Maybe we allow the younger brother in us to try to drown our sorrows, concerned with the wake but not the funeral service. The elder brother in us is dutiful and prudent, but inside is disappointed that he is not recognized for that. The elder brother in us is desperately concerned abut appearances but resentful of those who can live with a lighter grasp of the reins. The elder brother in us is judgmental toward how others grieve. How do you think the elder brother would handle grief? The father in us yearns for some sight of the loved one; One eye is scanning that far horizon. The father figure in us is forgiving toward the imperfections of the loved one, and the ones who remain with us. How would the father handle grief? If the younger son has changed, and some doubt it in the story, then he will look with real sympathy and

compassion. Being in the pig sty, he knows what it is like to be down and out. On the other hand, the younger brother may still be looking for any excuse for a party. We all face crisis, to some degree, in character. It may well be a mistake ot impose one form of coping on different characters.

188)Ps. 77:6 (Colin Parkes) Seeking behavior reminds me of searching for the pearl of great price. When we go out and think that we are seeing someone we know, especially when it is someone dead and gone, we may well be still seeking that person. It could be also that our minds tend to fill in gaps. When we see someone with some features similar to someone we know, we leap to a conclusion. We are hyper-vigilant keeping on the lookout for the loved one, like a sentry on guard. We may be looking for a bit of magic, that if we keep on the lookout the lost one will magically appear out of nowhere and be with us again. We all yearn for the loved one to return. Great dependence on the loved one heightens the feeling state. It is not an easy thing to learn to manage life alone, or to manage in their absence for that matter. When they occupy a central pivot point in one's life, we lose a sense of our bearings. We depend on people to manage tasks for us, to occupy roles within the family, to help us navigate our connections to others socially. Therese Rando even calls it "bondage of the deceased." Parkes describes searching as restless. Most grieving people go through searching and yearning for the lost loved one, at least unconsciously. We want the lost to return to us. Great dependence movement, as if you are scouring the environment for smoothing lost. People will revisit places they frequented, as if it is possible they will be found there. Some people call out the loved one's name; half hoping that they will respond to the call, that they will answer the voice and come back home. I will go out on a limb a bit and consider seeking behavior toward God. Loss may well entail the loss of our image of God. Sometimes we react by getting more rigid about the image we have carried with us, but we may well be now searching for the lost God when our mental structure for the way the world should work collapses. Indeed searching behavior as described by Parkes is a spiritual mainstay. That same God searches our hearts. (I think of it as a spiritual diagnosis). Jer. 17:10, Rom. 8:27, among others speak for this diligent God who can peer through our defenses and artifice and find things hidden even to ourselves or the most deft therapist. The French movie, the return of Martin Guerre (and redone as an American movie, Summersby) turns this notion on its head where a man returns to a village and now claims the mantle of a man gone to war. A similar ploy is used in the Jim Carrey movie, the Majestic. have you noticed elements of seeking behavior in yourself?

189) Grief does not permit us to think clearly for a while. We emphasize the depth of feelings so much that we forget how much our mental faculties are diminished or distorted. Our usual speed at comprehension is diminished in utter confusion.
See Year of Magical Thinking for a powerful description of the cognitive strain of loss. While her daughter was desperately ill, Joan Didion's husband died suddenly in their apartment. Her book describes some of the mental confusion that comes with grief, of trying to wrap one's cognition around the brute fact of loss. We don't normalize our difficulties in thinking during times of loss nearly enough. Grief takes a real toll on the thought process and concentration. Magical thinking is a small child's conception of causality. In the first days, it is an heroic effort to get one foot in front of another, and we often have to make some important decisions in that difficult time. What would usually take a moment's consideration leaves us in a quandary. We don't process what we hear very well. Later, we look for distraction in work, projects, or recreation, but our minds keep drifting off, lost in a fog. Our concentration lapses and it is difficult to give sustained attention to almost anything, let alone something difficult, complex, or analytical. We can try to read, but the words pass by and don't sink in. Simple tasks may give some relief in distraction, but complex ones leave us in neutral. we think we are hard at a task and then realize that we have been somewhere else for quite a few minutes. Volkan and Zintl (33) quote Helen Hayes speaking of two years of "total confusion" following the death of her husband. In our current time of rushing back to work, it is important for us to be gentle on ourselves when we

discover our concentration is not up to what it once was. this also applies to students of course who may find it difficult to focus on their studies as easily as they may have prior to a loss. In due course, it will not be such a struggle. Efficiency will be linked to effectiveness in your work life again, but it may take some time. The common advice to be gentle on oneself is fully appropriate for the struggle we have in returning to some semblance of a return to our accustomed mental faculties. At work we live embedded within all sorts of assumptions. One is that we should be able to place personal matters in a compartment and lock them up during work. Given that our cognitive capabilities do suffer as a result of loss, this puts us under even greater stress and strain.

190) Mk.1:40-5 Jesus healed others in Scripture-why not my loved one now? Jesus seems almost cavalier with the leper. One could translate the response of Jesus, as OK, I sure will, when he is approached for a healing. So, why did healing not come so easily for us? We may fear, secretly or overtly, that perhaps we did something wrong, asked improperly, kept a bad attitude. Bargaining is not only part of the grief processes of many, but it is a part of prayer life as well. When I stood over my brother's grave, I remember sobbing, in part, as I felt that God had let us down. I imagine that a number of us have prayed that we will make a commitment to do something if only this pall of grief would ease a bit. Many of us bargained in prayer if a loved one were ill in hopes of a healing. The pain of unanswered prayer is a deep wound for the faithful, or the merely desperate for that matter. Nicholas Wolterstorff in his lament for his son Eric starts to explore lament seriously as his prayer life felt off. He continues to pray that his family be protected, but then he comes up short, a she prayed for his son's protection as well. (70). Bargaining seeks a measure of control with an agent, God, who does not seem to exercise much individualized controls. Some of us imagine divine power as interventionist, available to directly change conditions. Some see it as operating indirectly, through intervening agents, including us. Bargaining assumes a quid pro quo relationship. I give you this, so you give me that. The older

Biblical and Presbyterian word for our relations is deeper than a contractual one, as it is covenant, an enduring relationship, a compact, a partnership. The God of grace does not seem to work on a quid pro quo basis. The Scriptures do not give many examples of Jesus not healing people, save for Mark's assertion that he could not do many deeds of power due to the people's obduracy. In Measure for Measure Shakespeare wrote:' the miserable have no other medicine, but only hope."

191) Death is a mythic force- Most of us are familiar with the image of Death as the Grim Reaper. Maybe we know of Bergmann's scene of playing chess with Death, or Woody Allen's badminton match with death. In All That Jazz Death had an alluring female aspect, where the protagonist flirted with her. Maybe some need to think of Death as the Dark side of the force. In his book on funerals, Accompany them With Singing, the noted preaching professor Thomas Long says that we always face 2 forms of death, as mortality, and as a force in its own right, the Serpent who strangles Life out of us, a leering negation. At funeral homes on occasion, I imagine Death as a preening celebrator of victory, dressed to the nines, like Fred Astaire. At the end of a Christian funeral, death sneaks out the side door in rags, defeated again. Death is portrayed often in earlier form as a skeleton, or a hooded figure, or the way the ghost of Christmas future is portrayed in some Christmas Carol productions. We feel helpless in the face of it. We often feel powerless in facing grief as well. We so want to help but lack the words or deeds. Even if we ask, the griever can't specify what would help, except the impossible of raising the loved one back to life. Fighting loss is a titanic struggle, and we feel ill-equipped to fight such an imperious force. I am stunned at what people can get though. The God of the grieving is on our side and empowers us to fight this fight.

192) Jonah 1 and running to Tarshish. I imagine it as a resort destination away from it all. Tarshish is the fantasy of escape, or

of a return to Eden, of living in a past when things were all right. As Joe Louis said, 'we can run but we can't hide." We could also think of it more in the psychological state of denial, or refusal to face reality by hiding in a haze of alcohol or by frenzied distraction to prevent unbidden thoughts of pain from surfacing. Jonah is fleeing from the very presence of the Lord, the calling of God. All we know is that Jonah is fleeing from a summons to preach to the capital city of the dreaded Assyrian empire. Only later do we uncover the reason for his flight. He is on the run from his vocation, his calling by trying to reach a vacation spot. When a storm hits, Jonah is sleeping. Sleep can be a way of trying to escape the pressures of life, to go to the Tarshish of dreamland. Have you been comforted or afflicted by dreams lately? How has your sleep been of late? He would rather die rather than go to Nineveh, the heart of the Assyrian empire, but we do not know why, as of yet. He virtually volunteers to be thrown overboard as a sacrifice to still the storm. Think of that. Jonah would rather be a victim of the waves than go into enemy territory under the call of God. The sleep of death would be preferable to life in foreign territory. If we blame God for a death, we may well want to hide form the presence of God, a presence that would be malevolent. We could go to the ends of the earth, but to no avail. In moments of deep despair, we too think we would much rather be with a loved one who has died, instead of facing another day of pain. The loving, insistent presence of God respects no time, no border. We devoutly wish that we could find a place to get away from it all, to set grief aside for a while. Of course, we need a respite but the way is through grief, not around it, not avoiding it. The trauma of grief may lead to sleep disturbances of nightmares, and that has a cascade effect of not finding oneself able to escape for eight hours in a peaceful slumber. Do you have a vision of Tarshish?

193) Job 3-Protest theodicy has my respect, even when that protest starts to flirt with being agnostic or even atheistic, at least for a time. It takes seriously the attribute of God's power and goodness. It wonders why God's power is not more evident for the good and against the evils we encounter. Protest shakes

its fist against the perceived power of God and asks why does God stand back and let a parade of evils move through unchecked? It takes God seriously enough to want to work through a real and meaningful fight with God as we have been led to understand. William Safire called Job a dissident, and that fits the profile of protest. Woody Allen in Stardust memories replied to someone: "to you I'm an atheist. To God, I'm the loyal opposition." Go through Elie Wiesel's play, "The Trial of God" for a literary meditation on theodicy. I move toward wondering if we misperceive the power of God, and we see power in terms of control, instead of the power of love. It is difficult for me to even begin to analyze the goodness of God, as that seems more axiomatic to me. If we say that God permits evil, protest wonders why, what good purpose does it serve? Some come to question if God is good, or if a mix of good and evil inhere with the character and purpose of God, at least from our perspective. Job's arguments are really a form of protest theodicy. Some argue against the question, or at least its formulation. Protest is at the root of asking, why. With every good intention, we construct ways of defending God's goodness and love and they are rarely convincing. Perhaps it is more palatable to speak of a lover's quarrel with God. I have heard some people say that God is going to answer a lot of questions for them when they get to heaven.

194) (I Sam. 17) Death is a Goliath. Goliath is a great symbol for death. Huge, brash, frightening, Goliath puts us under siege. Death taunts us, and we cower. There in the Valley of Elah is David by a brook, bearing taunts and selecting stones. On one side of him are the Philistines bearing insults with their weapons of war. On the other side are David's people demoralized, paralyzed with fear, unable to find a champion, until now. Goliath sneers at us, as we cower in fear before his brute strength. Instead of a great warrior, young David, a shepherd boy, takes on the role of champion. They try to give him the king's armor, but he swims in its size and casts it off. Sometimes, out of a desire to be helpful, we try to put ways to cope and attitudes about loss on to people, whether they fit or not. Most of us do face grief in character. Young David collects five smooth

stones. Even though crowds line the combatants, they face each other alone. David knows that he may face Goliath alone, but not unaided. Consider 5 resources available to us in the ordinary things we encounter or possess. It is a good exercise to wonder what five smooth stones we can employ against it. They don't have to be big things. They don't have to be items that require a pilgrimage to a far-off land. They could be easily accessible. Part of the anger in grief is the fight in the fight or flight response in the face of a fearsome enemy. Anger runs through grief like an undercurrent. Sometimes the anger is there and misplaced. When that happens, recall the Harry Truman model of writing a "circular file" letter for the wastebasket, not to be mailed. Tell them why you are angry and how angry you are and then dispose of the letter. Burning may be a good disposal method, or ripping it up in tiny pieces could work. Remember that Goliath sneered at little David. Remember who won and with what weapons. So often in Scripture, we hear the words fear not. I realize that is easier said than done. Fear paralyzes our powers. Fear can blind us to hope and options. David could fight his fear as being with the Lord. He could fight his fear by collecting the material at hand to fight, not flee or hide.

195) Biblical conversation Lamentations 1:2 v. Is. 40:1-Kuhn has a nice little book on the Bible as conversation. The Bible is not a consistent monologue. What he means is that it provides a way of hearing different approaches to the ways of God. Within its pages, the Bible has an internal debate going on as passages reflect on experience. when we read Scripture, we are drawn into a discussion that took perhaps a thousand years to produce, and readers have been drawn into its world for two thousand more years. Instead of seeing it as a monologue of God, it is a chorus of voices. Look at how the story of Ruth clashes with the rule of Ezra. Look at how Job is really arguing with the stream of tradition that says we can expect blessing if we stay well within the correct way from Proverbs or Deuteronomy and its histories. In a way, it gives us permission to argue with the differing, conflicting, ambivalent thoughts and feelings that surge through us. We can pray the Scriptures more easily perhaps when we see

that within its pages are already conversations with and about God. That opens a wide door for us to have conversation, dialogue, and arguments with Scripture as we meditate on it. The name Israel means to contend with, or wrestle with God. I take that to mean God's will and way in the world, the image of God we may hold from the words of the Bible itself. Personally, I not only like a diversity of divine images, but I do tend to downplay harsh ones. It is a bracing tonic for me to hear Rosanne Cash find God in both roses and thorns in "God Is in the Roses." I am suggesting that reading the Bible is a wrestling match of holds and counters, of gaining the upper hand, of a struggle to come to both understanding and means toward a richer, fuller life. The Bible includes what we would call arguing with the people and stories within its pages. I have long been enamored of the idea that we discover ourselves within the pages of Scripture. We can identify with, or argue with characters and situations throughout its pages. We can come to a new understanding, perhaps, only when we engage Biblical characters and ideas, less as answers, and more as invitations to grapple with them. Lamentations does not have one voice, but a number of them. God is silent in the midst of this welter of voices. For me, its structure gives a sense that people have a chance to fully express themselves and not be rushed toward a conclusion or attitude we may wish to hear. It is difficult to feel as if we get a full hearing, but this bustle of voices does lead me to think that this is a Biblical model for people getting a chance to speak their peace.

196) Prov. 15- Anger is one of the seven deadly traditional sins. Anger is also a typical component of grief. It gets expressed often at anyone within range. One may well want to be angry with God not intervening, or at least one's image of God, one that we may have carried with us since childhood, but we are afraid that it is inappropriate. so, we then avoid church, as that will show God. I've heard it said that God has tough skin and shoulders strong enough to lean on, but strong enough to take a pounding too. We get angry with those around us, even when they are trying to help. We may be looking for someone to give us an excuse to vent our spleen, funeral directors, doctors, and clergy. We may

come to admitting that we are angry at the departed, because we blame them for what has now happened ot our lives. How can one be angry at someone who has died? It does not make rational sense, but it does seem to have real emotional force to it. Anger does require a safety valve. On the other hand, dwelling on anger seems to feed it. Just because it feels good to let off steam does not mean it is a healthy habit to start indulging in it frequently, at the drop of a hat. It is especially important not to keep feeding the anger, so it starts to convert you into a constantly angry, aggrieved person. Twice in Scripture we read be angry, but do not sin. It assumes that we do get angry, but if it is left uncontrolled we run into serious trouble. (See a recent Thoughtful Christian piece by Farley on the topic). Anger kept boiling can and does result in saying things we cannot erase. Anger can push us to do things that we would never do if we were in better control of the impulses set in motion with anger. Just because something is a feeling does not somehow make it immune from the realm of self-control. We know well that anger affects our thought processes poorly. Certainly it is a spiritual impediment. Unresolved anger is clearly an obstacle to love. Few things turn someone into an object as easily as anger. We can learn from our anger as well. We can notice when we are being pushed toward anger, even baited. We can notice what situations tend too push us into anger. Then, we can take steps to find some ways to cool its presence and burning.

197) See text note for is. 63:9 God feels. Employing Greek philosophy, the early church saw God as above mere human feelings. It is of course always a danger to make God a larger version of the human. After all, God is divine, and we are but mortals. The Creator is not the same as the created. Yet, I harbor deep doubts about using philosophical categories as the interpretive frame on what God can or cannot be. It seems to me that we them are tempted to place God within containers of our choosing. It may well be convenient and important toward our understanding, but surely the Transcendent One cannot be captured within a set of categories that will soon be displaced when the next mode of interpretation rises. Why do so many of

us have no trouble with the wrath of an angry God toward sin and sinners, but balk at the thought of the power of love within God? If God is love, then God cannot be above all forms of feeling of which we are familiar, at least by analogy. Put another way, how could an intellectual or philosophical category push love down in a hierarchy of values? Scripture portrays God as in relationship with us, not a detached, impartial, disinterested, objective observer. No, the love of God has God on the side of our lives. Those categories threaten to make self-sufficiency, autonomy, and even isolation as regnant forms of being over love, relations, and connection. Process theology puts a premium on the responsive, sympathetic God. If Jesus 'sympathizes with us in our weakness" then surely Jesus sympathizes with us in our grief.

The theologian Amy Pantinga Pauw, a scholar of Jonathan Edwards, directed me to a 1741 sermon in a book review. There we see little evidence of the thunder of "Sinners in the Hands of an Angry God." Here he speaks of the bereaved spreading their grief before Christ. He speaks of the tenderness of Christ toward the bereaved, of the fellow-feeling Christ has with the bereaved. Jeremy Begbie wrote of a poem by George Herbert in <u>Interpretation</u> (1/12:41-54) where the poet, in The Temple, is thunderstruck by a line in Eph. 4: 30 where Paul command us not to grieve the spirit. Herbert than takes this as an affirmation that our sin causes God grief. I would go with his wondering and consider the grief of God for our grief. "art thou grieved, sweet and perfect dove, when i am sour...Grieved for me?....the God of love doth grieve...God doth groan."

198) Ec. 9:7-We lose the companionship of a loved one. When we lose a spouse, we lose the sheer warmth of togetherness. That does not define a relationship of course, but nor is it to be dismissed as a trivial matter. At a church coffee, I just heard a widower say that he never feels warm in bed, no matter how many electric blankets, now that his wife no longer shares their bed. It is yet another thing that we miss. Part of the wisdom of Ecclesiastes is imposing some order on his reflection on the meaningless search for big answers to the questions we raise about the course of our time here. Ch.4 moves in a linear 1-2-3

sequence. Organization takes some of the fear out of seeming chaos. This book challenges conventional pieties in large part because he takes an unblinking look at death. Death is perhaps the issue in his view that so much of life is a "vanity" better understood now as meaningless, absurd, a wasted breath, a mere shadow, a morning mist. One minute someone you've loved for years is here, then no longer there. We keep seeking that voice that asks us how our day was. Piece by piece such things fit into the mosaic of our lives. So much of what consider important seems less so, now. Still, we chase after those mists, as we don't know anything more substantial to work toward. We crave not only physical warmth, but the warmth of human contact, interaction, and companionship. That physical warmth is bolstered by the emotional warmth of having a close companion, the first you call out hello to the second you walk into the house. No electric blanket takes the place of the warmth of a body lying next to you. Here, we also need to tread carefully. With the loss of an intimate relationship, we may look to fill the gap. Someone who is a companion on the journey may fall into the need, and you both could get hurt more. This vulnerability applies to professional relationships as well, as it can feed the effects of transference. Some may even routinely fall prey to the temptation to cross boundaries that are there to protect both parties in a therapeutic relationship. As they say in Stephen's ministry, when someone is in a ditch they are looking for a helping hand out of the ditch, not for someone to jump down in the ditch with them. Joyce Carol Oates in A Widow's Story offers the basic advice of wearing socks to bed. (She also speaks of her loathing for the fruit baskets that come rolling in as expressions of sympathy.) Even though they are well-intentioned, tokens of sympathy underscore our loss.

199) The Spirit intercedes for us with sighs too deep for words (Rom. 8:26-8). We may well like to imagine ourselves being eloquent, moving, and helpful in times of loss, but words often fail us. I recall Thomas Long the noted preaching professor, speak of a suffering a death in his family, and the minister came back from a vacation, holding his Bible or prayer book, like a life

preserver at his chest, all the while wondering, "what to say, what to say, dear Lord, what to say?" In my experience, I bring along a prayer book, as I often say, "just to get my mouth moving again." I find it moving that the God who created with a word can be at a loss for words in the presence of the groaning of this creation. Sometimes words seem so frail, even if we can conjure some up. That's why a hug at the funeral home may mean so much. Silence seems to be the proper response as words seem inadequate, even cheap. Touch can be healing. A look can speak volumes, just as a picture speaks a thousand words. A gesture communicates, and sometimes with more clarity than words. Early Christian thinkers made the Spirit the bond of love between Father and Son. As the paraclete (Greek, one called along side-Jn. 14), the Spirit is our helper/advocate or counselor or comforter. I think of the verbal, erudite Judd Hirsch, as a counsellor in "Ordinary People" who can mutter only "oh, Jesus," when a tragedy befalls his young patient in crisis, before he can get him to somehow find his office. One of the reasons I am a fan of having a prayer book when visiting people is that it can give me a start when I am groping for words to pray. The prayers are often far more eloquent or deep than I could ever dream of coming up with, especially at the spur of the moment or caught in the grip of emotion myself. At times, we are inspired, and a thought or word comes to us that seems to appear more than being labored over. In the face of our stammering inability to say what we want, to pray as we would like, I find real comfort in the thought that within God's own self, continues to intercede for us. Even the Spirit seems to find words inadequate to the task. Instead the Spirit's sighs speak volumes.

200) On occasion, my imagination has Jesus at the 'right hand of the Father" enthroned in heaven. What are some of the activities for the ascended Jesus in the center of heaven? Jesus prays for us. When prayer will not come, Jesus prays for us Rom. 8:34). When I get frustrated at my own prayers, I find real comfort and release in the thought that my poor words can be interpreted and amplified in the divine realm. I wonder if it includes pleading, or debate, or relaxed conversation in this inner-divine

communication. Of course, the ascension indicates that Jesus went up, with the "two natures" in place. Those heavenly prayers are then made in full recognition of the human condition, as in the book of Hebrews. That is a comfort when grief seems to move in fits and starts. I just heard a woman speak of having grief attacks that come up on the way to work or embarrass her if she's with a group of friends or in public. The late Elizabeth Edwards wrote and spoke of a grief attack in a supermarket when she passed by the cereal they used to buy for their son. Alan Wolfelt calls them "griefbursts." If it is too hard to make a scene in public, excuse yourself to a rest room. Be gentle on yourself and see them as predictable part of the process. Jesus, who knows our needs before we ask, prays for us still. Part of the divine conversation includes prayer. We are not forgotten, we are prayed for. When we wonder if our prayers are heard, we can remind ourselves; that is all right; Jesus prays for us. Jesus prays with us. I assume the right hand of the Father is the position of power, an honored position. Surely Jesus has the ear of God. That pushes me to wonder if Jesus has to deal with unanswered prayers even in heaven. Prayer is not magic, even for Jesus.

201)Job 4- Tyron Inbody's The Transforming God has a good look at a variety of models for facing the theodicy issue, the issue of God and human suffering. To me, it seems the product of years in the classroom, as he worked hard to make difficult issues comprehensible. His examinations of a variety of ways we approach the issue seems to indict our conception of a God of control, if you will a controlling God. Some of the defenses of a "traditional" portrait of the divine are found wanting due to what he terms 'the damn proportionality problem." He means even if some good comes out of suffering it does not seem to square with the level of human misery all around us. Surely, we can progress without trudging through a veil of tears to get there. In his introduction he remarks that we may aspire to objectivity, but we live within a welter of personal and social experience. His view of an omnipotent God as a controlling deity was challenged by the suicide of his father when he was a young adult. Can any amount of beauty or harmony from the contrast of good and pain make up for the death of a child? Recently at a gathering, most of the males around the table were dealing with cancers of some sort. One of our members, to my utter astonishment, spoke of the aesthetic necessity of a world of suffering and blessings as necessary contrasts. This was coming from someone whose spouse had just undergone treatment for colon cancer. Just yesterday, a person in a Bible Study spoke of the need for the artistic resolution of harmonies and dissonance, and she had just cared for her dying mother in law as a hospice provider. So many of the intellectual defenses for God and human suffering seem tone-deaf to the emotional issues involved and also the dreadful reality of suffering. So, I cling to an image of the divine where sympathy and understanding live for each of us.

202) Eastman (Gal. 4:19-20) Recovering Paul's Mother Tongue. In his frustration with Galatians, Paul resembles the frustration of Moses. Moses wonders aloud how long is he to be like a nursing father to these people? Paul urges the Galatians to imitate him, but at the same time he reminds them he became like them. It is a way of introducing a different type of familial relationship. One thing they share is that they have both become new creations of the gospel. Paul realizes that the powers that be will continue to resist the fresh new world of the gospel. He maintains that he has become like the Galatians, even as he urges them to imitate him. He uses the intriguing image of labor pains (see link to the barren of Is. 54). The birth of new life has pain and birth throes. As Eastman notes, he speaks as a mother to a people here. Do not lose sight of the pain in labor pains. Eastman demonstrates that Paul presents himself as embodying hardship for others, including the Galatians (110). Christian life is moving toward a cruciform existence, even as it anticipates resurrection. After all of its angst about male circumcision, Paul adopts motherly language. (Well, at least I find it both amusing and strangely moving). Do we hear echoes of Moses as nursing father" here? Others see Is. 45:7-11. As Hays in his NIB commentary argues (296), Paul is concerned not only with individuals but the whole community learning to

form Christ, and part of that formation is in the suffering the labor pains of the new birth in Christ. Part of Paul's transformation is in being so courageous in the the face of death that he can use living and dying as metaphors for the spiritual experience of Christians. The pain one endures in grief can presage the birth of a new self, or at least bring to life previously untapped or unseen virtues. Now those may well not even show up on your screen now, as hindsight is able to see so much more clearly than we can in the throes of a difficulty.

203) Hab.2:2- For me, filmmakers have a vision made plain and public. Both of our daughters have taken a number of courses in mass media communications. A number of fairly recent films deal with grief in a variety of ways. Lately, they seem to emphasize ways of showing that the dead are still with us somehow, whether it is Ghost or the Bruce Willis movie, the Sixth Sense. A deep desire to connect with the dead shows up in these movies as much as a séance drew people in the 19th century. In the Harry Potter series, Harry catches glimpses of his parents through an "esired" (desire spelled backward). They join forces with other spirits who have been destroyed by Voldemort when Harry is dueling him. Dumbledore asks Harry if "the dead we loved ever truly leave us?" A significant move in grief studies has been a shift away from speaking of closure or reinvesting energies apart from a loved one to recognizing that we do carry our relationships with us beyond the grave. "To Gillian on her 37th Birthday" was a sort of love letter from the talented writer David Kelly to his spouse, Michelle Pfeiffer on imagining life without one's spouse. Public works of art provide a sense of being understood by an artist. It helps us to realize that we are not alone in our difficulties. It may even be reassuring to actually see that someone understands what I am going through. Pierce Brosnan came to the attention of American viewers in a romantic detective comedy, Remington Steele. His character used movies as a way to make analogies to a situation he was facing. In the popular NCIS, the character, Tony, makes constant references to movies in his conversation and search for evidence. Dialogue and scenes make a safe framework to build a bridge to experience but have

the advantage of being fiction. I often say that a contemporary Jesus would use video or movies as a medium to make visual parables as Ed McNulty calls them.

204) I Chr. 15:27, Ps. 137:3- Our youngest daughter took a class based on the Great American Songbook and the writers of those standards. Indeed, they were masters of the craft. Stephen Sondheim has written extensively on the sheer craft of writing songs, where lyrics and music blend into a work where neither should be expected to stand on their own. These gifted artists can lace experience into a memorable work for three or four minutes. Yes, inspiration is involved, but it seems that models and many anguished hours struggle to find just the right and fitting phrase, musical or literary. Internet sites have long lists of songs to hear when suffering with loss. I would suppose that some of us may want sad songs and others more uplifting ones. Just listening to these recordings (I typed records but that makes me even more of a troglodyte) gives permission to grieve and shows that art can touch chords within us. Listen to Tears in Heaven-the guitarist Eric Clapton lost a young son in a frightful fall when the boy was 4. The electric guitarist chooses a quiet acoustic accompaniment in much of it. The questions are important and obviously heartfelt. Years later, Clapton led a group of musicians to memorialize his friend George Harrison, even though they were married to the same woman successively. I prize a Biblically-tutored imagination to ask and wonder about ultimate issues. At the same time, the God who gave us the capacity for imagination as a creative power in its own right would not begrudge of its use, especially its healing use. After all, my own Presbyterian Book of Order speaks of time and space being sanctified through the Incarnation. A good song can go through alteration depending on the mood or situation we may find ourselves in. Our daughter told me how taken aback she was to hear a song with the thought of people separated by WWII such as White Christmas, or I'll Be Seeing You in Apple Blossom Time. The psalmist famously asks how we can sing a song in a foreign land. You will be able to sing again, yes a happy song, such as Here Comes the Sun, my favorite springtime song.

205) Col. 3:16- Hymns burrow deep into our spiritual nature. Sometimes they are remembered fondly from childhood. Sometimes they speak to us though the years, or we find a new one arresting. As a spiritual exercise, consider reading some hymns as religious devotional poetry. If you can, find the music alone, without the words, and live with the melodies for a while. It is your choice, of course, for what you are seeking. It may be to create a quiet meditative air, or a clashing sound to match turmoil inside, or the explicitly religious sound of a Gregorian chant. It can be an interesting exercise to pick hymns for one's own service. Amazing Grace shows up in most lists people present to me for a funeral service. I wonder what it is that speaks to people, or could it be that the "American Hymn" has become de rigueur for funeral services and we bow to the expectation of it? At present, I think I would like the hymns: Here I am Lord and the Celtic sounding Be Thou My Vision. Maybe you require a sense of reassurance or presence or the promise of heaven. Hymns could range from What a Friend, Abide with me. Can you recall the hymns that were selected, if any, at the services for a loved one? Do certain hymns come to mind that were especially moving or appropriate at different funeral services? Have you heard some singularly inappropriate songs or hymns that made you want to laugh? Secular music of different types is played more and more. Sarah McLachlan's "Angel" plays as well as a few songs, such as "You Raise Me Up or You're Still You" or "Where You Are" from the talented young singer Josh Groban. I am just now planning a funeral with a soloist offering Wind Beneath My Wings and I Can Only Imagine as features. Songs that meant a lot to the deceased may get played but sometimes require some background. What were some of your loved one's favorite songs? What songs remind you of them? What songs would you want to take with you, if you went on a vacation for a year? What are some of your favorite hymns in general? Have they changed over the years or in change of circumstances?

206) I Tim. 4:7-8 Grief and spiritual practice/spirituality-
Spirituality is quite the popular word. It can slip into an ethereal
state, a free-floating sense of seeking the beyond, but untethered
to daily life. Spiritual practices caught fire with the work of
Dorothy Bass and the good auspices of Craig Dykstra of the Lilly
Endowment. They match belief with action, theory with practice,
abstraction with action. Grief is a direct assault on the spirit, the
soul of one's life. It creates a spiritual crisis. Spiritual practices
are not to be seen as penance for a sin or failing, but methods to
try to deepen our virtues through the force of habit. They are not
trying to curry favor with God as in "works righteousness" as if
that is much of an issue in our time anyway, but a response to
felt spiritual needs. Could we even look at grief itself as a spiritual
practice? As I Thessalonians 4 tells us not to grieve as those who
have no hope, then it would seem that we are told to grieve as
those with hope. The blessing and charge in its close at 5:16-24
would stick in the throat a bit with its words of constant rejoicing
and thanksgiving in all circumstances. Between them lies the
famous injunction to "pray without ceasing.' Calvin famously
called prayer "the chief exercise of faith.' Part of his project was
to blow open the doors of the church sanctuaries so that we
would see ourselves living in the sacred space of creation, and
the mileposts of our lives leading on the road to redemption. Let's
go a bit further. In Scripture we see prayer paired with fasting. In
intense grief we may not have much of an appetite anyway, so
why not pair fasting with our prayers? After all, fasting could be a
manifestation of not taking food in when we feel so empty
anyway. it matches those times when as Geyl wrote, "the
sanctuary of the heart is empty.' Protestants have grown too
wary about words such as spiritual practices due to 500 years of
pounding that faith is a gift and not earned. We also fear "works
righteousness" and fear that our spiritual actions may not be
authentic expressions of our inner disposition. Spiritual practices
engage the mind and heart. they merge theory and practice.
They serve as exercises for our spirits day aafter day.

207) Ps. 28:1 winter of the soul-Martin Marty is an eminent,
prolific, church historian. Facing the death of his spouse, he wrote

a remarkable book of lament, <u>A Cry of Absence.</u> It seems to stand against the "springtime sunshine" so often offered, even expected, by Christians. Some expressions are sweet to one's spiritual taste and too sweet for the tastes of others. "In the bleak midwinter" applies to the cold days of the spirit as well as a Christmas favorite of choirs. Some of us need sweet words to help encourage them or to face hardships. I'm not one of them, but I certainly respect the feeling and the need. I may sometimes wish that sweetness and light could dispel the darkness. Too often, we try to use our own preferences as the template for everyone else. Some derive solace in going through the sentiments in some greeting cards. In an often bitter world, some sweetness leavens the effect. Sometimes we want to sleep to have some time of blissful unawareness. The group Green Day has a song that says 'wake me up when September ends." The writer Parker Palmer uses the seasons as an entry point into our spiritual moods and needs, in an introduction to the Center of Renewal in Michigan. He sees winter as sometimes bringing a stark clarity in its cold and clear days. He writes that in the winter of the grief over his father; some things are able to be in sharp focus in its short light. Winter is a time of dormancy. In our action-filled world, sometimes we need time to allow things to lie fallow. Things sometimes require time to settle, to steep, to have some time to ruminate and digest. Of course, winter is not the only season. The very nature of the seasons is movement one through another in a cycle. Winter gives time and space when we require a fallow period. Even in the depths of winter, we see signs of hope. The days start to lengthen almost immediately after the solstice. In England, people will note that the streams are not completely frozen, a small rivulet, a freshet may appear, and it is called winterbourne. Sleep is a daily winter for us. Every new morning is a new spring. As Ps. 3:5 "I lie down and sleep; I awake, because you sustain me."

208) A powerful look at parental loss is the philosopher Nicholas Woltersdorff's <u>Lament for a Son.</u> I had the opportunity to hear him speak about the book at Louisville Seminary maybe 20 years after its publication. When he walks into a room with people who

have read his cry of the heart and mind, he bears a heavy burden. Grieving parents look to him for answers, a pathway out of their enveloping, overwhelming pain. Some know he is a brother to them in suffering. His family learned that Eric had died in a mountain climbing accident when he was 25. I find it so moving as he does not let go of his great learning as a theologian, but he does not use it as a buffer against pain. Indeed his powerful mind may well give rise to even more imponderable questions to face in this terrible crisis of his family. Many, if not most, of his entries are laments, some shorter, some longer. His erudition, his great learning is no anodyne to his pain. At times, it increases it as he has so many questions and doesn't even begin to know where he can find the answers, and if any are to found. I suppose it is a bit like a therapist in personal pain and not finding relief by working with their colleagues. The questions don't end in his memoir of prayers. If anything, they may well mulitply as his mind clears a bit. He is wise enough to know that he may not find sufficient answers to his burgeoning list of questions, especially answers that could satisfy his brilliant intellect as an eminent philosopher. So, he knows the wisdom of learning to ask better sets of questions, and living with them. He knows that he will now go through life with tears affecting his vision. He wonders if he will now see "things that he could not see dry-eyed."

209) Mt.27:66- Joseph laid the stone against the tomb, but the opponents of Jesus sealed it. I keep thinking of sign, sealed, and delivered in contracts by way of Stevie Wonder. They thought they had sealed the fate of a putative messiah and his fledgling movement. They thought they had sealed another effort to inflame the passions of Rome against Israel. Of course, some things should stay buried. Some things deserve to stay buried and left behind. This is one more powerful point to grasp the power of the resurrection. We are not sealed off from death. The power of new life does not flinch in the face of a sealed tomb. The tomb may have been sealed from human entry, but it could not seal off the restorative power of the God of the living. What is sealed off by death? How do we try to seal ourselves off from its

effects? How does death seek to seal us in with our loved ones? That can be a real temptation, to leave our journey in this world and seal ourselves off with our loved one. What unseals us from a living death in the stone-cold tomb? To be human is to be a permeable creature. Events do not bounce off; they enter into our lives. Of course, the stone does not remain sealed. Even while the women worry that they will not be able to move it, the path is wide open. Somehow, the stone has been rolled away. Mausoleums always seem such cold places, and I usually have officiated at committals in the winter in them. The words of a 'stone-cold tomb' often enter my consciousness at some point. In his book on the death of his son in a mountain-climbing accident, Nicholas Woltersdorff realizes that part of himself was buried with his son, and that the stone slab slid over his life as well. He's right, of course. We cannot lift or move such a slab on our own. That is why the women worried on their way to anoint the body of Jesus. Part of resurrection's story is that the stone was rolled away from the tomb.

210) Hebrews ch.4:14-16-As I am reviewing this section, we are in primary election season. For reasons not entirely clear to me, an aspect of voting behavior seems to be related to seeing that a candidate resembles us in attitude and in understanding what people like me are like. In part, it is a response to mass society where we are known in a deluge of data mining, but we don't get a palpable notion that we are known and understood as and for ourselves. The preacher of Hebrews (if it is indeed a sermon) is working with the representative function of a priest in the temple liturgy. He declares Jesus to be a great High Priest. It is valuable to recall that Jesus "sympathizes with us in our weakness." Maybe we think we are weak when we find ourselves pushed beyond our limits. Maybe we feel faith is weak when we cannot stolidly accept loss. Here I see sympathy as feeling for our condition, not judging or condemning us for our weakness. Jesus is called a high priest as he is the bridge between heaven and earth. Indeed, his very life is that bridge. In Jesus Christ, the very hand of God touches us in our very human issues and needs. God's hand reaches out to console, to support. Jesus

knows what we go through. Jesus feels for us in our weakness. Jesus knows full well human weakness. Jesus is generous toward us in our weakness. That certainly includes the times of bereavement. One of the educational benefits of the arts is that it teaches us sympathy and even empathy. We can grow in appreciation of the circumstances and responses of others. Yes, sympathy is a product of the mind and the heart. This is after all the same God who heard the cries of the people in Egypt. Indeed the word, cries, could be almost synonymous with prayer. Is prayer not the primary mode of access to the divine? Jesus Christ is presented as the gateway to that access. We "draw near" to the very throne room of the divine, not in cowering fear, but boldness. The hymn, Blest Be the tie that binds, sings of the "sympathizing tear." I like to think it is shared in our ties to God as well. "Nearer My God to Thee" was played at McKinley's funeral and at the Titanic.

211) Patience is not a virtue in ready supply in this fast-paced, cell phone speed 21st Century. I find myself drumming my fingers in impatience at the ATM and waiting for a debit card to process at the store. Sometimes we hear the advice to "be patient." It is, on occasion, a polite way of asking someone to wait without complaint, at least complaints that they have to hear. For me, it is infuriating to be told to be patient when I am suffering and the speaker is not. I remember scratching my head at James speaking of the patience of Job. Job does not sound patient to me. He sounds understandably impatient at his condition. Here, translation issues and changes in meaning since the King James Version come into play. "Hyponome" has the sense of endurance more than passive patience, and that would be more like "makrothumia," an ability to endure unjust suffering, to be able to take what life dishes out. The KJV made it long-suffering. In public matters, I find it inducing rage when one privileged group tells a suffering group to employ patience, as the times are not right. So, they are told to wait, but as Martin Luther King answered, "we can't wait." In Revelation, the suffering people are being asked to hold on, to persevere, and to keep on keeping on. Trying times put that virtue to its limits. In moving, I

flipped through some material I hadn't consulted in a while, including some Theology Today back issues. One article was on the saving patience of Jesus. Job is not patient in the sense of passivity, but he certainly is patient in endurance, of holding on, of long-suffering. Job never lets go of his relationship with God, even though his words are hurt and indeed harsh. He never lets go of his sense of personal integrity (tam).

On the other hand, I do consider God to be infinitely, or perhaps better, eternally, patient. I think of God being as patient as Tom was in the Horse Whisperer where he spend the whole day looking at the horse on the other side of the meadow, until at dusk, the horse is able and willing to move near him. Patience is the virtue that may well counter some anger. It has the marvelous quality of adjusting our time horizon, and thus it eases the sense of crisis.

212) Ps. 104 27-30-Questioning God is considered doubting God by some, and they try to stop the process. Years ago, in our church, the pastor and the nuns forbade the young charges from asking questions, as he saw this as a time to be indoctrinated into the affirmations of the faith. Questions could come later, perhaps when they were adults, maybe never. I see our relational God less as a tough schoolmaster but more as a companion in Christ. Tillich delivered a sermon where he places faith and doubt together, not as polar opposites. We are part of the faith of Israel, of wrestling with God. It seems to me if we love God with everything we have, including our minds, then mental struggle is part of the relationship. Anyway, most of what we would characterize as doubt would often be easily exceeded by most of the lament psalms. Now, not all questions are good ones. They may not be capable of an answer; they may be confusing; they may be emotional outpourings with a question mark placed at the end. Christopher Morse quotes the great ethicist Paul Lehmann. He and his wife, Marion, lost their 27 year old only child. "Sooner or later we all find ourselves living between two prayers of Jesus. My God, why, and Father, into your hands I commend my spirit. Such times confirm the saying that "the dark is light enough." (Theology Today 1/08 p.502-3) Perhaps we do well to be wary of the answer to our questions.

Casting about in grief, we are not at our best intellectually. Sometimes, it is a sense of any port in the storm, and we grab at the first piece of flotsam that comes by and hang on for dear life. People wonder why they lack the overwhelming certainty and confidence promised by TV preachers. My dialogical notion of prayer fits into my dialogical view of Scripture. It invites questions. When working with a text, I feel as if I am praying the Scriptures like a monk. This passage I selected is an example. It sets me to ponder if God is such an active agent literally, who removes spirit, or breath, from each living creature. I resist the idea of the God of life, the Creator, being a God of life's end. Part of our lives as free people is the struggle with such large questions of our very existence.

213) Ps 88 is a lament psalm that does not end in an upbeat fashion. It is the dark companion to the previous psalm, full of light. Here we are in the "regions of darkness." Here we are in the valley of the shadow, a ravine deep and dark. Faced with some terrible evil, it ends in pain. Perhaps we can find a gospel message in that signal difference. It could be straight from the mouth of Job. Sometimes things do end badly, period, no better resolution, no pie in the sky, no upset win at the last moment. It stands as a sentry against easy answers, the presumption that we have the ways of the world all figured out, that we can give a convincing accounting of the great short prayer, "why, God?" Few psalms lay despair at the feet of God without having some sort of resolution or catharsis. Here, we see that the deepest pain can be laid at the feet of God in prayer. The liturgy of the church often shies away from lament, and it certainly would not have this dark psalm rival Ps. 23. Yet, what does this prayer do but elaborate on the sense of being in the valley of the shadow? In verses 4-6 it likens the condition of the psalmist with the condition of death, even being in the abode of the dead. It is picked up again in verses 10-12. The psalmist wonders if the abode of the dead is beyond the reach of God, there in the "land of forgetting." Some things do have a tragic end. Everything does not always turn out for the best. I heard a minister say that he never understood the psalm until the first time he had to deal with a suicide with a

family from his congregation. I think he meant that the usual words of comfort and hope do not readily apply in the face of such a tragic circumstance, especially in the first blush of facing it. Toward the end, one gets the sense of being hemmed in, surrounded by troubles. That is the exact opposite of the sense of salvation, where it has a sense of having plenty of room, unshackled, free to move, free to live. to be candid, I find some gospel in being able to lay such anguish at the throne , without the expected filigree of thanks, light, and hope. This psalm is a testament that anything, anything can be brought before the mercy seat. Praying a tragedy is a step toward starting to cope and deal with it. Walter Brueggemann (Theology of the Old Testament:399) reminds us that Israel matches the seeming silence of God with an insistence on speaking and an insistence on being heard, day after day, year after year. He footnotes (399) Elie Wiesel on rabbinic teaching that we pray and hope we are heard, but if we stop, then we are lost. It comes toward the end of a section of the Psalter. It does have the last word. Later in Ps. 139, we will hear that the 'darkness is not dark to you." Many, many more prayers follow. I'm glad it's there for some things do not have a resolution that we are capable of seeing into the future when we are having a hard time getting through minute by minute. We are hereby given permission to lay such pain at the doorstep of heaven. Notice that it has words in both the night and the morning. This is still persistent prayer to the God of salvation (v.1). God can heal utter heartbreak.

214) Ps. 51 Guilt is a heavy burden to carry. It seems to me that our culture has turned against guilt as a mode of social control, even as an emotion that is intrinsically wrong. For instance, the Church is accused of pushing guilt on to people. Erik Erikson, the psychological theorist, places guilt very early in the development of young people, so it is something we deal with for a very long time. Here in the prayer the feeling is so pervasive that it includes of sin from the very start of life, so it resonates with the later Christian espousal of original sin as part of the human condition within our very structure of life. Guilt is the sense of having broken a rule, an expectation, a duty. It is the signal of a

violation of conscience, or social oughts that have been internalized. Everyone has some regrets about things done or undone, words left unsaid or uttered in malice. Life is hard enough without carrying extra burdens, often self-imposed. Clinebell made a distinction between neurotic guilt and appropriate guilt. When we do something wrong, we should feel guilty. Guilt is a powerful deterrent to our temptations toward immoral behavior. As such, it is important for our life together. We should realize that we have done something wrong, not a mere mistake, something wrong. When we feel guilty when we don't do something harmful, then we have an issue. One of the elements of the Christian faith that I've always prized is its capacity to help us be relieved of guilt. I worry that some contemporary services don't include a prayer of confession, thereby falling into the pattern of excising sin from the vocabulary in place of mistakes or poor choices.

With guilt, we may be trying to keep the departed alive to us by feeling guilty about wrongs done or things left undone. One way to deal with the irrational component of things left undone is to list as many of them as you possibly can. then write down all of the ways you may have fulfilled them. Then simply ask if this is within the realm of possibility for anyone, even if they never ate or slept. When we do something wrong, of course we should feel guilty. When we feel guilty about something over which we have no control, no influence, no responsibility, then the guilt has become neurotic, dysfunctional, unhealthy. The Christian church is often blamed as a vehicle of guilt, of laying guilt brick by brick on to us. In some cases, I suppose this is a valid criticism. At its root, The Christian church offers release from guilt through the ritual of confession and declaration of pardon, or absolution as it is called in the Catholic Church. One could consider seeing that Jesus took on not only the weight of sin but guilt as well. Indeed, every Sunday in many churches we are absolved of guilt in the declaration of forgiveness and pardon at the close of prayers of confession. A sense of absolution is a gift to the grieiving as well.

215) Acts 9:36 Tabitha/Dorcas is a sterling reminder of a person

remembered for many acts of kindness. I love when Peter is shown all the articles of clothing she made. Think about the Tabithas who have graced your life. In the Presbyterian Book of Common Worship, we are asked "to give thanks for all in the departed that was good and kind and faithful." The grieving want to show tangible reminders of her. They remind me of the pictures and slide shows we now have at funeral homes to display, or the personal touches of items we place in and around the casket. Some speak of linking objects. They are instant reminders of something about the person. I was recently reminded that the word souvenir (French through Latin) means to remember, or more literally to come up (to mind). Sometimes we push others a bit too fast or too coercively about disposing of the belongings of the person who has died. On the other hand, sometimes it is just too painful to even look at some belongings and keepsakes. Dan Fogelberg in Souvenirs sang of a poem left by a lady love and a key to a boyhood home. At the end, "here is the sunrise to set on your sill...ghosts of the dawn moving near/ they pass through your sorrow and leave you quite still/sitting among your souvenirs." What are some of your most precious keepsakes? What makes them especially good reminders of a loved one? What pieces of them do you sense in the object? Did they put some of themselves in the keepsake somehow? What pictures have particular meaning for you? Why? Of course, merely having objects in one's possession doesn't keep us from missing them terribly. As Springsteen says in Missing "pictures on the nightstand, TV's on in the den/your house is waiting/for you to walk in." At the same time, we often deride material goods as "just things." Yard sales or estate sales are filled with folks getting rid of our "junk." One indicator of struggle with a keepsake is how long to keep the voice of the deceased on the answering machine at home. We associate things with loved ones, so they link us to them in significant ways.

216) 2 Tim. 4:6-8 uses religious imagery of offering, as his life is being poured out. (Could it reflect the emphasis on life being poured out in Lam. 2:18-19?) In a way, it is the opposite of the cup running over in Ps. 23. All of life can be seen as a gift. That

would mean we have no claims on the lives of others. Would it change your attitudes and actions if you saw them as gifts to God? Does it affect your view of your loved to see them as gifts from God? In a culture that admired athletic excellence, as does ours, the race and oath of an athlete is a natural metaphor. (See Phil 3:14, I Cor. 9:25). The race ends with a generous mercy. Then it moves into last requests. Sometimes, the death of someone who has fought illness long and hard for years is a relief. We are not always victorious, but we are not permitted to be destroyed. I think of the fisherman in the Old Man and the Sea. I think of those underdogs in the NCAA tournaments who give their all but can't claim victory. I think I love sports for those moments as much as the victory of the gifted when they play at their peak. The image of a crown would be fitting for the poor people who were attracted to Christianity but never knew much commendation or valuable prize. it also fits the imagery for the athletic contest, but here the spiritual race gets not a garland but one of righteousness, of right relation with God and each other, or maybe of final vindication and even "heavenly reward.". The rock star, Sting, made an album in regard to the passing of his father (Soul Cages). In a way, this is a last testament. In an Imperfect God, we read the story of George Washington's long struggle to figure out how to free his slaves under Virginia law. He exercised great financial care in making sure that they had the stake required by law and went laboriously through the will to try to make sure that his wishes would not be countermanded, an understandable point of view form the old general and president. What would you leave as a last testament, last words of advice or hope to your family, your church, your community?

217) I Cor. 13:12.- I've worn glasses most of my life due to being quite nearsighted. Sight has been a burden without glasses and wearing glasses helped make sight one of my preferred metaphors. Also, it could be part of my preferred set of metaphors within my own personality's structure. I say things like "getting the picture," or "not seeing the forest for the trees." When I understand something, I see it. When I don't get something, I don't see it, or I can't picture it, like waking up in

the morning fumbling for my glasses in the fog of half-light and myopia. "We see but in a mirror dimly, but then face to face." For all of our talk about being close to God, I do see a gulf, a chasm between us and the divine, the Wholly Other, as Barth said. Only Moses spoke to God as to a friend. Part of our limitation as human beings, mere creatures, is that we do not see clearly. We need light, and inside we need enlightenment. In our mystical moments, we may catch a glimpse of the Beyond, but that does not seem to be a constant companion of our consciousness. Since we are indeed limited creatures, we cannot trust our insights completely. This passage reminds us that we do not see clearly. Love indeed blinds, and it is the focus of this famous chapter. Grief blinds as well. It also means that we cannot accept what come off as full statements from others about answers to our questions or how we should face grief in its different stages and manifestations. Advice givers see through a mirror dimly too. Being human means that our vision is rarely 20/20. Especially when we are trying to peer into the depths of someone else's intentions or history, or into the depth of our own soul, we are limited. Getting another perspective often helps sharpen our lack of acuity; it could be friends, or in books, or in the hands of a therapist. At our best, we catch glimpses of the interior life of someone else.

218) John 10 Jesus as shepherd- This captures nicely a comforting image. At my aunt's house, a large picture of Jesus holding a lamb as the Good Shepherd dominated the landing at the stairs. I don't usually go for the image, as I am troubled by the thought of being a sheep, especially among wolves. The shepherd image in the Bible is one of failure to properly protect one's people. The word pastor is connected to shepherd, so these words of warning hit me between the eyes. I like the idea that a shepherd's crook is a pastoral image, so that it can reach into a crevice or water to rescue a lamb. It is an aid with our common walk. The staff can be a defensive weapon, I would think. On the other hand, grief is a time to embrace the image fully. If there is any time to need a sense of being cared for and protected, this is it. The image also deserves attention in our tendency to stray

away from the relative safety and security of the herd. Of course this picture of Jesus as the Good Shepherd fits nicely with the pastoral images of the 23rd psalm. I've liked the image that the shepherd's staff is curved at the top to help get a lamb out of a crevice in the rocks where it could get caught. Heaven can be pictured as a sheepfold. In a story of sheep, Jesus speaks of chasing after one lost sheep, while the 99 are left to stay together in the flock. Even if we fell lost and abandoned, the story tells us that God will search us out. Part of the danger is being left without the herd. So, the shepherd image may work as one for needed guidance and to stay engaged with others. After all, Ps. 23 reminds us that the Lord is our shepherd. That shepherd knows where the pasture and cool water are. That shepherd can guide us through the valley of the shadow of death, the deepest, darkest valley where trouble seems to hem us in. another image that comes through in this passage is the matter of a voice that is recognized. I talk to our adult daughters on the phone, and I think I can guess when they are distracted due to the tone of their voice, as 'they don't sound themselves.' A friend of mine grew up on a working farm and would try to imitate his father's voice, but the animals paid him no mind. When his father bellowed to them for feeding, oh did they come running. Keep your ears open. Lesser voices may clamor for your attention. Lesser voices may try to entice you into a quick and easy way to recover from loss. One day, that voice will gather us altogether, safe and sound.

219) I Cor. 1:18-25 Luther put the theology of the cross in opposition to the theology of glory. No one has done more to speak of the theology of the cross to North Americans more than Douglas John Hall of Canada. He realizes that it is a countercultural point, as we want to worship optimism and want to be blind to even the appearance of tragedy. Protestants rarely have a crucifix. Linking Easter to Good Friday, the cross is bare. Sometimes I think that we should still have a crucifix as a reminder of the suffering of Jesus, not only Easter triumph. Our triumphant cross makes it difficult for us to grasp that Paul is speaking of the cross in its terrible cost, as the last instrument

one could imagine as being the tool of salvation and deliverance from the sting of death. It loses at least some of its power as an instrument of torture and capital punishment. Is God's presence to be felt only in blessing, only in success only in positive experiences? Could God be hidden, precisely in the opposite of power and success, but also in the negative experience, experiences of failure, suffering, and loss? I want to be very careful at this point. I do not think it proper for us to glorify suffering as a path toward God. I don't think we should seek out martyrdom or some of its punishing aspects. My sense of the theology of the cross is descriptive, not prescriptive. In other words, it describes the dark night of the soul in suffering. The theology of the cross realizes that all of us suffer in some way, at some point. No one, no one is immune from it. It takes the doctrine of the Incarnation seriously and asserts that God's own did not dip a toe into part of the human condition but was immersed in it, including its tragic, painful aspects. Of course, God is the transcendent One. At the same time, God is the Immanent One. God is above, but not only in the great beyond, blithely above and beyond our experience. God is in the thick of life here, engaged and involved. Joan Osborne had a hit, with "What If God Were One of Us." For Christians, the Incarnation answers her question. We have to be careful that we speak of a theology of the cross, so that we don't glorify suffering. We have no right to try to impose this notion on the suffering but only share the human condition. Too much of our religion has deteriorated into a fetish of the blood of the cross. In our community, we have shared Lenten lunchtime services. This year, we were assigned to preach from a Lenten hymn. With a moment's thought I picked In the Cross of Christ I Glory. It sings of bane and blessing together. In its way it sounds like a marriage vow, for better or worse, in the last place we may expect.

220) I Cor. 2:9 (Is. 52:15, 64:4) -My mother always liked this passage that no eye has ever seen. It is a good reminder that we mortals cannot capture heaven in any precise way. Most of us then want a glimpse of what no other eye has seen. At times, I

wish we had more images of heaven to work with from Scripture. Of course, she was also infinitely fascinated by reports of out of body experiences, or near death experiences as well and would have been fascinated by the Clint Eastwood movie, Hereafter. Some look for some tangible evidence of an afterlife and seek out reports of a world beyond. Mary Todd Lincoln had séances in the White House to establish contact with her son. I showed a tape of near death experiences and views of heaven to a community college class on comparative religion. They were struck by the similarities and differences of many of the people interviewed and how little actual religious content could be found in the words. Images of heaven may well reflect not only our culture in general, but the particular hopes and anxieties that weigh on our hearts and minds. We want heaven to relieve those anxieties. Paul goes on to say that what has been hidden from us is indeed revealed by the Spirit of God. Basically, he says that just as a person knows what is inside them, so too does God's Spirit know the interior plans, intentions, and work of God. As he quotes Isaiah, no one can claim to know the mind of God, unless God chooses to reveal. Sometimes I worry that we have pushed heaven's wonders so much that people hide behind it as a way to hide their pain. I use that great time vacuum, Facebook, and notice that a number of Christians speak of a death only in terms of the glories of heaven and push away any other words, any painful thoughts or feelings, at least in what they decide to post publically. I almost get a sense of: "he doth protesteth too much."

221) I Cor. 3:16, 6:19- Here Paul calls us temples of the Spirit. It struck me recently that it is a more loaded word than I realized. After all, Solomon's temple was razed by Babylon and as soon as the great Herodian edifice was finished, then Rome destroyed it about 40 years after the death of Jesus. Of course, in our body-obsessed culture, calling the body a temple would be an invitation to worship its form all the more. A temple was a house of worship; and it was thought to house the presence of God. One could even say that Israel saw it as a meeting place, a portal, between heaven and earth, so God's "glory" could fill the

sanctuary. The presence of God could be pinpointed to a structure that was destroyed. This dwelling place of God within the church is then portable and impervious to a siege by military power, unless a mass slaughter of Christians would occur. It places a permanent presence within a shifting collection of mortal beings. On the other hand, when we speak of the spiritual, we often want to somehow "rise above" the material, the earthly. These bodies are focal points, dwellings for the Spirit, Paul seems to say. It certainly pushes us to respect the body more than we may normally to realize that these earthen vessels are a temple. The treasures they contain is the presence of God in and through us. While I am skittish about the belief in a separate "soul" as containing our spiritual essence, I do consider that our very selves, but including our experiences, our loves, our hopes persist into another dimension. That is a point of contact with the divine. I do not envision our buried bodies as being temples of the spirit, but I do see our lives as they have lived and loved as continuing to be temples of the Spirit, the gateway, the portal, the point of contact between us and God. Here I must admit that my Reformed background did not have issues with a soul, an immortal, soul as a distinct part of us. The Westminster divines certainly believed in it as an immortal substance (6.177), but then they return to the doctrine of the resurrection of the body at the close of the age. We are speaking of ineffable matters here, but it seems safe to sya that god will honor our temples at the close of our lives.

222) I Tim. 2:4 -If the path of Scripture bends toward a universal salvation, this would be one of the highlighted passages. I don't wish to get into an argument about universal salvation or not, but I do find it remarkable how easily we decide how to interpret the Bible and theology to take on the proper role of God in deciding the fate of billions of people. I like the phrase, "that is way above our pay grade." It is out of our hands to wonder if a loved one will be in heaven or not. It is arrogant presumption to anoint ourselves as caretakers of the heavenly gates. That certainly means that it is in the hands of God, not us. It is an act of arrogance to assign ourselves the role of God about the eternal disposition on someone's life. In the 19th century, we had quite

the argument if people could claim faith after death to get, in effect, a second chance to claim the love of the Forgiving One. The Lord's Prayer reminds us to be generous in our assessments of others, for we pray that the same measure of forgiveness be applied to us. Philip Gulley's, If Grace is True, addresses the issue in a fashion congenial to the general reader. Recently I went to a small conference, the Reformed Roundtable, where the author of a book on Calvin, Life in God was featured with its author the new CTS president, Matthew Boulton. He makes the surprising argument that one can take some of Calvin's own words and turn them against his insistence that only a small remnant of people will be saved. Calvin reminds us that we are not in any position to make determinations for divine decisions. Second, we should pray for the well-being of all. I tend to go back to the prologue of John's gospel where we know that the darkness does not overcome the Light. So many people fear about the heavenly salvation of their loved ones, if not themselves. In that case, throw your cares on the tender mercies of the Loving One, the tender mercies of god. Hope is always imbued with a divine aura, a sacred aura. Even the grave cannot shut out its light.

223) Miscarriage and stillbirth-(Ex. 21: 22-3)-Pregnancy is uncertain. I do know I distrust people who are certain that they know the precise moment a soul is present, at conception or birth or after the first month after birth as some rabbis had it. I've seen estimates that one of five pregnancies do not result in a live birth. Infertility continues to be a real issue for families, just as it was for the founding families of Abraham and his progeny, or Manoah and his wife, or Hannah and Elkanah. The early legal codes in Torah apply sanctions if someone would cause a miscarriage. In Numbers 5 we see a trial by ordeal that could result in miscarriage if a woman was suspected of carrying a child not her husband's. One of the holy moments of life is to hear the heartbeat during an ultrasound examination. I know a woman in her seventies, with three children and many grandchildren who speak of a miscarriage as if it were yesterday. We build up hopes for a new future. After all, we have nine full months to do so. Then the developing life is snuffed out. Hopes fall in tatters abut

an imagined future. What preparations have been made seem so futile. I don't know if we are even capable of preparing ourselves with an outline of our life's course that can include for that giant, looming fear. While this is another grief that does not have particular cultural sanction and respect, its effects are long-lasting need. I know a grandmother who speaks of her miscarriage with such freshness that one would think it was within the last couple of months. To some extent, miscarriage is an unacknowledged grief. If we have special rituals to mark the loss, I am not aware of many. Serene Jones, president of Union Seminary, created a makeshift ritual for a woman who visited her in distress over such a loss. Even if it is not properly acknowledged, this is a deep loss of an imagined future and potential not yet bourght to term. Heaven acknowledges such a loss.

224)-I Tim. 6:6-7 We brought nothing into this world (Job there too at 1:20-1) My maternal grandfather used to quote this when my grandmother would start off on a nagging rant about money being too tight. It has its counterpart in the phrase, "you can't take it with you." The one who dies with the most toys does not win. Our possessions cannot be allowed to define us. It has echoes of Jesus at the Sermon on the Mount. It is a call to embrace life as a gift, for we cannot control its duration with any certainty. Wealth inheres in life itself. This follows a notion that "Godliness with contentment (autarkeia) is great gain." Contentment could mean being self-sufficient as well. Contentment counters coveting, that difficult commandment. In the movie A Civil Action, the judge addresses the attorney forced into bankruptcy about all the things we use to measure a life. How should we measure a life? Have you heard anyone regret not spending more time on an office project? Not long ago, I heard an attorney make a presentation on elder law before a service organization. An amazing amount of it was a recitation of families cheating parents or businesses out of money. The other part was a series of suggestions to protect the wealth of parents for their children. Dealing with money is always an issue in relationships. Please monitor your spending and saving patterns to note if they have gotten way out of your normal budgeting. When we say things such as "not wanting to talk about something like money at a time like this" we are also signaling a need to do just the monitoring suggested. Money is not only important to live, but it is also a symbol of power, even as a demonstration of love. For some it is the symbol of abundance, but for most of us (the 99% of the Occupy movement) it is a symbol of lack and the anxiety it causes. I knew a generous man years ago who made it a habit to give money to those going through divorce or loss and always said "no one is thinking about how much money you are burning through right now and I hope this helps a bit." Ignatian spirituality aims at this same sense of detachment from circumstances. Accepting life as a gift, accepting dependence is a gateway toward contentment.

225) 2 Thes. 2:16-17, 3:5 -At some point we all say or think something along these ones: "this was the straw that breaks the camel's back, or it's too much for me; it's more than I can stand, or I'm sick and tired of being sick and tired." Admitting that we are at our wit's end is a good start. To keep at it, to endure, to persevere is a sign of great strength. While we often discover that within ourselves, that power also is transmitted through our connection to God. At times, when it has been a long struggle it is cruel to say that the person just stopped fighting. Instead, the words of Scripture to fight the good fight would be more appropriate. In the end, mental energy will not defeat the power of mortality, for anyone, no matter how much they possess the gift of perseverance. "Mind over matter" certainly meets its match in mortality. We cannot say that someone gave up fighting, as if they are responsible for their demise, as if they have a power we do not possess. Through it all we discover, or re-discover, the virtue of perseverance. We usually only use the word in relation to an arduous task or journey. Like a hero in an epic, we keep plugging away at the goal. Some social psychological research indicates that the mind and body indeed have loops that affect each other. Becoming upset has bodily reactions, as we all can observe. At times, those same bodily reactions will tell our minds that we must still be feeling a certain

way, and we will come up with rationale to back up the continuation of the physical responses. Perseverance develops with the force of habit and practice. Indeed, the whole notion of Christian spiritual practice has the notion of perseverance built into it, as it assumes that the practices are performed routinely over time. Bereavement challenges our perseverance, but it pushes us to keep on going against the odds.

226) Rev. 22 picks up the tree of life from Gen. 2:9 but it also refers more fully to the tree of Ezekiel's vision (47:12). It picks up a river of life from Gen.2:10, as well. We have access to the tree of life. The fruit is always in season of the sacred tree of life. The number twelve picks up the tribes of Israel as a number of Biblical wholeness. Here the leaves of the tree are for the healing of nations. The image has been vastly expanded to a world, not the chosen people alone. As Mirosalv Volf reminds us we need a sense of repair and restoration in a world filled with pain and injustice. Maybe the fruit is an image for ingesting something that heals our memories. We could certainly use those healing leaves to help us through the complicated griefs or the fears that we may hold within. When you receive Communion imagine that those healing leaves are entering into your system. I don't recall a tree of death. The other tree is the tree of the knowledge of good and evil. The tree of life is an image in other faiths as well. Indeed, it is astounding how prominent an image it is in Egypt, or Norse mythology, or the newer faiths of Mormonism or Bahai. The image figures in Proverbs where it is connected to Wisdom, and the rabbis linked it to the Torah as well as a whole. Eugene Boring, in his fine commentary on Revelation, insists that the story is not a return to Eden, but a gathering up of the good and goods of this world and transforming them into a new key (220)."Salvation is beyond but not without this world." I wonder if the river of life image is to be distinguished from other mythic images of the river of death, such as the river Styx in mythic accounts. In the end, we are ferried to a new dimension, one where life holds sway, beyond our best imagining.

227) Col. 1:5,11-13-We get lots of talk here of hope laid up for us in heaven, of sharing with the saints in light. Even if it doesn't always seem like it, we are transferred from the dominion of darkness to the kingdom of the Beloved Son. Light here serves as both an ethical point of approaching holiness but also movement into the divine realm of light. It could possibly be linked to life with the angels as well. The inheritance uses language applied to the Promised Land of Israel and now transfers it to the Promised Land of God's heaven. They are already being given access to that realm right now. That Son did die an excruciating death. It doesn't have to be made into a fetish, as in the Passion of the Christ. It was a death for us. Many Christians have turned against the notion of substitutionary propitiation, or a substitute for our deserved punishments. Certainly, we have a number of images to try to come to grips with the meaning of the death of Jesus on the cross. Later in the hymn (15-20) that same person willing to die for humanity holds all things together in him. When things feel as if they are flying apart, Christ is the glue that holds those pieces of our lives together. That can be a most comforting thought when it seems as if the center of our lives is threatening to split wide open. In other places, we see the architectural image of Christ as the cornerstone or even keystone. I wonder at times if that hope laid up in heaven is a reward, or the fulfillment of our hopes for a better life, a dream no longer deferred but made actual.

228) Is. 4:5-6- I grew up in southwestern Pennsylvania toward the end of the coal for coke for steel era. A book about the region was entitled Cloud by Day. Coke ovens still roared not far from my house when young, and the mothers had to be careful when to put out the wash. An old saying was to appreciate when the sky was dirty, because that meant people were working. Of course, in Isaiah's hands, we have a reference to the presence of God in the wilderness experience of freed Israel (Ex. 13:21). The cloud both obscured and guided Israel on their journey and became an image for the presence of God of light and darkness. The Loving One is present with you now. The Guiding One was present with you every step of the way of your life. In covenant, God has made that pledge to you, to us. You can and will flourish

again. As the hymn says, our lives may "blossom and flourish like leaves on a tree." The myth of Persephone has real power as it links grief to the natural cycle of the seasons. Spring would come when the mother got to see her daughter. Winter descended when she could not see her lost in the gloom of Hades. "Bloom where you are planted" goes the old saying. You may not want to be in this particular soil but here you are. You can be open to blossoming again. In other words, winter does not last forever. Already by Christmas the length of the dark night grows shorter. Yes, it is impressive that we can get through a day at a time. It is an accomplishment to survive. Those are but pre-requisites to making it through. We are not condemned to be in constant autumn and winter. We are not made to exist only in their half light. Maybe before we can have a chance to flourish, we need a place of safety, a place to gather strength. Dylan's song, "Shelter From the Storm" evokes the sense of the hospitality and allure of that promise, "in a world of steel-eyed death." (This is picked up again in Is. 25:4). Carrie Newcomer touches on the same sense in her song, A Safe Place. "seemed the darkness was doggin' my heels/ but every time a light from the center said/follow me home right here." That sense of shelter requires a sense of hospitality, some safe space to be able to get what we need, rest, or warmth, or a chance to swap stories. We need room to move, to explore, and to have some elbow room to break through our often self-imposed confines.

229) Col 2:5, 15, 3:4 In the time of Jesus, the powers were quasi-divine forces, say Fate, that affected human life. Some placed the powers as correlative with the stars, as in astrology. Due to the work of Walter Wink and others, I link the powers to any impersonal large force that touches our lives and over which we have little direct control or even influence. Think of the "powers that be" or "the Power", or even what was called the "Establishment" when I was young, or perhaps "the Man." Jesus not only disarms the powers but crosses out, Xs out, at the cross their power. One of the more effective spiritual practices or rituals I have come across is in the Grief Recovery Handbook, where its process leads to writing a letter to the deceased. One could also

write to oneself. One could write of the anger and then throwing it away or destroying it. I'm loath to say closure, but it does of the benefit of placing some limit to one's mourning. One could write a letter to God spilling one's soul. If you did not want it to be seen, destroy it. Harry Truman used to dash off angry letters and tell his secretary to place them in the circular file, the wastepaper basket. the very process of writing may help to clarify and organize thoughts and feelings, so they are not so chaotic and threatening. I recall a gentleman whose talented daughter was murdered by her estranged husband. He wrote page after page in his grief. He kept going, in part, because he was able to put some form, some boundary in his grief on all of those legal-sized pages. Alan Wolfelt suggest writing a letter with a format "I used to be....and now I'm... or to consider writing a note on what you miss most and least, or things I wish I said or had done, or what is easiest and hardest for me, or what you would most like to ask your loved one. For me, the powers have the force of ideology, what is expected and permissible. When that power grows malevolent, we can resist.

230) Phil. 1:20-30- Paul hopes that to be with Christ exalted by life or by death. The great commentator Luria said that in reference to a mourner leading worship that "the King of Kings prefers broken vessels," as he drew from the Psalms that God does not despise a broken and contrite heart (Wieseltier:367). Here Paul is torn between two competing goods, to be with Christ in death but also in doing the work of Christ here and now. He knows to be with Christ is better, but calls his work with the churches necessary. Death can have a siren's allure in its call at times. The Beach Boys sang in God Only Knows: "if you should ever leave me/life would go on believe me/the world would show nothing to me/so what good would livin' do me?" Freud even speculated on a "death instinct." At the end of the chapter Paul puts belief in the good news of grace at the same level as suffering for the gospel. He even calls it a gift from God. We are in the territory that our loved ones are 'in a better place." It is a real art to know when and to whom that can be said. Charles de Gaulle and his wife cared for their children, and one of them had

Downs Syndrome. His wife so prayed that she could be like the rest of the children. When she died, the grieving mother could not wrench herself from the grave. With exquisite tenderness, the great man told his wife "come; now she is like the others."

231) Col. 3:13-To condole has the sense of sharing sorrow, a dolorous feeling. Not for nothing is the path to the cross called the Via Dolorosa. The root of the word has the sense of hurt, of pain as well. It is as if we have lost someone close to us. Giving condolences has come to take on a more formal, impersonal expression of sorrow. Perhaps no better condolence is than to sit with someone in their suffering. To be able to listen to the same tape over and over as someone struggles to gain their footing against such an act. To me condolences are less feeling sorry for someone, than feeling sorrow with someone. One of the advantages of grief groups is sharing sorrow, often without judgment. Grief groups are great examples of communities in suffering. At their best, everyone get their turn. The grief is not measured by others on some sort of scale. People get the chance to tell their account of events in there life, and they know that they will be heard with respect. In that sacred space, people may well share thoughts and feelings not before expressed. How many times, someone will notice and say "I have never told this to anyone before." Grief groups can serve the dual purpose of helping out an individual, but those individuals also are looking out for the other members of the group. Bound by loss, they can be joined together in a common search for healing.

232) Phil 2:7-8 may be part of an early Christian hymn, where it speaks of Jesus "emptying/nullifying himself (of privilege), of humbling himself." Naomi said that she was full but came back empty. Part of the Incarnation is for divinity to have a deeper sense of life without power over things. To love is not to control. I have a fundamental disagreement with the Reformed tradition in lifting up the so-called sovereignty of God over against the love of God. It leads to an over-emphasis on the power and control of

God. Indeed this self-emptying of the trappings of divinity is in itself a sign of love.

Morna Hooker in the NIB (508) says "in his self-emptying and humiliation, he reveals what God is like." For the life of me, I cannot square control with the God of love. It does not seem to fit the narrative of Scripture, with the exceptions of the cycle of punishments in Judges and the sense Jesus had of the divine imperative often translated as must. Some struggle with this by understanding that in the very act of creation, God then undergoes a sort of self-limitation. Creation itself needs room to breathe, room to grow, room to just be. In a spiritual sense, when we are empty, we are capable of being filled with spiritual virtue. Emptiness is similar to the declaration in 12-step programs that we are powerless over something that has enslaved us. In turning oneself over to God, a "higher power" is a plea to be filled with a new way of life. The recognition of emptiness, of being powerless, is prelude to a conversion experience.

233) Phil. 2:17 -I read this differently than some other writers on this passage. I read it as an extension of the emptying earlier in the kenotic section on Christ. Now Paul too is being emptied. I read it as an admission of weakness, that his strength and energy are spent, spilling out like blood. Paul says he is being poured out like a drink offering, a libation, common to sacrificial rites (Ex. 29:38-41). Not only are our lives an offering, a gift, to the service of God and each other, but here our death can too be seen as an offering. I am more than a little skittish about speaking of offering suffering to God. I don't think that I've quite grasped the concept. After all, are not sacrifices to be our best? Maybe our grief can be seen as an offering as well. In a sense it is an offering of our deep love. Still, we can and do speak of our lives, the entirety of our lives, being a sacrifice, an offering, of praise to God. Paul emphasizes the phrase, living sacrifice. Wait, maybe grief is the best of us after a loss. It is a good thing to pour psychic blood on the ground. Our actions can be seen as enacted prayers. They too communicate our attitudes. Paul speaks to the

extent of speaking of making oneself as nothing. Indeed Paul could be seeing the heart of Christian action as being self-giving, even self-sacrificial, for the good of the whole. In grief, we may feel as if we have lost the best part of our life with the loss.

234) Phil. 3:10 Paul keeps cross and resurrection together. One could almost see it as the summary of the gospel itself. Not only does he want to know the power of resurrection, but he also shares in the sufferings of Christ. Christians are joined to the life, death, and resurrection of Jesus. For Paul, nothing matters that much except for this signal relationship. (Earlier he can call anything else, refuse, actually something more vulgar than garbage). We are not immune from suffering. Indeed Paul uses the word koinonia, a fellowship, a community of suffering. Paul's linkage keeps us from becoming solely Good Friday Christians. By that I mean those who emphasize the crucifixion and atonement to the near-exclusion of all else. It may prevent a fixation on the wounds themselves, and the spiritual masochism that can result. At the same time, it prevents Easter Christians from being overly involved in the sunshine of life, while ignoring or even denying its shadows and darkness. The power of the resurrection will work on us after death of course, but Paul sees its power coursing through the Christian experience in this world. In the last of the American Recordings (Vol. 6) of Johnny Cash, some of the songs were penned by Cash himself. Part of the reason I find them so moving is that Cash faces death with the courage of his younger self, but he has the assurance to face his frailty head-on. Paul tries so hard to keep the darkness and the light in balance. He does not promise more than this life may deliver. In his anticipation of God's coming triumph over all evil, he is more than willing to extol the glories of the coming triumph in contrast to the troubles of the present. All these years later, it is still quite the struggle, butit is at the core of the Christian life.

235) Phil.3:14 Paul keeps his eyes on the prize. This was a phrase of the hope of the Civil Rights Movement in our time. For

the grieving, one way to speak of the eye on the prize is coming to health, of feeling who and restored again. Our eye could be kept on heaven. In the verse before, he speaks of straining toward it. I picture a runner leaning for the finish line. We are not sure of the dimensions of the prize, and perhaps it is best left a bit vague. Is the prize the same as "that beautiful shore in the sweet by and by?" Some know that it is heaven, but I would wish to keep it more earthbound as well. Paul's athletic metaphor is interesting in that athletic endeavors require training and effort. We can practice disciplines and virtues that strengthen us, make us more resilient.

I was going through some material in these pages and was stunned to see that the Reformed watchword, providence, did not appear in the pages so far. Recently, Rev. Janet Riley asked me to help with a class on the confessions, affirmations of faith, of the church. Our second class was on providence. I was struck by how confessional material can use the doctrine to be secure in God's love and provision in times of plenty and want, sickness and health, joy and sorrow. The early Reformers saw not just blessing but everything as contained in the hand of God. God was constantly making discrete decisions about us, for us. Yes, our vision cannot see providence in tragedy and pain. Paul is able to keep his eyes on the prize, because God always keeps an eye on the prize. God is always at work trying to bring some good even out of the worst circumstances. Still, we sometimes mistake Providence for pre-determination. Some use this verse to say, in effect, if we keep our eye on heaven, we will be spared the pains of this life, through the power of the comparison of the joys of heaven that await us. Not so fast, as not long before this passage, Paul is grateful that an associate's life has been spared. In that recovery, Paul says he is spared "sorrow upon sorrow" (2:27-8). Sorrows present themselves always, but may Providence provide guidance, shelter, and relief.

236) Phil.3:20 "our citizenship is in heaven." Paul uses a basic word for politics: citizenship. In a way, our loyalties are divided,

as we have one foot on earth and another in the world to come. Maybe better put, we have dual citizenship. We will not be aliens there. We already have our citizenship papers. We will be at home there. Elsewhere, Paul speaks, as does Peter, as if we are already strangers, aliens, in this world, as we are 'apart from the Lord." I grasp the power of the image for a beleaguered minority. Grief is an alienating experience. We feel as if we have become strangers to others, and even our narrative script doesn't fit us anymore. Still, if God "so loved the world" as to give us the Incarnation, then surely we are at home here as well. I resist "pie in the sky, by and by" and neglect the hard of salvation right here on earth. Heaven is our heart's true home. When we feel fully at home, we are in a "thin place" a place "near to the heart of God." Right after that, he speaks of the work of Christ in transformation from a body of humiliation to one of glory. Earlier the phrase "becoming like him" has a sense of metamorphosis (v.10). now our lowly body will be changed (metaschematize). We will be "conformed to Christ (the same word show us in Rom. 12:2) with a sense of changing with. The schema of our being will change, in less vivid but closer English. Paul is struggling to try to speak of a fundamental structural transformation. We will move to a body of glory that I assume is similar to the spiritual body of I Corinthians. This event will include the body of believers as well, as Paul says we form Christ in Ga. 4:19. It is as if we are holding dual passports. Citizenship implies other citizens. This is a welcome image in America, where our individualism makes salvation sound like an individual ticket, instead of a shared polity. Our heavenly papers may not lessen our commitment to this world, however. We are rooted to this good earth. When we get frustrated we may dream of a better world in flight from this one. Alternately, we can look toward the onrushing way of God. As Christina Rossetti said, "as the wind is your symbol, forward our goings/as the dove so launch us heavenwards...as a cloud abate our temptations/as dew, revive our languor"(BCW:21).

237) Phil. 4:11-4 speaks of learning to be content (self-sufficient) in all circumstances. Can we consistently rise above circumstances in order to be better balanced, to be contented? It

is a hurtful thing to be told to be contented in all circumstances when we have lost someone close to us. This sounds to me to be in the same ballpark as the Stoic desire to rise above circumstance, or detachment in the sense of some Eastern religions. Do circumstances have to govern our mood, our stance toward life? Does it imply that we are then captives to the quality of our circumstances for the quality of our lives? Grief isolates, so community keeps us engaged with others and with living in the shadows. So, Paul can say this. "It was kind of you to share my trouble." It has a sense of being partners in sharing. I think it is close to what people mean when they say that someone is there for them. It is one thing to share in a business partnership. it is another thing to share resources, but to share the emotional and mental resources, one to another, is powerful. This is what community can offer the grieving, a chance to share one's troubles. That can be clear in grief groups or in Bible studies that may choose to examine grief for a season. Still, we need boundaries stable enough to try to not absorb someone's troubles as our own. Notice that Paul places this call to self-possession in the same breath as sharing trouble.

238) Ps. 25:16-18 "I am lonely and afflicted/relieve the troubles of my heart/and bring me out of my distress/consider my affliction and my trouble." The entire psalm is in an acrostic form, so we move through A to Z, if it were in English. Limburg (WBC p. 80) sees a classroom in the background, but I see this as a plea for guidance, like a park ranger guiding someone along a tricky trail or else one would be hopelessly lost. Some commentators then say the psalm lacks a coherent structure, due to the impact of the acrostic form. I think not. The psalm is disjointed as that is how people talk when they are troubled. The acrostic tries to put some sort of structure for unstructured feelings to finds a vessel in which to be poured. We may wonder if anyone is capable of understanding us, even those closest to us, even those who have been through similar circumstance. As unique people, we process things differently. No two circumstances are precise3ly the same, so a full grasp of what we go through is at a premium now. We may feel the need to unburden ourselves too readily. Yes, we want a sense of God's

kindly presence with us in troubles. Some of us may well want more. We want more than a sympathetic companion; we want help, real help, to lift us out of the pit and on to solid ground again. we want more than a tissue; we want our tears to stop flowing. At the same time, our passage wants that pain not only to be assuaged but to be acknowledged, maybe even seen as legitimate, that the condition is noticed. It starts from a position of trust, and out of the trust the psalmist dares to state a case of complaint. I would note that the psalm uses three different Hebrew words that deal with sin, one means missing the target, one has a sense of rebellion, of transgressing limits, and one deals with guilt with a sense of being twisted out of shape, distorted out of alignment. Reconciliation puts us back into shape; it clears distorted vision, and allows us the sincere pleasure of a clear focus once again.

239) Gen. 27:46, Job. 10:1, Is. 50:4, Ps. 6:6- Grief can make us so tired, bone-weary. In that way it reflects its similarity to depression. We see that grief work is difficult and exhausting labor. Carrying its load makes the other normal activity of life seem even more difficult. I have a friend who checks in regularly. When things have been stressful or hectic, I know that the word, exhausted, is going to be spoken very soon. Sometimes, it seems a heroic effort just to get out of bed in the morning. We feel and act robotically, just existing one day, maybe one hour, one minute to the next. As Therese said, just for today, Lord, what does it matter if the future is dark?" After numbness subsides, that protective sheath of mind and heart, we notice that we are feeling again. We notice how little feeling has been present; it hasn't burrowed to consciousness much. We also notice how little energy we have, and what effort even basic things can take. At some point energy starts to kick in, and not just for distractions. Focus at work starts to improve. When it is difficult just getting out of bed, the future seems to be enveloped in mist. So, the prayer is fitting: just for today, maybe just for the night, maybe just for the next hour. When time seems to be a burden, when we feel at the end of our rope, what gives you energy? Do you have a set of 'pick-me-ups" that tend to help

you? Does your diet have an effect on your feelings of lethargy or energy? Do you have the seemingly contradictory experience of being tired from emotional stress and then finding that physical exercise then actually seems to increase your energy level?

240) 2 Cor.12:1-4- This passage goes to the mountaintop and the valley of human experience. (See Alan Segal's works on the afterlife). In the first part, Paul speaks of a visionary experience and so gives some oblique hints about the ineffable glories of heaven. His visionary experience is used to buttress his authentic spiritual standing. Scripture tends to give hints of the advent world we call heaven. In Paul's time, we spoke of levels of heaven, with the highest heaven being in the presence of God. My sense of this is less of being in higher levels due to reward but more of proximity. I read this as another form of the visions of Is. 6 or Ezek. 1. Extra-biblical material spoke of transport into paradise, an Edenic place of peace (I and II Enoch, Baruch). Like Enoch, Paul is seized into the heavenly places. In Acts 22:17 Paul describes a trance-like state in the Temple. Paul won't or can't give much insight into the mechanism of the vision, "in the body or not," but it is certainly a religious experience. Like Thomas, we want to know more. The words about levels of heaven lead us right away to surmise that maybe we will be in the very topmost part of heaven, and we wonder who will be in the lower levels. We want some tangible proof. We want more precise description. On the other hand, "post-modern" thought is not so empirical. We realize that we are moved by things that cannot be measured. We have grown to see a variety of ways to reach for the beyond as an asset. We are not so quick to label a visionary experience as a hallucination but an image of an altered state of consciousness. Have you noticed that so many things can trigger a reverie? It may be the timbre of a voice, the smell of a cookie, the click of a lock. Are you someone who has a mystical bent and experiences visions?

241) Prov. 31-I've been hearing this read at more memorial

services lately. It makes sense as it describes a woman at home in the private and the public spheres, and more and more women have the opportunity to demonstrate the same sort of skill and versatility to do the same. It gets at a sense of honoring someone's reputation in the family and in the community. We read this at my aunt's funeral some years ago, and it was a fitting tribute to her. Recently, I heard it read at the service of a woman who raised a family and helped manage a grocery in town. The part that brought tears to my eyes was her uncommon generosity in helping people out who needed food or just a little more patience with their bill to help keep their family together and fed. It is a marvel of combining the two spheres of life. Great people can make us feel inadequate, however. I just spoke with a woman who absolutely adored her father to the point of idolizing him. That is admirable, but it poses the danger of no one ever coming close to living up to his example. This reading may pose the same problems for those who think that they could never like up to the ideal character described here. I was listening to a woman in her fifties (I hasten to add she looks 15 years younger) and speak of a real regret that she thought she could be superwoman and "do it all." Something had to give, and she feared it was her capacity for relationships, especially deep, enriching, fulfilling ones. All of the tasks made it so difficult. We never really let go of the view of our parents as super beings, even through the difficult teenaged years when their frailty collides with that idealized vision. What qualities do you most admire of your parents?

242) 2 Cor:12:14-I do not wish to be a burden to you. I heard that phrase a lot and still continue to hear it when people contemplate being in a nursing home or a facing a prolonged illness. It even helps some of us face death, as opposed to being a burden on our loved ones. (Our youngest daughter assures me that I will be taken care of, with the caveat that if she lives in Maine, I will be placed in San Diego). Part of it emerges from our distaste for every seeming dependent, every needing help. I find it much easier to offer help than to receive it, especially physically. Many of us find it far easier to try to be of help than to

be recipients of help. Sometimes we keep our feelings and needs private as we do not wish to be a burden to others. One way family gatherings or time with friends can become problematic is when people won't dare breathe the name of the departed out of a sincere desire not to stir things up, not to upset us. It is right and proper to use the name of your loved one, and to use it with someone who has undergone loss. Yes, it may upset folks at first, but it starts to make the loss more bearable, as we come to know that they are not forgotten. In bereavement our love does seem like a burden. Its burden only seems to increase when we need to make a thousand decisions about money, property, and goods of all types. With Paul, we cry that we are not interested in things, but we want the person back. Then, families get caught up in possessions as emblems of love and care and may fall into squabbling over them. Some feel as if payment is owed them for being burdened with the care of the loved one. Others sees it as a duty, others a privilege. Would you prefer to be cared for or to care for a loved one?

243) 2 Cor. 13:4-5 In southeastern Indiana, I encountered a new word, flustrated. I heard it as a mix of being flustered and being frustrated. Circumstances do flustrate us, but we do not have to remain that way always. Many men find even the suspicion of weakness as anti-masculine, so they hate grief all the more for exposing some vulnerability and weaknesses. When one is already frustrated, flustered, and flustrated, small alterations in a plan, little disappointments may set us off. I remember a lady yelling in a cafeteria line, what you mean I have to wait for more peas. She was in a fury, as if she was the graduate of some bizarre assertiveness training academy. She was a few months after the loss of a loved one. The Bible loves reversals. Weakness can be a source of strength. Admitting to weakness closes down our insistence on self-sufficiency and independence and opens us for a helping hand and our dependence on God and our interdependent relationships with others. It is no sin to admit that one feels weak, or even as if "at the end of my rope." Indeed it may well open the door to the discovery of new strength and new resources from within and

without once we push through the psychological barrier of trying to present an image of stolid, unmovable self. For Paul, signs of weakness puts us in community with each other, as we all share human frailty. Moreover, it establishes identification with Christ in the crucifixion. That is not grounds for being a victim; as such weakness is then moved into the realm of resurrection power. If I understand him here, we are tempted to being strong and self-sufficient and thus lose our sense of dependence and identification with God. When have you had moments of being flustrated?

244) Mk. 12:18-24- The question about resurrection hit the Sadducees, as they were religious conservatives. They held tightly to the words of Scripture and distrusted the newer interpretations of others. This included a belief in resurrection that we see Martha had in John 11. They believed that death was the end. They held to the words that widows needed protection by being able to marry a brother-in-law. To try and show the difficulties in belief in an afterlife, they drew on this earthbound principle and wondered what would happen if a woman were married multiple times. Would one worry if progeny were our link to the future? Some folks expound on this passage and fear that they will not know their loved ones anymore. This angelic notion does seem to be at variance with the notion of the resurrection of the body, but Jesus does speak of the dead being raised here. I keep going back to the resurrection appearances. Jesus went to his friends for appearances, those whom he loved, and those who loved him. They recognized him, even though his was a transformed visage. Perhaps, wrapped in God's light, our mutual bonds grow stronger toward everyone. Perhaps, all Jesus was trying to do was to get at the transformation inherent in a resurrected state. Placher, in his Mark commentary, (173) sees the afterlife as a way to give hope to all of us who have received too much pain and hardship in life. "Death cannot be the end of their stories." For Jesus, God is the God of "the living not the dead." He takes the vision at the burning bush as the God of Abraham, not as a title from the past but a living reality. For Jesus, concern about the structure of gender relationships,

property, and rights is a sterile application, a deadening of the life we live now and the life-giving new future. He sees anew age intersecting the present age. Life here and life in the realm of God's presence beyond death is within the province of the God of life.

245) Mark 4:35-41-Reaction to loss does feel as if we are in the midst of a storm. Our little boat is getting swamped in the dark. Where is Jesus? Is Jesus asleep? They were in real danger, did Jesus "not care?" I love this version of the story because here Jesus says, Peace, be still. That may well be an excellent breath prayer, or a sort of mantra during the day" peace, be still. We may not be able to weather a storm on our own. The little boat was a symbol of the early church. It may seem frail, but it was an ark to hold us together. We cannot still storms on our own. The storms of grief are not predictable. Sure, they may touch phases as in the Kubler-Ross pattern of denial, anger, bargaining, depression, and acceptance. Those phases do not go in lockstep, and they do not disappear when we are in another phase. I remember hearing a chaplain arguing with a woman in a hospital as the chaplain was convinced that she had concluded one phase, so had to be fully in the next one, with no overlap. C.S. Lewis said that grief was getting the same leg cut over and over again; the same knife plunged in again. Instead see them as waves, often intertwined, as they swell and move into each other. We do hope the waves grow smaller in time and less frequent. Let those words enter into the depths of your soul. Peace, be still. Consider making them a sort of mantra. Lewis also notoriously said the human pain was God's megaphone to get our attention, but that was long before he lost his wife to cancer. Maybe we could think of our pain as a megaphone to waken a seemingly sleeping God? When we get depressed, we sometimes get told to pull ourselves up by our bootstraps. I tend to picture depression as being in a bog or quicksand, and if you struggle, you just go down quicker. We may require a helping hand out of the mire, and that helping hand is part of divine care and healing. Some doctors are very quick to prescribe anti-depressants for people in grief. I'm not so sure. Depression is dangerous as it seems to often come out of

the blue, with no discernible reason. Being sad and depressed due to a loss seems to me to be part of dealing with the loss. It's the appropriate and proper response to loss. In a similar story that seems to be added to Mark's account, Matthew has Jesus walking on the water. Peter leaves the boat, to go to meet Jesus. Peter is OK for a bit but then the reality of his action sinks in and he starts to sink. His excellent quick prayer is Lord, help me. Jesus take shim by the and and they walk together into the boat, the symbol of the early church. then the wind ceases. Jesus says do not be afraid. Yes, storms assail us, but they are not ultimate. We are in the little ship with others. Even if it appears that Jesus sleeps, Jesus is with us. Jesus does care that it feels as if we would perish in the storm. Peace, be still

246)   Mark 5:3 The Gerasene Demoniac lived among the tombs. He truly was experiencing a living death. He lived in a liminal state, caught between life and death. Sometimes, when folks start to worry about the duration or intensity of our grief, they will beg us to return to the land of the living. Besides, we aren't really sure of the location of this story. That adds to its uncertain situation. My sense is that the people were able to project their troubles on to him, which is why they were alarmed when he was freed of his affliction. He was an emblem of warning to some and a stark reminder of what can happen to us...that could be me. He had become the carrier of a social dysfunction into his own personality. So, perhaps, it would be better to say that he absorbed the pain of others, and it was eating him up inside. In some family systems, it is as if one member is appointed to carry the grief for the rest of the family, as if they are consigned to live in the tombs. Sometimes the dying person leaves a virtual set of instructions for their expectations of feeling and behavior following their death. Those final wishes can take on an almost sacred quality, of being set in stone as firmly as the name inscribed on a tombstone. Even when it is done with the best of intentions, I wonder about the ethics of trying to control another's reactions from beyond the grave, even if they are as bland an instruction as be strong. Control is a major issue in grief. All of its many symptoms come at us so fast and chaotically

that we feel as if we are losing our own self-control. We look to God to control events to protect our loved ones and then find that control absent, especially in facing accidental death. When we make a point of visiting a grave everyday, that can be a most comforting ritual, but for some, it can be residing with the dead more than continuing to engage life.

247) Spiritual types and grief-when I was a kid, a popular song went: "Different strokes for different folks." A one size fits all approach to spiritual life in grief can heed that sage advice. for instance, some people need a more action-oriented spirituality, while others are of a more meditative, mystical bent. some need a communal experience. One style or type is not to be considered better, more religious, more spiritual than another type; they are merely "varieties of religious experience." (See Urban Holmes and Corrine Ware) We could take them a step further and consider that different spiritual types of people may require different types of spiritual material and aid in facing grief. At the very least, they may find some types of material more appealing than others. Mystical types of Christians may need a lot of time alone in meditation and prayer. Activist Christians may need to find some public action related to their loss. People who move into their faith "head first" may will do some "bibliotherapy" and read of others facing grief. I think of John Adams and his books filled with his arguments and comments about the passages that threaten to overwhelm the texts themselves. Heart-first Christians may find it most difficult after they have spoken often to others about finding solace in God now finding that the well seems dry for them when they are in crisis. They may well need to pour their hearts out to you others and indeed to God in prayer. Spiritual direction is no substitute for grief therapy. I do want to commend it however. Its basic question asks, "where is God in our lives today?" It is a good question always, but a most important one as we travel through the dark, uncharted valley called grief. We tread carefully in prescribing spiritual tools for the grieving, for what works for one type of person may not be fitting for another. Naturally, one may think that the pieces of the soul require all types of these to become fully formed and you

may well be correct. I would say that some of us have decided tendencies in certain direction. Still, the point is well taken. Contemplation may well open the heart and mind toward compassion that results in just the sort of social action desired by justice-oriented people. We do well not to judge different spiritual types and accept them as part of our diversity.

248)   Mt. 14:13- According to Luke (ch. 1), the Baptist was family for Jesus. Even in the womb, the Baptist responds to the presence of the mother of Jesus and the life within her womb. So Jesus undergoes the loss of an important person in his life. Jesus was not somehow rendered immune from loss. The reality of the Incarnation means that he was indeed "acquainted with our grief." After all, the ministry of Jesus starts with his baptism by John in the synoptic gospels. Obviously, the Baptist is an important figure in his life. Jesus learns that a family member has been martyred by Herod. His response is go to a lonely place. I bet he wanted to pray by himself, to process the loss. Instead, he is beset by needy people. I think of Jesus Christ Superstar where he cries out, "there's not enough of me." Even in this private moment, duty calls. In the mini-series Jesus of Nazareth, it seems that Jesus catches but short breaks to rest and always gets disturbed when trying to regain some energy. Most of the time, we do not want to be bearer of bad news. We don't wish to be intrusive; we do want to give people their needed space. Sometimes, that distance gets problematic. We don't want to upset people, so we sometimes don't mention the name of the deceased. We aren't sure when we should bring up a memory. If someone is busy, would the pressure of it be too much? At times, the mention of a name does elicit a reaction. At other times, it triggers a desire to withdraw from the mention of the name or places associated with the loved one. On the other hand, it may assuage their fears that the love done is being forgotten, even by them, when they cannot conjure up a specific image of them or a specific memory at a moment's beck and call. That is a difficult burden. As Joan Didion writes, "what is lost is already behind locked doors." So, Jesus knew a terrible loss within his extended family. We have yet another example of Jesus being able to

sympathize with us.

249)   Mark 6: 45-56 Mark likes doublets. After the feeding of the multitude, Jesus sends the disciples to cross the sea on their own, when he goes off to pray. This is the second perilous sea crossing. Jesus walks on the water when the disciples were rowing hard against a strong wind. I think of the painting the boy spies in the movie Good Will Hunting of the fisherman rowing in the midst of a gale. Mark says that Jesus was going to pass them by. In other words, Jesus has a focus and moves toward it. We do often feel as if God is passing us by, perhaps busy with other things. Mark may be echoing the sense of god's presence with Moses as passing him by to protect him from direct contact with the full experience of divinity (Ex.33:19,22) He comes near them and says, "it is I; do not be afraid." After the miraculous crossing what does Jesus do? He helped out people who were in need of help. Recall that the sea is often a biblical symbol for death, chaos, uncertainty. It has mythic overtones all the way back to the creation accounts of the ancient Near East. God strides over the sea (Ps. 77).I always think of being in a rowboat on the sea in the dark when you cannot see the shoreline nor the stars. It feels so utterly lost to me. Some churches are built to remind one of being in the hold of a ship. That is why we speak of a nave in church, after all. Jesus can stride over that trouble on the way to meet the disciples. John 6:15-21 has it in similar fashion, but Matthew (14;22-33 adds the great part about Peter getting out of the boat to meet Jesus. He stays on top of the waves for a bit, but then sink and cries help me, Lord. Jesus gives him a hand and they enter the boat together. The wind then ceased. I love the short prayers in the New Testament such as Peter's. Those desperate breaths may be the best we can do under the circumstances. The worst storms can be navigated. Look at how it seems to reflect Ps. 107:12-31. Jesus enacts this passage in mark. Jesus continues to enact this passage as we try to weather storms in our little boats.

250) Ps. 116:13 Console comes from Latin to soothe. To me it has the sense of a mother saying, there, there, or a hand on a fevered forehead. Who doesn't need consolation at one time or another? As usual, what soothes one may not soothe another. I would think that we could call the Spirit, the Paraclete, of John 14 could be called a Consoler, in the sense of being there alongside you. What soothes you in anxious, troubled moments? It is said that music soothes. Does it for you? Some move toward food or drink they regard as soothing, such as a "nice cup of tea, or maybe "chicken soup for the soul." Some find it consoling to realize that others are in the same condition, while others find consolation in a book or even in solitude. Do some words of consolation stay with you? Have some people consistently been consoling toward you? Have those consolers changed over time, perhaps? Do certain times, people, or things tend to push you into a disconsolate mood? We try to bring words of consolation, but they usually seem to fail. At best, they may be recalled later down the road. Jer. 16:7 speaks of a cup of consolation as the antidote to the cup of wrath, but it was being forbidden. Oh to have a cup like that and drink it down, or as the Irish blessing would say that the dregs have no sorrow left at the bottom of the cup. Do you have favorite drinks? Are there soothing ones for you that are the liquid version of comfort food? What ingredients do you think should be in your cup of consolation? Have you been tried by wanting to drown sorrows in cups of alcohol to excess? The Paraclete may not be able to provide all consolation wanted or needed at the present moment. The Spirit will "lead them into all truth." Jesus realizes that they and we are not able to take in everything at once. We need to sit with it, to live with, to let our understanding emerge and grow over time.

251) Sympathy has a sense of fellow feeling, sensitivity toward the feelings of another, indeed to feel for another. It's an English word that comes straight from Greek. (At times, I feel the need to remind myself about taking intensive Greek in seminary). In a way, we can recognize the feelings someone has through the prism of our reaction to a similar experience. Sympathy crosses the boundary of the self to grasp, albeit partially, the condition of

someone else. Hebrews has Jesus sympathizing with us in our weaknesses. This is the same Jesus who prayed with loud cries and tears. Not only is the humanity of Jesus involved in sympathy, is sympathy a divine quality as well. Notice Jesus does not condemn our weakness here, Jesus sympathizes with us in our very weakness. I got teary on my mother's birthday, in this first year without her, and was more than a bit embarrassed. That's OK we can hear in the passage. Jesus sympathizes with me in my perceived weakness. This is the God who heard Israel's cries and was moved to call Moses to begin the exodus. "Blest Be the Ties" sings of the "sympathizing tear." I Peter 4:7-11 speaks of us having sympathy for each other. It extends family feeling to the new spiritual family of which they are a part. It extends previously feelings among intimates to a much wider sphere. It seems that we may resent when sympathy becomes pity. Too often, we do sympathize, but we do not let people know of our sympathies after their first, pained expression. We may well mean it when we say to call if there is anything we can do, but the recipients aren't sure when to call, for what they can call, and if they are being intrusive. In time, being able to offer sympathy to others who are grieving can be a real vehicle of health and healing for us when we are downcast.

252)Jer. 31:15-22 Compassion and mercy are twinned in the Bible, even in the character of God. Compassion means to feel with someone, to share in their suffering. In Hebrew it is connected to the word for womb (ruhamah and rehem). Compassion then has the sense of motherly love in the OT. (See Trible, ch. 2 in God and the Rhetoric of Sexuality for a detailed discussion on compassion.) It suggests that the very process of carrying a new life to term develops that sense of compassion. It is a shared experience. We are often clumsy in trying to offer or show compassion. Swinton speaks of "raging with compassion." It can become a determination not to allow others to suffer as I did. for many of us, discomfort or feeling uncomfortable seems to trump that feeling of compassion. As U2 sings, "we carry each other" or at Boys' Town: he ain't heavy; he's my brother." Sometimes we act as if someone has to go through the same experience to be able to demonstrate compassion. It does seem often the case that someone who has suffered discovers deep new wells of compassion within. Mercy tempers the abstract aims of justice to treat us alike when in similar circumstances. Its disposition is toward forgiveness, generosity, leniency, kindness. Calvin saw this divine benevolence as a merciful tolerance for our incapacity in prayer, and that mercy gives us leave to pray and pray fully. I pray for that same mercy when I stumble about trying to console those in grief. Compassion so wants to ease the pain of another. I pray for that mercy to be felt within when I fail to offer the comfort I so want to provide. I hope others can be merciful to my efforts to see compassion transmute into acts of charity and justice. In other words, compassion felt is a human response. Mercy, compassion in action, puts those feelings into motion.

253) John 17-Jesus's prayer for unity seems to include a capacity, a gift, for empathy. Empathy is the capacity to walk in another's shoes. It is more than sympathy, it appears to me. Thoreau spoke of the miracle of seeing through another person's eyes. A number of people have remarked that evil stems from the inability or the refusal to discover empathy. We resent it when people assume empathy when they tell us that they know what we are going through. On the other hand, we are a bit more willing to accept it when we know that they have undergone a similar situation. When Lincoln's son Robert asked him about tension between the president and Sen. Trumbull, Lincoln replied that the they agreed completely, except Lincoln looked down Pennsylvania Avenue and the senator looked toward the White House from his office. It is a deep imaginative capacity to walk in another's shoes. In To Kill a Mockingbird, Atticus struggles to give his children that sense of empathy, of trying to see the world from the perspective of another, from their point of view, to get inside another's skin.. We want an empathetic person, and we assume that going through loss themselves can help in that regard. At the same time, we consider our grief unique, so we think that no one can really understand what we go through. Often, we can achieve an empathetic breakthrough if we just slow

down and listen to the story someone has to tell us. Perhaps, when Jesus said those blessed/happy/fortunate are those who mourn, he looks to the blessing of empathy, that rare sense to break through the separation of self. Perhaps it helps us to become open to others, even in their pain. Recently, we were asked in an otherwise dreary presbytery planning meeting to reflect on events where we became aware and then moved toward a commitment. I was struck by my going back to my youth, and that all of the events involved photographs. Now Susan Sontag feared that photographs were too distancing, that they could make us callous toward the suffering of others, as an artifact. I don't know if our empathy can easily reach beyond our circles of intimates, or if it weakens with distance, as it does decay with time. Empathy has its dangers, of course. I don't think it can be healthy to absorb someone's pain, as if it were one's own. Do you think that some distance is part of the human experience?

254) Acts 17:23-4 Shrines are kept when we really expect someone to return after they have died. It is a refusal, or an incapacity, to admit that the death really happened. We try to freeze time. A shrine is set up as if nothing has really changed, as if the death is not irrevocable or permanent. We have not yet integrated their death into the fabric of our lives. I knew a man whose kitchen was unchanged for 15 years, as he associated his wife with it. A woman kept her daughter's room untouched for years, as if waiting for the little girl to return. After many years, we keep many things, in the vague belief that somehow they will come back and wear the same clothes, play with the same toys. One of the reasons it may be hard to give away the clothes of a loved one is that we think that they may need them, say when the weather gets cold. To me, it is a sign of movement when we are able to part with things that signal an expectation of return. I do not think that we have a right to tell someone when that should be, as if our schedule should rule. A hospice worker told me recently that it should be honored as long as it is not interfering with their basic functioning. For me, the standard is set too low. It is all to the good that a shrine is not keeping

someone from eating, bathing, and other essentials. OK, but I do see long-standing shrines as an indicator that the person has a long way to go in coming to grips with the loss and connecting with them in a new way. Put differently, I have never seen a shrine that tries to freeze time where the person has moved through various tasks of grief well. Trying to freeze time before someone died also freezes grieving and keeps it too potent a force over too long a period of time. Enshrining frozen time can and does inhibit the hard work of grief; including the full realization that time's arrow flies toward the future.

255) In the KJV, Lev. 26:39 speaks of people pining away. (See also Lam. 4:9 and Ezek. 33:10) Is. 24:14-16 has a speaker note that "they lift up their voices, but I pine away." Pining/yearning/searching- I became aware of these words through some British research with widows. Bowlby wrote of it being an expected reaction, as it shows an awareness of a precious person being lost. Parkes wrote of the persistence of pain frequently intruding on someone, of being so preoccupied with the loss that other thoughts seem to be the distraction. Our minds play tricks on us. We are searching our environment for the one we've lost, as if we are trying to find something we misplaced. We walk through a crowd and something looks familiar and we fill in the gaps and make it appear to be our lost loves. When we are in unfamiliar territory the same thing occurs and we place people into familiar locales. Since the departed are weighing on our minds, it is then not surprising that we will be reminded of them in the features of strangers. I remember a widower telling me that the hard time for him was the morning. He had always prepared breakfast for his later-waking wife. Now that she was gone, he found himself wondering, day after day, why she was so late for breakfast this morning. We have the phrase, at least among the elderly; of pining away, of neglecting even basic duties so great is our focus on a loved one. Pining comes through Latin, with a sense of pain and shares the root with penalty. The penalty for love and loss is to pine for their return, their presence, the unrequited desire to have them back here with us. Emmylou Harris sings of it "I would

walk from Boulder to Birmingham, just to see your face, just to see your face." Pining has a sense of wasting away in grief, of losing the capacity to properly take care of one's basic needs.

256) Keepsakes are important. In Acts 9, the people show the things that Tabitha made for them. Could we call the relics in the tabernacle as keepsakes (Ex.40:20)? They don't have to be important or valuable in money. They are little sacramental tangible items that connect us to the person who has died. They are small incarnations of love. What are some keepsakes that mean the most to you? In the movie of the recent fable, Hugo, the orphaned boy wants to repair an automaton that his father tried to fix before his death in a fire. Did arguments ensue over who would get certain keepsakes? Why do you prize certain keepsakes? Do they pick up an interest, a quality of your loved one? I saw a piece of Tim Allen's sitcom Home Improvement where Ernest Borgnine plays a widower who spoke of arguing with his wife over some ugly knickknacks she kept on the kitchen counter .He hid them, and she put them back. Did you get rid of them when she died? "No, you don't have to understand a woman, all you have to do is love her", he said in bemused resignation. A teller at a bank I used kept a picture of her son who died as a teenager up on her counter. It is not only a marker, as it is an invitation to ask her about her son. Otherwise she would not put it in a public place. We may feel pressure to get rid of belongings quickly after a death. Speed is not of the essence here. At the same time when you do choose to start to clean out belongings, don't just pitch everything. After all, some items may be of real value to different people in your circle. It was always important to my mother to give things away to people who could use them, so I filled the car a few times with some of her items and gave them to Goodwill. If your loved one had a favorite charity, have a yard sale of some items and donate the money to it. While you are having the sale, you may also note that you do not want to part with some things, so keep them. In the movie, The Descendants, we see a family faced with continuing shocks as they come to grips with the coma of a wife

and mother tha twill lead to dying. A yellow blanket is over her the last time the family sees her to say goodbye in the hospital. In a coda, the ten year old daughter is watching TV with the blanket. She is joined by her father and then her angry teen sister. They all share the blanket and the 2 bowls of different ice cream. I could well be reading too much into this ending, but I do wonder why that particular keepsake and who selected it?

257) Joel 2:28, Dan. 1:17- Apparitions- A good number of people report sensing a loved one after death. The senses include a touch, a sight, a voice, a fragrance. Stairs seem to be a common site for them. Those who sense a presence may spark a question if we are going crazy. I doubt it, as when something is on our mind and heart all of the time, we are going to have a sense of it. They do seem to come out of the blue at times as well. Once many months after a cousin had been killed in a car wreck, my mother, brother, and I were picking berries in different spots. When we rejoined to dump the berries into a larger container, we mentioned that we all sensed him. He had been a devoted berry picker when he was young. In the last Harry Potter movie, the young man asks his mentor if this is real or in his head. Of course, it's in your head, the mentor replies, what makes you think that makes it any less real? Carrie Newcomer sings of sensing a presence in There Is a Tree "last night I dreamt you very near...I knew you left before I woke/but you fogged the window when you passed." The fairly recent survey by the online magazine, slate, reported a fair percentage of respondents having some sort of felt contact. This can be an alarming experience, especially for those of us who are naturally skeptical. It may trigger a real fear that our minds are slipping away from us. it may be a most comforting experience, as it heightens a suspicion that the dead are still with us in some way. Christopher Reid in Late (from The Scattering collection of poems) writes of being in bed waiting for his wife to come home to bed. He had forgotten she had died. He tells of hearing her come in, undress, and come under the covers, with the mattress and headboard reacting to her weight. Then she is gone before he can feel her caress.

258) Acts 10:4, Jos.4:7, Zech. 6:14-Making a living memory-It is a good idea to make a memorial with and for our memories. When Christmas seems like the last thing we want to face, one could consider getting an ornament to symbolize the person who is gone. A local farmer was a John Deere fanatic, so his family put up a John Deere ornament, maybe it was a toy tractor, on the tree. In time, that was the first ornament set up on the tree. Scrapbooks have become popular again, and one could make different ones from themes of a life. With computers, we can make slide shows and recordings of pictures and even put them to music. Re-membering Lives includes material like decorating the urn of ashes, of eating a piece of cake for them on their birthday, making a flower garden or tree plantings, of lighting a candle for each story told by them or about the loved ones. Stories are vital in keeping a memory alive. I so admire those who seek to make some public good through loss, such as the founder of MADD. Making public good out of a tragedy seeks significance to a loss on the public stage. It moves from the private to the social concern. It realizes that a community shares in grief and in reconstruction of a life, of life, after a loss. As they work through a death, people discover new skills and interests in themselves. Plus, doing some public good takes some of our inward focus away, has us see that others have a hard time too. Plus, it feels good to be of help to someone else. It moves us out of our own self-focus, out of isolation, and into society again. As I was reviewing material, Valentine's Day just passed. We were talking about men feeling at a loss at what a proper Valentine's present is. One lady, married over 50 years, was bragging about her husband's exquisite care in gifts. Then she said that he always picks a perfect card. We talked that women seem to appreciate that a card took time and effort to select by it seeming to fit the person to whom a card is sent well, fittingly. Creating a memory, cherishing a memory could be a trigger for making a memorial as it should fit the interests, or character, of the person to elicit memories of those who knew them along those very same lines as appropriate.

259) I was raised Roman Catholic, and the maternal spiritual image was filled by Mary, the mother of Jesus, and the many compassionate female saints. Protestants either lack the image, or we have transferred it to Jesus, the Holy spirit, or human role models. The maternal image of God is not frequent in the Bible, but it is clearly present. Later portions of Isaiah use both paternal and maternal images to get at a sense of comfort that begins at chapter 40. .Nowhere is it more powerful than in Is.66:13, as a "mother comforts her children, so shall I comfort you." When we are little and hurt, we run to our mothers for comfort. I heard a radio commercial where they hire a mother to deliver bad news and then to seal it with some fresh-baked cookies. If one's image of God is overtly paternal, it could be that this is a refreshing expansion of one's image of the divine. God is the rock of our birth in Dt. 32:18. Many of us experienced our mothers as the emotional center of our households, so to me it makes emotional sense to project some of those qualities on to God. for instance, when little, we often cried out to mother when sick or hurt. It may well take a shift in one's image of God to be able to sense the consoling presence of God in a difficult time. Again in Isaiah (49:14-26), the people feel forgotten. God responds that a nursing mother cannot forget a child and not have motherly love, compassion on the child. When a nursing mother even hears her child cry, she can feel the milk start to flow. Her ability to give matches the child's need. Even if that nursing mother could forget, but not God. Even if God could forget, our names are engraved on the hands of God. the word, character, has the sense of engraving or stamping, like a coin. God is stamped with our names, as if God needs a string around the divine finger. Patricia Tull (Willey) in Remember the Former Things sees this portion of Isaiah in dialog with other Biblical material, as the passage is awfully similar to Lam. 5:20. Only in this case, the prophet answers the pain in Lamentations in a positive vein. Have you sought, or received, a maternal side of compassion, including a spirutal sense of it?

260) In the Bible wailing was individual response to death, of course, but also a communal one (Es. 4:3-4, Jer. 9, Am. 5:16) Keening is an old word from Celtic tradition. Apparently it had set

ritual elements of postures or organization, where some singers took the lead and at times the whole crowd responded with a chorus. It seems to include elements of asking why, of eulogy, of woe for the survivors wrapped into this outdoor event. For me it can be the heart-rending cry of loss or a more formal set piece of a public crying over a death. All my life, I have seen images of women wailing over a child in too many wars. In Scripture, we see examples of mourners wailing over a death. In the movie, the Apostle, the Robert Duval character shouts, I love you Lord, but I'm mad at you." He could be candid with the God who loves him. I envy that openness, as I sometimes fear that I am too reserved in my prayers. Worse, I fear that some of that reserve is less from personality and more from a nagging fear of God as punisher. Do I trust God enough to be candid, or do I need to coat things with a veneer of piety, civility, and euphemism? I speculate that the women in Scripture who wailed at a funeral were doing a Middle Eastern version of keening. It's a release to be able to weep and wail. It expresses where the words themselves fall short. In our current insistence of making only positive feelings public, I wonder why we cannot be candid with ourselves. We do use symbols, the yellow ribbon around the tree, flags at half staff, quiet public displays. We would not even have a clue where to begin to create a public ritual of abject mourning such as keening in our time. Where would you start?

261) Ps. 77 starts with a protest to God about the way of the world. I am taken with the idea that prayer can be forceful protest to God. I heard Thomas Long say that it is a basis for trust to see that we are not consumed for such speech. It is Biblically authorized prayer to ask where was God, where is God in the midst of our travails? It is part of the faith to recognize that the word is not the way it is supposed to be. Here, the inmost self has refused to be comforted (In v. 4 the psalmist cannot sleep and can't speak, although speech in prayer is evident). Then, v. 10 has the grief being changed or undergoing a transition. The remembrance of things past brings both pain and hope. Why does God not act in a big way now? Has God forgotten about us? If you are feeling the need to shake a fist at God but are not sure where

to start, please consider using a psalm such as this as a model. Use it as your basic form, or consider rewriting it in your own words and for your own condition. It may be helpful to use it as a daily prayer for while and note the different elements of the prayer that hit you as you go over it day by day. By v. 19 the psalmist finds hope in the old stories of deliverance from Egypt, but even there God's footprints were unseen. We may well spend too much time hoping for a miracle, "counting on a miracle" as Bruce Springsteen says. God works in different ways. God's hand may well be hidden, working behind the scenes, but working nonetheless. In Mt. 13: 34 the female baker hides some leaving into a large batch of flour, enough to feed one hundred. My guess is that part of the parable's message is that God does not always work on a grand scale but works almost invisibly, but nonetheless throughout and thoroughly, to bring about transformation, as a starter leaven a whole batch of flour for baking.

262) Rabbi Kushner's book was so popular, in part, due to its arresting title, <u>When Bad Things Happen to Good People</u>. He certainly knew of the position of a grieving person, as his son was stricken with a disease that made him age far too rapidly, and he lost his life at a terribly young age. Some of us have a sense of an implicit contract with God. "If I am good, then I should be immune from trouble." After all, some parts of Scripture make fairly explicit links to behavior and blessings or curses. In a basic sense, we expect good to be rewarded and bad to be punished. It is part of the reason why the suffering of children is so affecting, as we consider them innocent, in other words, they have done nothing deserving of suffering. That implicit contract is part of the cry, 'I don't deserve this." We wonder what we could have possibly done to be treated this way. We can try to find some condign sense of punishment according to the wrongs we have done. Then, when we can't find anything that matches our troubles, we start to wonder about the level of divine justice, or divine goodness for that matter. That is a sobbing cry from someone who wonders if loss could possibly be some form of direct punishment. The rabbi tries to square the goodness of God and the power of God. His solution is to downplay the power of

God. While he can worship a God who works within limitations, he cannot worship a God "who chooses to make children suffer and die, for whatever exalted reason"(134). He is not interested in what he perceives as defending God's honor at the expense of our "bewilderment and anguish" (p.4). His notion that divine power is circumscribed fits, apparently independently, the movement of process theology, as both are concerned about God and human suffering and the nature of divine power. That power is empowering, more than control, a field of forces in relationship.

263)Dt. 32:39- Kenneth Surin in <u>Theology and the Problem of Evil</u> reacts against the run to make evil a philosophical problem instead of facing it in practical terms based on situations and the context in which it develops. In other words, instead of abstraction, he wants us to go into the heart of the beast of suffering as it is experienced and see what theology can offer. He moves toward people such as Jurgen Moltmann, or for a North American, Douglas John Hall, in lifting up a theology of the cross. Put another way, he doubts that a satisfying intellectual response to the theology of evil can be made practical or workable for those suffering right now. Even there, our situations differ so much that I doubt that a one size fits all approach can be comforting. One does hear people speak of something done or said that lodged in their mind. Not every question of theodicy (God and human suffering) is a hidden way of asking for emotional solace. At times, they are honest questions. At times, people will share something they read or something they have composed that strikes them as a satisfying answer to their questions. Theodicy is a response to very real questions, religious questions, which confront us. Tragedy does put religious convictions to the test. I am not sure how much good it does to be told that are questions need to be reformulated. As I have reflected on this, I move back to the middle of the book of poems in Lamentations, here 3:32-3.It sounds Reformed in its emphasis as God as a causing agent, but it quickly moves toward God's compassion and love, but then it continues to say that God does not "willingly afflict or grieve anyone." The phrase literally is "from the heart." This is said after some of the most heartrending pieces in all of Scripture about seeing destruction as punishment for the misdoings of the people. God's silence in this book could be the proper response to God, too, being caught in this immense human tragedy.

264) I lived in a farming community for 15 years. Our commercial time in the early morning had dueling products to fight the eternal struggle between weeds and useful crops. Pre-emergent and post-emergent herbicide commercials promised room and resources for bumper crops. The noted preacher and homiletics professor Thomas Long alerted me to the parable in Mt.13:24-30, 36-43, the wheat and weeds, in his fine commentary on the gospel and a powerful speech he gave at Northminster Presbyterian Church in Indianapolis on suffering. The wheat and weeds grow together. The parable speaks of the church being a "mixed body" as Augustine said, where good and bad are mixed together. In part, this story tells us that trouble and good times grow together in this life, this field of the world, in the church or outside of the church. As Jesus said, the rain falls on the just and unjust alike. It is difficult to clear the weeds without destroying the wheat. If it is correct that the weed is darnel, it looks like wheat when sprouting. So, if one tried to weed it out, you would take a big chance that you were weeding out the wheat and leaving in the weeds. At harvest time, it needs to be culled, as it is poisonous. So, only at harvest time can they be properly separated. Of course, wheat and weeds grow within each one of us as well. Forces vie within us to be healthy and unhealthful all of the time. In trying to eradicate the weed, we could be in danger of puling out potential good as well. They are all tangled together as they grow. The parable also tells us about time. If we look at the wheat and weeds too early, we are liable to make a mistake. Only at harvest, when the wheat and the weed can be more easily distinguished is it time to act to separate them with care. We can push the image a bit more and see that each one of us is a field of wheat and weeds, a mixture where good and evil, healthy and unhealthy attitudes and actions are all tangled within. While we are told that we should not speak ill of the dead, as they cannot defend themselves, I think it is a sign of health

and movement in grief to see our loved ones as a mixture of wheat and weeds as well.

265) Difficult deaths-(Saul- I Sam. 31, II Sam. 1; and Judas, Acts 1:17-20, Mt. 27:3-10)-A friend was complaining that they wish their divorce was easier, more business-like, more controlled. I asked if he were aware of any of these easy divorces. He replied that some just had to be easier than this. I suppose he has a point, as child custody arrangements continue to bedevil their family after some years. In similar fashion, every death is difficult, but some have particular complicating factors.
Suicide brings out a sense of shame and guilt. Both are feelings deeply rooted in the psyche from early ages. Shame has a sense of being a failure, of one's whole self not measuring up, while guilt is a failure, a transgression against a standard. Our impulse is often to hide the cause of the death, even to concoct a cover story, a fig leaf, for it. Some wonder if it is indeed an unforgivable sin. Within hours of my brother's suicide, my aunt and mother had concocted a cover story for his death. For once, I was inspired enough to say, "the truth may well be easier." Guilt is a companion to death, especially difficult ones. the parade of if only I did such and such flood in an unrelenting stream. I don't like to compare the intensity and difficulty of grief. Each grief has plenty of pain on its own, without having to go through the minimizing pressure of having one's grief placed on some arbitrary scale. It almost begs for the pronouncement, "you don't have it so bad." The grief of suicide seems to me to bring up acres of shame and guilt. Shame shows in the desire to cover up, to keep secret and private. When we have an impulse to create cover stories, we can be assured that shame is present. Public exposure is too painful both for the family and the reputation and memory of the deceased, in that awful phrase, the successful suicide. Maybe it is good to examine patterns of different deaths and some of the crisis points and issues it may bring up as opposed to others. Of this I am sure. God understands fully what drives people to take their own life. God's abundant sympathy goes out to those who struggle with the impact of a particularly difficult death.

266) Mt. 2:13 and Lam. 2:11-12-At Christmas we often avoid reading the part after the visit of the Wise Men in chapter 2, as the young boys are killed on orders of Herod in his maniacal search for a baby he thinks could be a threat to his throne. We can get competitive even about losses, about who has suffered more, so I don't like to compare grief on some sort of scale, but the death of a child does seem to be the hardest to bear. We imagine a future as a series of milestones that we get to witness. Every time one of those comes up, a graduation for instance, we are again reminded of our deprivation. Time has changed, and many date their lives before and after someone's death. (David in II Sam 12) Remember that in biblical times the rate of infant mortality and child mortality was much higher than in our developed world. Go through an old cemetery and note all of the tiny grave markers. Of course, such losses scar us still. In the popular CBS shows Criminal Minds and NCIS major characters have lost children. It seems to be a way for writers to signal a deep vulnerability of the implacable advocates of justice. In Criminal Minds one of the profilers stays with his long-divorced wife as she lays dying. She asks him if she will see David again. He replies that he is certain of it. At the end, he sips a glass of wine to salute her at the grave and the son, David, his namesake, whose burial site is next to hers. Part of our difficulty lies in our depiction of children as innocent. In the back of our minds, someone older could well have done something deserving of death, but surely not a child. It could be possible that vague memories of limbo or fear about an unbaptized child's eternal habitation may lie in the background as well. Our eldest daughter was talking about limbo as a doctrine to try to get at the notion of original sin and sins for which one could be counted as responsible. Part of the immense heartbreak expressed in Lamentations is the wailing over the children of the city (2:12). In some ways, it could be seen as the nadir of the depths of a despairing city. The loss of an imagined future is hard to bear. It leads to the famous dictum of Irving Greenberg: "no statement, theological or otherwise, should be made that is not credible in the presence of burning children.' As in Ps. 79 we want revenge. We shake our heads at lasses, especially when they move past

our capacity to absorb the number.

267) Ruth 1-death of an adult child-Naomi is not only widowed but she loses two adult sons to death. Her security, her link to the future is snapped. In earlier days, the threat to a life was the many illnesses of childhood. We have now been spared many of those. It seems to flow against the natural, proper course or sequence of things to lose an adult child before we ourselves have passed on. In the Harry Potter series, we witness a moment when the young heroic Cedric's father grasps that his son's body has returned to the contest field. In the movie the actor lets out a terrifying spasm of pain. We can be grandparents who lose a member of the family, and this is sometimes an unrecognized grief. Some of us are better grandparents than we were parents. I've told our daughters that being a parent is like living in a time tunnel. At one point we see the person in front of us, and at another point we are back to when they are small. Even though our offspring are grown and may have children of their own, we still feel the urge to be responsible for them, to protect them. If they die before us, we may well be nagged by the sense that we failed in our duty to protect. It seems no matter the age, part of us wants to shield our children from danger and trouble. An early death stands as a proof that they were not ready to take on this hard world. Maybe we could have raised them better, warned them better, made them more careful. How many times I have heard an older parent say that they wish they had died, as they have lived a full life, instead of an adult child who still had so many potentially good years ahead of them. Over the years I have attended a number of workshops. I've noticed that almost as soon as the presenter mentions grief's impact, a series of comments will come up where different folks are looking for a forum to tell their own story of their personal grief. They also strike me as looking for some free grief counselling. To be more charitable, their pain is so intense that they seek help wherever and whenever they may find a listening ear and some wisdom to help them on their way.

268-2 Sam. 1:11, John 15:13-15 death of friends strikes me as a form of disenfranchised, unnoticed grief. Friends are part of the crucible of our lives. Sometimes, we have deeper relations with friends than family. Defining moments of life are more often than not with friends. I think of the Stephen King story, The Body, that was made into a movie, Stand by Me, or the return of the Secaucus Seven, or the Four Seasons, the Alan Alda movie. Ps.35:14. In the Big Chill, one of the characters looks at his old college friends and tells that, "I was at my best with you." Bruce Springsteen ends an album with a song in memory of his longtime bandmate, Danny Federici. He even has Danny's son play accordion on the piece. Recently, I marked my brother's birthday on Facebook, and was delighted to see two of his best friends growing up offer warm and gracious memories of their childhood friend. One of our earliest surviving myths is about Gilgamesh and Enkidu. (By the way, the story has some parallels to Scripture). Enkidu dies from a fight or from a disease. Gilgamesh mourns his friends and roams the earth in fear of death. In the Iliad Homer demonstrates the depth of Achilles's grief of his friend Patroclus. When the grief is first reported he receives it without a word. Then he goes through a paroxysm of grief. At our congregation, one of the members found that his longtime friend was diagnosed with advanced cancer. Just in time, they had a reunion of friends who came a distance to enjoy a weekend with their fried. They even got to see him play a gig. Not long after they returned, a heart attack felled him before the cancer did. He felt he acted just in time, out of an intuition. Have you lost some friends to death? What has been hard about that loss? With the advent of Facebook, many of us have established some reach back to old friends in the parade of people in our lives who have fallen by the wayside. I was struck by my real sadness that two classmates whom I like had passed away around Christmas time. I admit that neither had crossed my mind in years and years. I think I kicked the memories of youth off my feet more than most folks. To be charitable to myself, maybe it was because I moved away and spent time back home to visit my mother and brother. I wrote the families of both of my classmates, partly to cope with those feelings of regret and real loss. When my mother died, one of the men with whom I grew up made a point of coming to her visitation, and I was moved beyond words. The parents of two brothers with whom we had grown up made the journey too, even as they were both facing health issues themselves. Small town bonds persist.

269) Gen. 25, 50 -We know that in the course of time, the chances are that we will bury our parents. Nonetheless, we feel orphaned. We have a lot of "unfinished business" with our parents. Regrets pile up. We think of all the horrible things we said or did, and our failure to say or recognize them enough. In Leader of the Band, Dan Fogelberg sings "poppa I don't think I said I love you near enough." I don't know if we could ever expect "closure" with a lifetime of things done or not done, things said or unsaid. For a younger child, it is a devastating loss that marks us with scars of pain in our very identity. Parents are the emblem of safety, security, and stability. What becomes of those when their lives seem snatched away. A child may well blame themselves in a sort of magical thinking that something they did caused their grievous loss. In the movie Clara's Heart, a caregiver guides a child through coming to grips with the loss of a baby as his parents stumble through their grief. I once heard someone say that after his parents died, he felt rootless, as if all the stability of his own life had been thrust aside. I've heard other adults realize that they are orphaned, even when they themselves are grandparents. To whom will we turn for advice, for family history, for a recipe? For my baby boomer generation, it comes as a shock to realize that we now represent the elders in our family. (I think of the actress Goldie Hawn not wanting to be Grandma, so she is GlamMa in her house). I always am touched when people bring up their deceased parents easily in conversation, as illustration for a story, or remembering advice, or even using them as a negative example. We have so many regrets we should bury with our parents. Some of our attitudes need to be dead and buried as well. No, our parents were not perfect. Here's a news flash, no one has perfect parents. If you have children, you are not a perfect parent. If have not worked through some of the multitude of conflicting emotions and

thoughts surrounding them, their loss may well trigger all sorts of conflicting feelings. Deborah Tannen has explored the communication struggles in the mother -daughter relationship. In all candor, I think that the field of parent -child relationships is rife with joys and troubles no matter the gender issues in particular cultural settings. We may think that losing our second parent may be easier than losing the first parent to death. That may well be, but the sense of being orphaned may be heightened. The sense of going home to visit irrevocably changes when you are now in the surviving generation. We sometimes consign prayer to the realm of magical thinking. If only we say the right formula, or have the proper spirit, or better words, then my prayer will be answered. Religious interest is prone to fads. A while ago, the prayer of Jabez caught fire among evangelical circles as just such a magical prayer (I Chr. 4:10). All it speaks of is to enlarge one's borders and protect from hurt and harm. Patrick Miller realizes (They Cried to the Lord:379) that Jabez's very name deals with pain. The prayer could be a desperate plea that he will not live out the meaning of his name, so harm and pain could be in the past and not always portend a future.

270) Num. 20:1, 29, death of brother or sister- We do not accord the loss of sister or brother the respect of other family deaths. Yet, we know that siblings hold deep attachment for us. Few are privy to our growing up, our secrets, and our dreams. In some ways, no one knows our childhood better than our sisters and brothers, as we share many things out of the sight or earshot of our parents. They often represent for us the roads not taken and the roads taken, for good or ill. They have seen us at our best and worst. Sharing parents, we know the family system well. That means that we may have acquired roles in the family drama that we never requested. Sharing experiences, we know our reactions. When we think of family, sisters and brothers are often at the center of our memories. Sometimes our families try to see the lost one in us. It is not uncommon for families to start to compare us to the dead offspring. Few of us can compare to the often idealized portrait of a loved one that starts to emerge. Sometimes we are tempted to take on some of their

characteristics and live our lives through their lens. I heard of a brother who was asked to bury a Playboy key in his brother's casket. Then, he started acting out in ways that were not in his character. It did not take him long to realize that he was over-identifying with his dead brother. Look at how Mary and Martha bewailed the loss of Lazarus. Years ago, MASH had a haunting episode, the Billfold Syndrome. When a young man needed treatment, it emerged that he had promised his parents that he would take care of his brother, but he saw his brother die in combat. I wonder if birth order has any impact on how we mourn the loss of a sister or brother, or if we the same gender or not? Deborah Tannen has done some good work on the communication issues between sisters. They are fraught with subtext, family roles, and birth order that develop, overdevelop, and create static in the words, gestures, and perceived intent of messages. What do you miss, or not miss, about your brothers or sisters?

271)Is.45:7 -Is God responsible for the evils that befall us? A professor at my old seminary, Diogenes Allen (great name for a philosopher, no?) in Traces of God resolutely refuses to put such responsibility before God. Burton Cooper finds this phrase important in his book, "Why God?" I'm not entirely clear about the word, responsible in death and grief. Does it mean that God "feels responsible" for us? (see Harmon and White book on this topic) Part of me thinks that it is a way of moving from fault to learning to bear or shoulder a measure of responsibility. Is it a way of shifting a sense of responsibility from our shoulders? Is it a nicer way of speaking about someone being at fault? Does it mean responsible in some higher sense, as in responsible for the structure of creation that has so many tragedies befall us, that has room for so much evil, that has mortality at its core? How should be distinguish between responsible and culpable? I think of a story Thomas Long told in a sermon about a young pastor going through her list of parishioners and went to a home where a mother's young child had toddled off into the swimming pool. Part of her issue in not returning to church was if she could not blame God for the death of the child, then would she have to blame herself? The Bible does place blame directly at the feet of God for disaster or tragedy. Naomi does it in Ruth 1. Further, Ps. 80 :5 says that God has "fed them the bread of tears, and given them tears to drink in full measure." How much responsibility for what happens in life do you lay at the feet of God? When is it a denial of our own responsibilities or an admission that we cannot control the world around us? God interacts with creation. In that alone, we can find a measure of responsibility.

272) Num. 36 Inheritance and Legacy-When we speak of inheritance, we usually mean money, property, and possessions. I have been repeatedly struck by the accuracy of memory, the precision of it, when people start to recite who received what keepsake or what gift from their parent's estate. Often, there is a bit of envy over what someone received when the unspoken complaint is that they were the rightful, proper ones to receive it. Not long ago, I saw a family trying to hash out their share of the funeral expenses on the roof of the funeral coach as we prepared to lay the remains in the ground. Indeed the Hebrew word nahalah, has a sense of a precious inheritance of family land. Beyond that, we bear a legacy from our family. Family is the crucible of our lives. What were the core values in your family? What were some explicit lessons that your parents tried to instill in you, either by speaking or through reflected experience? What values do you wish to transmit to the next generations? What are some family stories that get passed around like a peace pipe when your family gets together? What are some unhealthy, negative patterns from your family of origin? I was just talking to a man, slightly older than me, and he had been through a good bit of therapy. He noticed that he had married the precise number of time as had his mother. He felt compelled, but learned to fight it, her practice of chasing people down in arguments until they would bend to her opinion and will. How have you tried to break those patterns? What patterns do you maintain, either by conscious choice or by reflex? In family systems models, we learn that family patterns tend to persist. They resist attempts to change assigned roles or the usual way of dealing with issues. It is based on the premise that we try to

keep things in rough balance, and we fear, perhaps rightly, the effects of upsetting what is often a most precarious balance.

273-I Peter 1:22-5-Beker in <u>Suffering and Hope</u> affirms that suffering needs to be allied with hope for its meaning or it becomes even more destructive. If they are separated, hope becomes wishful thinking, but suffering can degenerate into despair. He knew suffering as he was separated from his family in WWII and forced into labor. In some ways, he was haunted by that experience all of his life. Somehow, we think that a brilliant religious scholar should somehow be above such feelings, but the assumption is wrong, not the person. The key to the book is in the title, as he thought suffering could be bearable only if it existed within, were bounded by, hope. The book cites Biblical passages to amplify the theme, especially Paul in Romans. Paul sees suffering as an evil, and apocalyptic hope sees the death of evil on the horizon. At the same time, in the present, suffering is a part of our experience, and we pray that it can serve a redemptive purpose. He speaks of the integration of suffering and hope, but I think he may mean that they must be kept in a tensive relationship; otherwise they tend to fly apart. So often we search for one big answer to the question of suffering and evil. We look for Scripture to provide an axiom that flows through it consistently. That desire to make experience fit a geometric proof is understandable, but wrong-headed. As suffering and evil appear in many forms, as hope and good appear in many forms, we perhaps should expect a variegated approach in Scripture. Toward the end of the book, he dismisses all attempts at consolation as banal when we try to demonstrate that others suffer more than we (116). Emily Dickinson wrote: "hope is a thing with feathers." Yes, like a bird it can soar over the bad weather and see the blazing sun. It can fly over troubles and move into the future. Without meaning, hope is difficult to maintain. Meaningless suffering may become unbearable. When we cannot find meaning in it, we may well force meaning on to it, for we are determined to try to make sense of the senseless, to find pattern even amid the random events that befall us.

274)-Ezra 3-4-Our expectations cause us no end of trouble in bereavement. At a basic level we imagine an implicit contract with God. if I am good, I deserve to be immune from trouble. As Jesus said the rain falls on the just and unjust alike. One of the reasons holidays or anniversaries or birthdays are hard is that we carry a picture of bliss in our minds, and it has irrevocably changed. We wonder if it is even proper to celebrate a birthday or a holiday ever again. Is it crazy to want to mark the birthday of the deceased? I recently heard a woman in a program say that she dreaded the holidays because she knows that she will never live up to the cheer of Christmas commercials. My mind raced to all of the holiday programs that show the time of togetherness to be one of disasters and tension, like National Lampoon's Christmas Vacation, Home Alone, 4 Christmases. We may well dread the anniversary more than its actual appearance. Make some plans for an important date. Consider some ways to make it ceremony with it. At the same time, please don't avoid going to important events out of fear of how you will react. You are always able to excuse yourself early if need be. About a week after we buried my brother, my wife had her 10th high school reunion. I didn't want to go, but the thought of wasting a ticket was even more painful. I did not mingle with her much, but hid in the bar watching sports. If I did not go, I would not have seen her look over the large room and sniff, "I don't remember this many blonds." To a large degree that line alone made the painful trip almost worth it. We may well expect too much or too little of ourselves. We may be constantly comparing ourselves to how we thought we would react and lose sight of the reality of our position today, here and now. Maybe worse, we seek to place our expectations about grief on to other people. If they don't live up to our expectations, they are failing a test of our own devising. Parents may place this burden on children, and spouses may well expect each other to approach the loss in similar, or even identical, ways. Religiously, we may expect faith to be a magic weapon that can eliminate grief. Indeed some would measure faith by this criterion. We may absorb the expectations of others during this time as well. We can be vigilant about not rushing to get back to normal, to get over it, when friends and family and coworkers have decided that we should. After all, role expectations are shared expectations. Part of adult choice is not falling in line with the expectations of others without some reflection of propriety and a proper fit for our own gifts, interests, and abilities.

275)Ec. 12- Tragic expectation-We Americans seem to have a sense that we have a right to be happy, an expectation of it. Where do we get that notion? At times, it does come from the positive thinking-religion as motivational speaking wing of the church. We are quick to find a scapegoat to blame if we are not as happy as we think we should be. In some ways, it is an offshoot of Christian Science that denies the reality of illness as a reality. This newer blessing is all movement ascribes that illusory quality to all issues. Its great flaw then is that it opens the door to tragedy as being the fault of one's mental processes being weak in being a beacon for blessing. I don't wish to deny that a positive mental attitude can be helpful. I do think that it can be an ease to those around someone as much as to them. I do reject firmly that it should be seen as a panacea, and it should not be placed on a burdened soul as yet another expectation of how we can judge they are doing.

I would think that while happiness is an aspiration, to see it as one's due is to set us up for continual disappointment. Where do we even get the idea that we should be able to ride along the ridge of one mountaintop experience after another? Where do we get the notion that evil events are somehow personal affronts directed at us from some cosmic force? One of the great things the cosmic tour in Job 38-41 does for Job is a demonstration that the rules of the cosmos may apply to him, but they are neutral toward him, not for his benefit or struggle personally. Put differently, Job is introduced by the Creator to the tragic dimension in creation. That tragic dimension may go a long way in adjusting what we think is what we deserve, or owed, should expect in our life span.

276) Lk.20:27-40 some people worry that this passage would

mean that they will not recognize their loved ones, perhaps especially a spouse. This is a frightening prospect for anyone, but especially for those who have been widowed and married again. My sense is that Jesus is turning the question of opponents around a bit. He seems to be saying that in the resurrected life, we have immortality, so we have no concern with needing progeny. Marriage is a holy estate for those of us on earth. Jesus seems to suggest that a different order of relationship would be present in the new dimension. We may be a little lower than the angels to start, but it sounds as if we are closer to them in heaven by this example. I don't want to build a whole structure for heaven out of a clever response in another type scene where Jesus bests his opponents yet again. We should be careful when we want to over-generalize from single Scripture texts, especially in an area where scripture is reticent about providing us with a veritable blueprint, such as the afterlife. I do think Jesus is saying that the resurrected life is not to be equated with life here. It is uncertain if we interpret the passage in God's perspective, or in the full life of the Living One, where we are risen by the power of God. Perhaps we could read it as: in the presence of The Life Giver all are alive. I do not notice this lovely phrase, children of the resurrection, very often. That is linked directly to be children of God. Luke Timothy Johnson in his commentary on Luke (318) says that our imaginations are impoverished when faced with the new life in Christ. What artistic resources help us to fill our empty imaginations?

277) Mk. 12:40-One of the Presbyterian Confessions warns pastors about long prayers that get to the point of becoming "vexsome." My brother and I about burst at an anniversary party when a former Catholic had to demonstrate new found capacity for public prayer and went on and on with a grace before meals. Once my younger daughter attended a service where the minister typed out prayers, she informed me that I should do the same, not for memory or quality, but because his pastoral prayer was shorter than what she termed "that long prayer you do." When

we are at a low point our patience and tolerance wear thin as well. Sometimes these get directed against long prayers, religious bromides, or showy public piety. I was just with a family before the visiting started at the funeral homes, and one of the relatives loudly announced that someone was taking the death hard because "she didn't know Jesus." Perhaps the long train of citing some of the same passages for the grieving has left some of them exhausted, and the passages themselves need some fallow time to regain their freshness and immediacy. In our time, I think that the danger is less long prayers but the attempt to comfort that becomes either testifying about one's own faith experience and commitments or the sermons that pour out of people's mouth determined to impose their particular, even idiosyncratic views of the faith on the the grieving. The message unspoken, or even loud and clear goes like this: "if you believe exactly as I believe you will be spared much grief. If you don't you deserve your misery." Some prayers for the deceiving may not be too long, but they may well promise too much. Prayers feel like such weak offerings sometimes. They seem to pale before some physical act, some tangible help. On the other hand, I do not see prayers as substitutes for action, or a reflex response to feeling powerless and useless. I see prayer as providing the inner resources and power to continue to do the work that needs to be done with less threat of burnout. Please don't take this in terms of an attack on one's own prayer life, as this passage deals with communal worship and being cognizant of the sacred gift of the time of others. I notice in church that those who complain loudest about service length go on to great lengths when they present a prayer joy or concern themselves. In prayer, take all of the time you desire or need.

279) Mk. 9:29-Preparing for death was a spiritual practice during the Middle Ages with the "ars moriendi" In its way this devotional could be a preparing for grief. They ran imagined conversations between the patient and the figure of death about the anxiety of leaving this world. a short version even had woodcut pictures of the devil presenting various temptations and the response to these temptations. They instructed the family on behavior at the

bedside and supplied a group of prayers toward the end. Forewarned is forearmed. The pop singer Dan Fogelberg left his wife a set of recordings to be released after his death. He wanted to provide some more money, but I think he wanted to communicate his thoughts as well, as the end drew near. (The album cover reveals the boundary of life and death). I just spoke with a widow who had a conversation with her spouse about making a life after one of them would die. Since he had a serious illness, the odds were that he would die first, and he gave his blessing for her to live her life as fully as she could. Ingmar Bergmann famously showed a chess match with death, and Woody Allen satirized it by having a badminton match with death. I wonder if something like this devotional set could be a preparation for grief, to face more abstractly some of the expected issues in coping with loss and grief. I imagine a dialogue with Grief and with an angel going back and forth. Sometimes we send prayer up as a last resort or send to God as a plea for magic. In some manuscripts Jesus says prayer and fasting to his disciples' query about their inability to expel a demon. Perhaps we can read this as the necessity of praying to align ourselves and resources with God's intentions for healing. In other words, prayer cements a partnership between us and God and empowers us to be agents of God's healing touch. Prayer creates a "meeting of the minds" to accomplish that partnership. Years ago, we had last wills and testaments. Consider writing out some of your spiritual advice to your loved ones. In our ritually deficient time, one could consider some personal or social rituals.

280) Ps.130 "Out of the depths" certainly touches the experience of loss. We are rarely in lower depths than in the face of grief. Sometimes it seems so far down that we are not going to be able to climb out. As time passes, we try to wall off the deep because we are afraid that we still may fall in. Even out of the depths God hears us. No place is too far from God. "My soul waits" (v. 5-6) brings out an anxious sort of patience and perseverance in prayer. With the Lord is unfailing love. It is one constant is a sea of trouble. This prayer may start out of the depths, in the depth, but it also a vehicle to move out of those deep caverns and climb

into the light. Waiting can seem to be a deep a hole as depression at times. Some worry that if we pray from the depths, we are liable to stay in the depths and make matters worse. Part of climbing out or getting lifted from the depths is recognizing that is precisely our location at times. To deny it just wastes energy. As too most of the lament psalms, this one ends on a note of uplift, of confidence, of hope. It speaks of unfailing love. One of the things to keep alert in the depths is a sign, any sign that the wave that came crashing down on you is now starting its lifting patterns. Of course, the depths don't only mean to be down low with the blues. To go into the deep means diving down to the heart of things, to stop skimming the surface and really explore. We can go so far down that we get the bends coming back up unless we get some help and take our time surfacing. Some of the healing stories in the gospels touch on that terrible time of waiting. We've looked at John 5, but Lk.13:10-17 too involves a healing from the depths. She was crippled, bent over and unable to straighten up. In its way, it is a physical manifestation of a grief posture, with a woman who had suffered for 18 years. Indeed she is disabled by a "spirit of weakness." The story also points out the danger of "oughts." The religious opponents point out that Jesus may be violating the Sabbath command that we ought to work but six days a week. Jesus replies that should a child of Abraham suffer all these years, so she ought to be healed.

281) Ps. 71, (See also Is. 46:3-4 is one of the few psalms from the perspective of being older. We pile up too many losses by the time we grow old. From that long perspective, in both passages, we hear of being protected from youth to grey hair. Sometimes, the fragility of age breaks down some of our resilience. My mother quit reading the obituaries as she said that she saw too many people close to her in age. If someone important to her passed, she said she would hear abut it. How hard it can be to lose the partner of a lifetime. Kenneth Doka has edited a number of books for the Hospice Foundation of America. He draws together admirable sources to include the effect of accumulated griefs as we grow into old age, and we may start to lack the

resilience of youth. According to Erikson, we develop the virtues of care and wisdom as we age. The accumulating losses are part of the last great piece of the life cycle, integrity v. despair. Melancholy, tristitia, spiritual sadness, strike at our virtues. We are sorely tempted to give up and ask what's the use? Here the psalmist sees the signs of age, of grey hair, as a sign of the continuity of the care of God and our response to it. It realizes that we do not have as much power, so the psalmist pleads with God to stay close when "my strength is spent." Ps.42 asks "why are you in despair, o my soul?" Notice that the psalmist is in dialogue with the inmost self. Ps. 71 realizes that our life can be a portent to others, and youth's response may be "hope I die before I get old." It directly addresses the fear that while God may have been a constant companion, would that now change as grey hair appears and death draws near? I have heard too many of the elderly say things such as: "why was I not taken first," or I'm tired of living, why not me, or "I see no reason to go on living." Yes, these words come from people in nursing homes, but also assisted living centers, and people in their own homes. To the extent that we may become a bit more dependent as we become aged, the words to the graying in Isaiah are noteworthy. In the eyes of the Ancient of Days (Dan. 12) , we are carried from youth to grey hair. Just as the people of foreign lands had to carry the idols, God tells Israel that God carries, and god saves. God is not burdensome. No, God lifts our burdens off our shoulders, and that includes our heaviest burdens, the emotional ones that weigh us down, even grief.

282) Tears in a bottle (Ps. 56:8) . Tears do flow in grief. Tears do have a comforting release for hearts and spirits at the breaking point. They seem to me to be some sort of escape valve. Men do not have as much trouble with tears as they once did, but I do sense some stigma with them in a very short period of time for any gender, any age, for any loss. We are particularly uncomfortable at public tears. We say that someone is doing well when they are not crying. At some point, our patience with tears starts to wither, and sympathy may transmute into annoyance. I wonder if there are different types of tears in loss. We know that

the tears that form in emotion are of a different chemical nature than the ones that occur when a foreign body irritates the eye. Would we want to preserve some of them? Augustine wrote in the Confessions: "The tears streamed down...and I let them flow as freely as they would, making of them a pillow for my heart. On them it rested." Ps. 6:6-7 speaks of so many tears flowing that the bed is soaked....my eyes waste away because of grief." Extreme and volatile reactions are part of grief. In the book, the Shack, tears are softly brushed into a crystal bottle. "don't ever discount the wonder of your tears." In the last Harry Potter movie, Harry captures Snape's dying tear in a bottle. Snape's tear contains memories that open up a world of Harry's destiny, as well as a new, accurate understanding of the perilous journey of his life, especially on Snape's unrequited love for Harry's mother. Instead of being spilled or dried, what is precious about tears that we hear a desire for them to be kept? What do your tears measure?

283) Ec. 7:2-4 Recently, I heard the baby boomer rule at the funeral service, that it was to be a celebration of life. This one went further by having us feel guilty if we were sad because the deceased would not want us to be sad. (I heard Wayne Dyer say that he has already told his family he expects waterworks at his funeral). We deny the impact of death; we repress its proper feelings at our peril. I also find it controlling, as if we should be able to dictate to others their expression of feeling. Indeed, we have gotten to the point where the only proper expression of feeling is celebration. A service should give people permission to grieve. It should not be a place where this vital need is forbidden. Church is the one place where we may let down our guard, admit to ourselves that we are not independent and depend on God. In a seminar, famed Christian educator and Synod Executive Carol McDonald introduced to us to a bit of English research that indicated that one of the few places we independent people ever admit that we are dependent is in church. That pushes us to let down our guard and may be one of the primary reasons why tears flow in church when they have not been shed in quite some time anywhere else. Prayers of confession admit that we are not

perfect, always strong, always put together well. Still, as Casting Crowns sing "church can be a stained glass masquerade" of putting 'walls around our weakness and smiles to hide our pain." Where better than church to let our guard down and admit our dependence on God? I am not saying that laughter and celebration are excluded from a funeral. After all, in Presbyterian circles the service is of witness to the resurrection. Eulogy is part of the service, but it is not the only part. Ecclesiastes knows full well that we are tempted to find only good things to be our proper lot. In a way, he lives in an Ash Wednesday mood. We are mortal, and as much as we seek to deny or flee from that reality, we evade the gates of wisdom.

284) Titus 1: 13, Rev. 21:21 2:2 - "Have faith, or your faith is so strong." Sometimes I think we say this out of a reflex, or it is one of those clichés that shut down critical thinking, and we just mutely nod our heads in agreement. If in a less than charitable mood, I wonder if we say this as a polite way of saying that we don't want to witness the troubles of loss. I wonder if we mean that strong faith will not grieve openly, will not question the justice of a death, but can stand in acceptance of what some term God's will. Perhaps the best response is "I believe; help my unbelief." What sort of faith are we being urged to have? I fear that it is advertising more than is promised in the faith. I do dread that we may be promising that a certain level of faith will protect us from the ravages of loss. I fear that it is an invitation to a sort of magic surcease from pain. We can have faith and confidence that things will get better with time and effort. I fear that faith, no matter its strength, will have a hard time making sense of the senseless. Faith is less an anodyne but more a baseline for resilience, for the capacity to find a new equilibrium. Put differently, instead of emphasizing the amount or intensity of faith, we may do better to note that just a little bit of faith is plenty. I have heard too many people say things on the order of: "I guess my faith isn't as strong as I would have thought, or else I would not be taking this so hard." The Reformers insisted that faith is to be equated with a trusting relationship, less than a collection of dogma. We will always run into critical people who

wish to correct our mistakes across the board, even in grieving. So, they could well seek to use grief as an occasion to correct one's weak faith or to build you up so high that you are incapable of staying at that level. As I grow older, I have noticed that people trying to use funerals as a time to trumpet their religious beliefs and push them on others manages to press my buttons, even when I am prepared for it. It is difficult for me to use a time of extreme sadness as a wedge into spreading the gospel.

285) Ps. 69:1-3 describes the experience of grief, as the numbness starts to pass, and we grow tired of its pain. Look at v. 8: "I have become a stranger to my kindred"-even family does not what to say and they may signal their anxiety by absence. Move down to v. 11-"sackcloth as clothing." Nothing is comfortable, so one may as well wear clothing of repentance and discomfort, funeral clothes if you will, all of the time. Verse 14 moves to "sinking in the mire-don't let the deep swallow me up" (15). To me it is an accurate and evocative sense of being stuck in grief. The psalmist finds new words to name the turmoil, v. 17's distress and despair. We often feel no solid ground beneath us and the sense is of sinking into a pool of trouble. How can you pull yourself up by the bootstraps when you can't find the boots in the first place- how do you get your feet under you when you can't find a solid place to stand? The isolation sinks in at v. 20-"I looked for pity, there was none." Toward the end (33) comes the affirmation: "God hears the needy." Recently, I heard a gentleman whose family had suffered through four consecutive miscarriages speak of "stacking" of losses and everyone in the group picked up on that phrase. He meant some things are the straw that breaks the camel's back, after too much has already been stacked on top of it. We all have cumulative losses, and at some point, it seems too much. Death always has layers of loss. A new loss refreshes older ones. Multiply the losses and we are faced with a glacier of levels. Further, those levels get bent and folded like old rock formations. Instead of a layer cake, it resembles a large marble cake where all sort of issues get interspersed. The psalmist wants a responsive, active God, with a sense of being close and knowing the actions of God. This will lift

up someone brought low, needy, and lowly and in pain (33, 29). In a way, this psalm is a compendium of grief reactions folded in prayerful hands.

286 Tender Mercies is one of my favorite movies. The great Robert Duvall won an a Academy Award for his portrayal of a down and out country singer/songwriter. The love and acceptance of a widow allows him to start to recover, and they marry. When Mac and his adopted son have been baptized, the boy looks in the rear view mirror to see if he looks any different. Later, a terrible tragedy befalls Mac. He says that "he can't trust happiness"). When he sees his estranged daughter after years she remembers that he used to sing about a dove, and he says he doesn't recall. When she leaves he starts to sing, on the wings of a snow white dove/you send your precious love). The daughter later dies in an automobile accident. He wonders aloud about the tragedies that befall us in life. Why, he keeps barking. His new wife uses the phrase tender mercies when she speaks with Mac, her husband. Indeed, she is the vehicle of God's tender mercies, to offer Mac the chance of redemption. The psalms use the phrase tender mercies ten times. In each case tender has the sense of a soft new bud that a deer would love. The father of John the Baptist uses it in his great prayer when he can speak again when his son is born (Lk. 1:78).

Martin Seligman wrote a book on authentic happiness and a new book on well-being, called Flourishing. He launched a program to help soldiers deal with the terrible things they do and witness to help alleviate post traumatic stress disorders (ch 8). A good deal of his program could apply to preparing for grief as well. First, trauma "shatters beliefs about the self... and the future." Instead of holding it all in soldiers are taught to share the experience in a narrative form but pay attention to the event as causing both grief and gratitude of life at the same time. You are encouraged to identify the personal resources that helped you. Instead of living as a survivor of trauma, new sources of power are encouraged, such as becoming more giving, more caring, that are more robust than thought previously (162). Even trauma does not have to rule our future, for we can learn to flourish once again.

287) Rev. 21:21 The imaginative vision of Revelation gives us the base for the pearly gates. Heaven is portrayed in movies in imaginative ways that still reflect cultural hopes and dreams. After the Civil War, heaven was portrayed as a place of Victorian domesticity. In The Gates Ajar and subsequent books, heaven has gingersnaps and strawberries. Old Hollywood had fluffy clouds and harp music. What Dreams May Come offers an artistic wonder, with the color and splash of a child with finger paints. The Robin Williams character paints his own heaven. While in "my Father's house are many mansions" (or rooms/dwelling places), this has the sense that we decorate our own piece of heaven. The movie Stairway to Heaven (1946) has earth in color, but heaven is pictured in a gauzy black and white. (OK, how many of you thought of Led Zeppelin as soon as you saw Stairway?) Albert Brooks in Defending Your Life has the interesting premise that we can only grasp heaven if we can conquer our fear. (On the other hand, calories don't count in his version of heaven, similar to Woody Allen's notion that a good future will show the health benefits of cigarettes and bacon).We have a lot of artistic license as we get just glimmers from Scripture. This is a move as wise as the decision not to portray the resurrection itself in the Easter accounts. In Reversed Thunder (177) Eugene Peterson sees the emphasis in heaven on symmetry, fertility, and in a city, not a new Eden, no less) and light. In other words, it is the opposite of chaos, emptiness, and darkness. After we encounter so much heartache in this world, the promise of a better world offers a hope for recompense.

288) James Limburg titles Ps. 73, "when good things happen to bad people" (244). It is a cute flip on the famous book by Rabbi Kushner. Douglas John Hall criticized the book with its implicit claim that we are to be the judge of our relative goodness and the blessings we deserve. This psalm has a spiritual struggler

amazed to find blessings at all. Ps. 73 looks back in amazement at survival, especially spiritual survival. "When my soul was embittered/ when I was grieved in my heart." This is not spiritual soldier, the psalmist remind me of most of us who have our struggles with the faith, and throw up our hands and ask, what's the use? While bitterness can be an element in response to loss, it is an exceedingly dangerous one to nurture and keep alive. It has away of draining the life force from us, making us blind to the good, cynical to the point of drying up inside. Then, in v. 23, nevertheless, I am continually with you (meaning with God). Move to v.26- "my flesh and my heart may fail." Maybe that bitterness also goes a bit in helping us understand the many foolish and cruel things people say and do during hard times. My charitable side calls it a response to anxiety, but bitterness seems to love to try to spread and share its poison as much as possible.

Look back at your time in mourning. Were there days that seemed to hard to survive? What sort of things have you been able to do that you never thought you would be able to do? Are you too a bit surprised that you have survived? The motto of "one day at a time" certainly helps many to get through such difficult times as trying to look into the future seems impossible and a crushing burden. In the movie War Horse, Spielberg's great eye breaks our hearts in seeing horses, used to the pastoral work of plowing at most, are reduced to falling by the wayside due to the crushing burden of pulling the burdens of the war machine in WWI. Later, the stallion, Joey, the title horse, is caught in a field of barbed wire in the no-man's land of the trench warfare. Sometimes we recoil at what happens to human beings, so we are able to sympathize more easily with an animal. When have you felt caught like Joey?

289) Lam. 1:4, Ps. 38:6-11 -The movie 4 Weddings and a Funeral has a heartbreaking scene at the title funeral, where one of the bereaved recites a poem from Auden, "Funeral Blues." It sometimes goes by the first line-"stop all the clocks." Its last two stanzas go: He was my north, my south, my east and west/my working week and Sunday rest/my noon, my midnight, my talk,

my song/I thought love would last forever/I was wrong/ The stars are not wanted now, put out every one/pack up the moon and dismantle the sun/pour away the ocean and sweep up the wood/for nothing now can ever come to good." In a much less elegant way, the Rolling Stones sang, I see a red door and I want it painted black/no colors anywhere, I want them to turn black." At the epilogue of the movie, we see that same heartbroken person finding love again, as life moves on for the rest of their gang. Do not be afraid to be yourself with God. Do not be afraid to be open, candid, and truthful with God about what is going on in the entire self, one's entire life. As I was reviewing the passages, the stark difference between what was and what appears in the present is galling. Loss has a way of making the past seem even more glittering and the future look more foreboding. The two readings citied both see prayer as a deep form of communication. Our trust in God can certainly to handle words that reflect spiritual crisis. Sometimes, I fear that the contemporary praise service provides a vitalizing aspect of worship, but they tend to give short shrift to the troubles we all face that should be included in our communication with God as well. Look for some metaphors, some images that capture your feelings. With these passages, you may feel the need to go beyond one's personal words and enlist the world around to share your condition. A structure of a lament may make it possible to place your thoughts and feelings into a container.

290) Thanksgiving psalms (50:14, 95:2, 100:4, 147:7, for instance) and thoughts are not an obvious place to go during grief. Sometimes we may encounter God in the last place we would think to go or to look. At some point, they are precisely where one should go. They can give us a frame for being grateful to God for the life we have known and loved. We get at it a bit in eulogies. As usual, the psalms give us a framework to be able to organize prayers of thanksgiving. Maybe this is especially important when we want to go silent in even considering prayers of gratitude and thanksgiving for the life we have shared. A good way to go at it is to think about what we most miss about them. Tell some stories about how they enriched your life. In a

documentary about the late singer and songwriter Harry Nilsson, all of the witnesses look so sad when they recall his self-destructive decline, but all of them brighten up when they start telling Harry stories, usually ones about him getting them into trouble, often for days at a time. Stories fill in the portrait of a life. Stories allow us to inhabit a section of a life. Stories allow us to share in a moment beyond mere data. When the stories are shared, we get a more varied picture of someone. Over the years, I realized that thanksgiving prayer did not come to me as easily and fully as say, supplication, as I seem to have lots and lots of wants and needs. Following the advice of Eugene Peterson, I used the psalms as a prayer book to teach me how to pray in thanksgiving. I suggest that we utter a prayer of thanks for stories. We can attach a prayer of thanks for every story we hear about our love done. Thanksgiving psalms often highlight certain aspects of God's character, especially God's steadfast love. They often close with an act of worship. They are often prayers in the first person singular, I, prayers. It is easy to fall into the trap of abstraction or too great a generalization in prayers of thanksgiving. I am not sure how helpful it may be to speak about being thankful for just everything, and it may be start to lessen a sense of gratitude. I would encourage some real care with specificity. Use your sense to recreate some specific moments, act, or qualities for which to be grateful. Consider taking a story and using it as a story of lament but also a story of thanksgiving. What happens in that distinction? Do some things get deleted, lessened, or emphasized?

291) John 20-19-31The folks in my mother's assisted living center found out that I was a minister. They had a meeting and then asked me, well surrounded me and coerced me, to do a series on some questions about the afterlife, from the Bible of course, they were quick to add.. Almost all of them revolved around the issue of recognizing our loved ones in heaven. Part of it came from their fears about starting to forget their loved ones a bit, such as not being able to conjure up their face on a moment's notice. Part of it also stemmed from their fear that they would be forgotten by their loved ones. Like most of us, they

found themselves reflected in the desire of Thomas for proof. They wanted the Bible to be much more explicit about the content of heaven. Almost all of them could recite accounts of near death experiences, as they sought tangible proof for heaven. We may imagine it less for what it could be than what it would not be: that is, it would be a relief of the tribulations of this life. Johnny Cash, with the Carter family, deals with their concerns in "Meet Me in Heaven." They will know each other. After all, Jesus is recognized by the disciples. Now we are alerted to a significant difference, as Jesus can appear without bothering opening locked doors. Now a striking thing occurs. For the second time, Jesus identifies himself to the disciples, or maybe presenting credential would be a way of speaking of this visit from the other side, by showing them his wounds. I usually think of them as scars, but they are wounds are they not? We speak too loosely about doubting Thomas. After all, the word is closer to disbelieving, not doubt. Like most of us, he wants some tangible proof. Maybe he desires the same experience the other disciples had, and he feels a bit cheated. After all, they got to see Jesus, but Thomas is operating on their report alone. That means, we are all in the same position as he is over the years. Jesus gives him just the proof he requires. Thomas has boldly stated that he wants to place his own hands in the wounds of the crucified Jesus. Notice that Jesus does not push Thomas on his questions but says don't be disbelieving, but believing (my translation). Notice that Jesus is able to show him scars. He invites Thomas to do just what he had declared he needed to establish some empirical proof of the reports he heard. Thomas then does not take Jesus up on the offer. The life of Jesus has not disappeared, but it continues in this new, beyond physical body, but body it is nonetheless. God is gentle on us for our Thomas moments of desiring some Missouri-style show me proof.

292) Is. 40:27-31 evokes soaring confidence. Few sections match this as an affirmation of receiving needed strength and power. Aging seems to mean a lessening of energy, so it is wonderful not only to be compared to a youth but to exceed a youth in endurance. Yet, this soaring affirmation gains it strength as a

response to the despair of being ignored by God. For most of us, turmoil and anxiety drain our energy. Grief leaves us exhausted. We wonder if we will have the power to go another step, to make it through another hour, let alone another day, as time yawns out before us as a dreaded weight. For mere mortals, it is to tax our limited resources to trying to figure out the way of the world, and the ways of the creator God. Here God renews strength. To mount up on wings like eagle is to soar above the mundane, to glide on the breeze with little seeming effort. Perhaps, it has us fly over our futile desire to try to figure out the huge questions in life, an in death. To run the race and not be weary, to walk the long pilgrimage road of life is a psychic as well as physical aspiration. God does not grow faint or weary. God transmits power to the powerless and faint. Those whose lives have already taken flight don't need that infusion of energy. Since I've seen the great Lord of the Rings trilogy, I think of the eagles or other birds saving the day in moments of peril for the Fellowship of the Ring. The road in grief is long. To be able to walk it without fainting, without growing weary, is a miracle, not a minor one either. Some interim pastors speak of taking in the view from the balcony. They mean that we do well to take in a view synoptically, to see the forest for the trees, from a vantage point that allows us to see things as a whole. In a sermon after his daughter had another bout with leukemia on this passage, "Strength Not To Faint," John Claypool could report no ecstatic view from the clouds, no ability to run in the cramped hospital room, bu the did have the power to walk and not faint, to do what little he could for his ill daughter through the night. To walk and not faint may be the most we can expect of ourselves on tough days. When we are stronger, we can find the energy to keep going, to keep pushing.

293) Ps. 84:7 "they go from strength to strength in the presence of God." In grief we discover strengths that we did not know we possess. In adversity we may discover previously unknown, hidden strengths. The Wall Street Journal (10/19/10) carried a

piece that facing everyday adversity increases our coping skills and making us tougher. The same article goes on to cite a study that deep adversity can overtax our coping skills and take a toll on our overall mental health. In other words, facing smaller troubles can toughen us out of being Pollyanna, but radical suffering, suffering at the root of our lives, can uproot even the strongest of us. We come to realize that we were stronger than we gave ourselves credit for, stronger than others could imagine. We do not have to rely on our own resources alone, especially when we feel that our resources are tapped out, that it is all too much for us. Through the Spirit we tap into the healing energies of God to help us through. Imagine your prayer as tapping into a current that surges through you to give you energy or some virtue you need at the present moment. What sort of strength do you require at this point? Images in this psalm may be of some help here. God is portrayed as powerful, but is still a personal strength, as a shield. In v. 3, I hear an echo of "His Eye Is on the Sparrow." If the sparrow can find a nesting place in the temple, the place of the Holy Presence, surely we too can nest there as well. (I wonder if this is an image drawn after the temple was ruined or in its lesser reconstruction. The birds there may have been a sign for dejection but are made glorious in the presence of God) Donald Capps talks about the resourceful self. He draws on Erikson's schedule of crises and attendant virtues through the life cycle. We have within us a vast pool of power. Lately, I have been taken with making a distinction with rigid or flexible, supple strength. A bulwark is impressive, but it can get breached. In our emotional life, I fear that a bulwark may be a rigid defense, but it is as vulnerable as a glass figurine, as easily cracked as eggshell. I think that bridges need to be flexible or they will snap. No, in emotional life, the supple, elastic strength seems to be what is required.

294) 2 Cor. 4:3-6 would have slipped past me, had not it been of the selections for Transfiguration Sunday, the Sunday before Lent. It speaks of a veil. When I was a boy, women would wear black veils to a funeral. They obscure our look into the eyes of the mourning. When Moses returned from Sinai, his close contact

with God had his face shine, so he wore a veil to allow himself to be more approachable, I suppose. Earlier in 3:18 Paul talks about being changed in Christ's likeness. Paul is looking toward and for transformation. Christ is present as the very presence of God. In the popular X-men series, transformation isn't chosen; it appears. The transformation brings powers, but they have to learn to marshal those forces and learn to channel them. They learn to adjust to the transformation within and learn to negotiate the changes brought to bear socially. Obviously, it is a metaphor for all sorts of human experience. I suggest that transformation or transfiguration is a matter of perception: how we view others as a result of an experience and how we are viewed by others. Even here, we do well to be prudent. I know someone who was able to look at others through the transfigured eyes of compassion, but she tended to project her experience on to others, whether their situation fit her circumstance or not. Still, it is a gift to be able to view someone with the eyes of compassion. As we move through grief, it is a gift to see the new person we are becoming, even while maintaining our basic personality structure and identity. Paul may say that we walk through life as if we are veiled to ourselves and to the realities of the world. We all wear a veil and are unable to see as clearly as we would like. Those we encounter are veiled to our sight as well, not physically but inwardly. While God is able to see deeply into our intentions, the vision is much cloudier for us.

295) -When our eldest daughter was little, she played the violin, and it was difficult. One day someone showed her how to play "Heart and Soul" on a piano keyboard, and she had a delighted new sense of confidence and basically taught herself to play some piano. The psalmist belongs heart and soul to God, but the experience has gone off track. Ps. 63 is a good look at the desperate longing we have for the presence of God in comfort when we struggle. We want a sense of divine care and concern. Instead of seeming absent or distant, we want a palpable sense of God being close. I so admire those who seem to have almost a casual sense of God as a companion. I often say that I have more static on the line when attempting conversations with God. Our

souls, our inmost being does thirst for God as if we are parched in a "dry and thirsty or weary land." When it says, "My soul clings to you," I think of a child's tight grip on a parent's hand, or a couple locked in a loving embrace. In the "shadow of your wings" is a wonderful maternal image of protections. It is a commonplace among Christian mystics to work with the notion that a sense of absence is part of the spiritual experience. John of the Cross, a major figure for John Paul II, spoke of the "dark night of the soul." The journey metaphor is such a powerful one, since journeys are part of any hero's tale of growth.. They encounter difficulties and surprises. We are having a Lenten series at lunchtime in our community. This year, pastors were asked to use a Lenten hymn as a sermon text. I thought of Beneath the Cross and its words have resonance with this ancient hymn. How we hope with Elizabeth Douglas Clephane for "a shadow of a mighty rock within a weary land/a home within the wilderness, a rest upon the way." Speaking to reconciliation, Isaiah has words that admit of being abandoned "for a brief moment". I hid my face from you," but with everlasting love I will have compassion on you." Does that final line have resonance for you?

296) Hopes of the dying in Christian Century 2/23/10-see I Kings 2, but Jn. 14-17-Sometimes we try to walk in the shoes of the dying and try to relieve their thoughts and feelings. We lose family history in their loss. To add to family lore, consider making tapes of memories, not only at the last of course. If we have a chance, it may be a good idea to ask them about how they would wish to be remembered, what is important to them, what were turning point moments in their lives, what qualities, stories, events help to encapsulate a life. Going through pictures so we can note who is on them is a smart case for aids to memory, We all have some family pictures and have no idea who are in them. Can we move this into a frame of "hopes for the grieving?" Hospice would see basic dignity, the offer of comfort and respect for one's wishes as paramount. It seems that many folks want to not pass away with all of the machines, technical hardware, and constant monitoring that is a part of hospital stays. If we are unreconciled to some people, we may hope that a beautiful,

tearful scene of reunion may come, but that is not always the case is it? I hate to think that people will carry even more regrets if we are unable to help realize the fond hopes of the dying. Tim Madigan writes of his estrangement from his beloved brother Steve, even when Steve was diagnosed with inoperable lung cancer. For a year they were stiff and formal with each other, but in a year, Tim drove 17 hours to see his brother and the ice thawed. Steve, a tough guy, had his eyes mist over when Tim told him that his friend Fred Rogers, prayed for him and his family by name every morning. (Rogers awoke at 6AM to pray for scores of people, by name, daily) "Mister Rogers prays for me" (I'm Proud of You: 109). Jane Kenyon ended her poem Let Evening Come with: "let it come, as it will, and don't be afraid. God does not leave us comfortless. So, let evening come."

297) Mk. 1-Look at how Mark's gospel starts with healing after healing as Jesus travels. The good news is enacted in all of these healings. Different needs present themselves, and Jesus responds to them. As they are described, we encounter one of Mark's favorite words, immediately. No patience seems to be required once Jesus goes into action. The healing power of Jesus Christ persists in the face of grief. Unfortunately, it does not always grant relief immediately often. People do survive. They do love again. They seem "themselves" again. The pulses of pain seem less frequent and less deep in the valleys. In time, it seems we take two or three steps forward and but one step back. It does get better. Maybe not every day is on the constant ascent, but the tend line certainly is moving upward. In the Presbyterian Church, the key theme of our Confession of 1967 is reconciliation. The wounds are not incurable. Look around. People may be affected by loss deeply, but they do live. They do more than survive. They flourish. They may well be transformed in the experience, but they do more than not give up on life. They live. At this point, can you identify some places in your life where you have been healed? I don't mean a lessening of symptoms; I don't mean coping better. I mean has the issue itself disappeared? Has the cause itself of pain been not limited but eliminated? Even if you haven't, have you noticed some signs that your becoming

reconciled to the loss?

298) Four sections of Isaiah are called servant songs (42, 49, 50, and 52). They are images of a suffering servant. This figure is the reverse of the powerful political Messiah that it seems at least some expected at the time of Jesus. It seems to be a fluid image of both a representative person and a suffering group, maybe the whole nation of Israel. When Israel was entering the Promised Land, correlation with a powerful deity makes good sense. The servant represents a major religious move, as it affirms the working of god in the midst of hard times for Judah, especially the destruction of the temple. The figure of the servant is alternated with the figure of Dame Zion. I'm not sure how to read them together, but I do have a sense we are making a mistake when we so analyze the servant passages and virtually ignore the Lady Zion passages. When Israel was on the losing end, its basic notions of God and power were challenged, even threatened. Many Christians use the suffering servant image and apply it to Jesus Christ, especially as the last of the servant hymns in Is. 52 seems to fit the story of the Passion of Christ. Mel Gibson used it to open his movie on the passion. What if that representative function of Christ goes beyond atoning for the sins of this broken world? What if somehow the wounds of Christ also help the wounds of a broken heart? He has borne our griefs takes on a different sense. Maybe not only our sins were cancelled out at the cross. Maybe Jesus carried our grief over death into his own death. No only the cross's weight bore down on his long walk, but guilt and grief as well. Even if the cross has a forensic function of dealing with sin, punishment, and guilt, it may well have a therapeutic function as well. At the very least, we do not carry our griefs alone. No matter how much they weigh us down, the suffering servant has borne them with us and for us. As Christians have appropriated this material to Jesus, we are pushed to look at the Holy One's participation in our suffering. As Moltmann said in The Crucified God" that "God is not more glorious than in this self-surrender (of the cross). God is not more powerful than in this helplessness. God is not more divine than in this humanity" (205)." At the cross, we see love at its weakest

and strongest point. The cross is like a stake pushed into the notion that power is the ultimate force. Power does not coerce love. Love can topple power. The selflessness that love can engender can defeat the selfishness of power, control, and coercion.

299)2 Tim. 3:5 Denial is invisible but its power is potent. Denial shows its face in all sorts of ways. (As they say in AA denial (da Nile) is not just a river in Egypt). Freud warned of the danger of rejecting something or someone we have lost. By saying things like, "I'm better off without it, or it was no good anyway, we are really in the territory of denial of the reality of the pain of the loss. (See Capps, The Poet's Gift) At a holiday gathering, if we decide that everything has to try to be exactly the same, as if nothing's happened, it too is a face of denial. Not mentioning the loved one's name, not telling any stories abut them is an attempt to wall of memory and pain. Theodore Roosevelt walled off discussion about his wife when he was widowed, even to their daughter, even when he went off to the West to try his hand as a rancher and to try to flee from his pain. Denial does make it easier, at least for a while, but reality has a way of intruding on our most cherished illusions. Working through the temptation of denial results in a stronger person in facing grief and in rebuilding the rest of one's life. I am convinced that the demand that funerals be celebrations are part of trying to wall off the pain of grief, so we act as if a funeral is more like honoring someone at their retirement than burying them in the ground. A generation ago, Ernest Becker wrote The Denial of Death. Bravely, he indicts our culture as erecting a solid wall of repressions and denials that effectively blind us to the sufferings of others and prevent us from recognizing our own fear of death. For all of our vaunted courage and confidence, we rarely muster the courage to face death in the eye. In perhaps the best of the Star Trek movies, the Wrath of Khan, Captain Kirk realizes that he has always tried to cheat death, not looking it in the eye. O'Connor notes in Lamentations and the Tears of the World that consumerism, addictions, violence may be, in part, responses to the rampant denial in our culture. The series of poems wonder if God is blind to their sufferings. Repeatedly, God is told to look at them, to see their distress. If God's eyes were open, would God then not respond to alleviate their pain? Facing loss takes courage. We may spend a lifetime building up defenses that prevent an easy look into ourselves and our relationships. It is no easy task to face a relationship and begin to admit its imperfections, and the problems within the one lost to death and the one lost in grief. The virtues of courage and endurance allow us to face candidly the panoply of issues set before us.

300) I Chr. 17-18 - After a while, the need to idealize starts to lessen. It may be well to start to admit that they were not perfection incarnate. What were some annoying habits of your loved one? What were some of their weaknesses as well as strengths? Did they know how to push your buttons? What did they do, or not do, that drove you nuts? What do you not miss about them or what they did in your experiences? Not everything is harder is it? Are not some things easier? Certainly the relief that they are not suffering is palpable, no? Have you been able to make some positive changes in your living area, in your diet, in activities? I'm often struck by how bold Israel was in its collective memory and national narrative. No sugar-coated Parson Weems fables about the morality of young George Washington, with the possible exception of Chronicles and David. No, they were willing to present the patriarchs or their greatest king, David, warts and all. It is a powerfully human founding narrative, these great figures that were recognizable to us mere mortals. When we arrive at the point at admitting some of the imperfections of the deceased, we are moving toward some health. It is no sign of disrespect for someone to be a fuller person in memory. You can be more balanced in your view in time. Know that they loved you as they could. Know that they were proud of you, and they wanted to brag on you. it takes immense amounts of energy and courage to face reality head-on. I'm not sure that we can even manage it in more than very small doses. To make it more manageable, we break it down into bite-sized pieces. We hold them together with stories, with narrative. to survive all of the emotional surges, those stories may not be,

perhaps cannot be accurate. Instead, character, events, shadings are introduced to make them easier to handle. When did they embarrass you? When were you proud of them? I wonder if one of the great honors we pay to the deceased is to be able to view them in full. Yes, we would immediately get some significant push back from those who would say that we should never speak ill of the dead, but try to preserve only their noble features. Still, it seems that then they are being made in sculpted saints and not the person we knew and loved in this life.

301) Ps. 35- So often, people hear the constant call from American culture: move on, get over it, start living again. People sometimes look to replace their loss in an attempt to avoid some of the pain of loss. Human life is irreplaceable. Sometimes, we try to replace the role instead of a real personal relationship. The sheer intensity in which we throw ourselves into a new relationship can be most attractive in some situations. The danger is that we are using someone as an extension of the person we have lost, not for themselves. Sometimes we try to replace elements of a relationship, say with time at work or a new project. In its way, it is an extension of trying to stay in denial of the pain of death. Leaping into a new romantic relationship with the intent of marriage is probably ill-advised. This is especially crucial when an attempt is being made to dull the pain of grief with the thrill of a new romantic relationship. Another issue is that some folks seek to replace the roles occupied by the deceased, and they are not really looking at the new person. So, it's doubtful they are being fair to them. So deep is our desire for stasis that we will look to qualities of the deceased and seek them out in the remaining members of a family. Elizabeth and John Edwards made a decision to "bring some life into this house" after their teenage son was killed in a car accident. They made the risky decision to pursue a pregnancy well into middle age for her. I do respect the motivation. A widow told me how she threw herself into a relationship after her spouse's death because" being in love was a whole lot more fun and easier than facing the loss of my first husband." Hear these words from Wendell Berry's Hannah Coulter: "there are people lying awake grieving, and

every morning there are people waking up to absences that will never be filled. But we shut our mouths and go ahead. How we are is "Fine."

302) Joel 2: 12-17- I was raised as a Roman Catholic, the last of the Latin Mass altar boys. After the turbulent sixties, I rejected that tradition as a teen, as a mode of rebellion, more than anything else, so it is definitely not some perverse form of pride about it, no great rational breakthrough or critique.. After a while, i ended up with the Presbyterians, whom I found 'least objectionable." Over time, I did grow to reject a background sound in my birth faith, around mortification. It struck me that some elements of it, the saints who flogged themselves, went over the edge. It seemed to me that the notion was capable of great and grave misunderstanding that did not square with the central dogma of Genesis. 1:27 that we are made in the image and likeness of God. Even though mortification is easily abused, it does have some merit. It can and does for many stifle some of the egotism and arrogance that lives within us. Certainly, some vices need to be mortified within us. Nicholas Wolstersdorff quotes a section of Henri Nouwen's Letter of Consolation (p. 95 in his lament). "Our lives can indeed by seen as a process of becoming familiar with death...I do not mean this in a morbid way. On the contrary, when we see life constantly relativized by death, we can enjoy it for what it is: a free gift....All of these times have passed us like friendly visitors, leaving us with dear memories, but also with the sad recognition of the shortness of life. In every arrival there is a leavetaking...All living is dying and all celebration is mortification too." Recently, I saw a Simone Weil quote about treasuring both joy and suffering in one's spiritual life. I admire its balance but have a hard time accepting it.

303) Neh. 8-Translation is so difficult, as it is so taxing to try to recreate the sense of a word from one language to another. We rightly use a word to cover other words in the bible, but it may be well to do a little background work and see if the same word has

different uses and nuance in original tongues. The translators of the King James Version of the Bible, now over 400 years old knew well its rigors and hoped that their work would allow

"Translation it is that openeth the window, to let in the light; that breaketh the shell, that we may eat the kernel; that putteth aside the curtain, that we may look into the most Holy place; that removeth the cover of the well, that we may come by the water."   Comfort, comforted, comforting have a number of words in both Biblical languages. In the Old Testament, one word comes from a root meaning to sigh. Perhaps that means that comfort can elicit a sigh of relief or contentment. Blest Be the Tie sings of "our comforts and our cares." Maybe the sense of being comforted is similar to the sigh of slipping into a bath at the right temperature after a long, hot day, or slipping under a comforter, interesting name, on a cold winter's night. It provides warmth. Comfort may well give a sense of warmth after struggling with the cold chill of death. In its way, all forms of human communication require some translation. Language approximates, but rarely can express exactly what one is trying to say or express. When we get anxious, it often makes matters worse, so we stammer, or know the words are not coming out right, and then we get more nervous and more tongue-tied, even when we try to pray. Where have you sought comfort and found none? Where have you found comfort?

304) Rom5:3-4, Heb. 6:12, II Pet. 1:6, II Tim. 3:10- We get impatient with ourselves when intense grief bubbles up. we may say that" I thought I was doing so well." Friends and family find their patience growing thin when we feel the need to go over details yet again. God, however, is infinitely patient with us. He starts with some scenes from the Peter DeVries novel the Blood of the Lamb, a searing look at parental loss and religious crisis. Its lead character, Wanderhope, bereft and furious, throws a cake at a crucifix and throws a cross into the woods. He seeks consolation and finds none. Eventually, he starts to see that his desire for consolation gets transmuted into compassion for others, all of us who sit together on at the long mourner's bench we all share as survivors. Lauber (article on patience of Christ in

Theology Today) moves from there to a consideration of the "redeeming patience" of Jesus Christ. Following von Balthasar, Lauber asserts of a God of "absolute love, not absolute power." God's power is of love and acts always through the prism of live. For Jesus, that divine patience is shown in a willingness to be utterly available to the call to live, the call of life, to be wiling to absorb what we hurl at God. In a way, the cross disarms evil by exhausting its assaults. How ever you want to describe hell, utter separation from God, death, spiritlessness, the ten thousand hells of everyday life and those yawning caves of crisis, God is with us,; God stays with us; Jesus Christ remains a faithful companion. We may grow weary, but the Patient One does not. Easter does not erase that. He recalls the scene in Stegner's novel, Crossing to Safety, where the travelers see a painting of the resurrected Christ. Instead of a face of triumph, it is a picture of a man risen but whose recent life was torture and death, so he carries on his face "terrible eyes." Those terrible eyes look with complete identification with what we go through. perhaps, the silence is not distance, far deeper than uncaring or ignoring us, but is the only proper response in being present in situations where there are no words.

305) Jos. 1:13, II chr. 6:32, Is. 44:21, 3 John 10-"Re-membering" lives of others plays off of the difficult word, dismember. Its sense is stitching our present together with our memories, of pulling the shards and tatters of the past into a coherent fabric for our new situation. Some of the more recent work in grief uses the metaphor that we do not, cannot, and should not "cut off" a life from ours. Indeed trying to cut someone out of our memory, out of our life, also cuts us off from the very crucible of our lives. The task then is how to weave the import of that life into our own, even though they are no longer with us. Sometimes this method flirts with not coming to grips with the full reality of loss, but that may be a reflection of training and personal reflection, and I must be careful not to generalize unnecessarily. I do find some wisdom in not always emphasizing the loss but emphasizing the relationship. After all, that is not a private possession, but an attachment that is not cut off by

death. Families maintain that attachment by telling and keeping stories about a loved one. Some take a favorite story and place it in an Easter basket or in individual stocking at Christmas. Some creative people name a drink, a dish, an art work after a loved one. In the one of the churches I served, we had some talented quilters, and our church is opening some space for a group of folks to set up their tables. I have been moved at the sight of the AIDS quilt that has toured the country, and I have seen talented quilters piece together fragments of a life together into the presentation of a quilt. Francisco Goldman wonders aloud if forgetting is sometimes better than memory. "Sometimes it's like juggling a hundred thousand crystal balls in the air at once, trying to keep all these memories going. Every time one falls to the floor and shatters into dust, another crevice cracks open inside me, through which another chunk of who we were disappears forever" (from Say Her Name). We grow tired of the tide of memory that brings someone back for a moment and then ceaselessly sends them out again.

306) Lk. 18:1-8-Persistent prayer- I am not saying this is easy. Especially in our instant society, we want a solution to our problem more than an answer to our prayer. Repetition builds habit. Repetition creates an island of stability in a chaotic world.

Persistent prayer is a key spiritual practice at any time, but especially in times of grief. It keeps us in constant contact with the God who is with us at all times, including deep adversity. Just as the widow in the story pleads and pleads with the corrupt judge to obtain a hearing, we keep banging on the gates of heaven for our case to be heard. It has been said that knowing persistence in prayer is to have calloused hands from beating on heaven's door. If the corrupt judge would eventually listen, how much more so the God who wants good for us? Pray, pray hard, every day. It does not need to be the same prayer, or the same type of prayer. On the other hand, you may find comfort in a prepared prayer, a familiar one as an anchor. After all, it is your prayer. In my view, every tear shed is a prayer. Every choked word at the gravesite is a prayer. So, the very persistence of grief can be seen as a persistent prayer in itself, a communication with

God about the state of our heart, mind, and spirit. Sometimes when I am asked to preach at a nursing home, I like to say that the contemporary nursing home may be the current analogue to the monastery. It can be a place of intense prayer. For so many people in nursing homes, time feels like a burden. Even as life is ebbing a way, the seeming surplus of time weighs on the residents. I tell them that some of the wonderful changes that I have seen in my life may well be due to the persistent prayers of people such as themselves blasting down the gates of heaven.

307) Jonah 3:9. Num.14, Hos. 11- Process pts-I find the vocabulary of process theology impenetrable, but I do like where it ends up often. I appreciate its emphasis on a responsive God. In its conception divine force attracts all creation toward good. God works through other agencies but still respects and work through other actions and actors. Nothing lost that is worth saving. In process thought, imagine the love of God as a magnet that draws everything toward God. In their view, God is not a God of power over everything. Instead, God empowers. God frees. God works with the creation that infinite space allows. God's power, then, affects the world, but the world touches the heart of God as well. God is always at work drawing the good out of situations. God's will is difficult to see clearly as it is mediated not by discrete acts like a thunderbolt, but through the complex interplay of the multitude of experiences in our world.   The God of love rarely commands, but instructs. God's primary attributes are: love, compassion, sympathy. This is very much a relational God, not a despot riding herd over puppets. Andrew Park speaks of God having a wounded heart. That wounded heart of love may well act like a magnetic field to draw us into the vision God has for drawing the best out of us and our situation. We are brought into the memory of God, the life of God, in this life, and the next. Pope Benedict spoke at his friend Manuela Camagni's service:" we...preserve a shadow of the people we have loved. the memory of God...it is the origin of life; here the dead are alive, in his life and with his life they have entered the memory of God which is life." No way of trying to reach the Ineffable One can ever be full and complete. In his wonderful book <u>What shall We Say,</u> the

noted preaching professor Thomas Long sees its view as too weak for his tastes, not enough to summon up the awe due the Divine One. Yes, might is a divine attribute, but so is compassion. God's love does not change, even as we do.

308) In the Reformed tradition, we speak of Jesus as priest, prophet, and king. Priests intercede to God for the needs of the people. Jesus intercedes for us (Heb.7:25). There Jesus is a perfect priest as representative, as Jesus does indeed represent us fully, but Jesus is no mortal priest going through the prescribed cycles of Temple work. Jesus lives in the presence of the heavenly temple forever. Indeed Hebrews sees Jesus as the embodiment and the culmination of the sacrificial system that was designed to join heaven and earth, human and divine realities. We sometimes worry that our prayers are ill-formed or poorly worded. Sometimes we cannot bring ourselves to pray. Here we see a wonder. Jesus himself intercedes for us; the priestly role of Jesus continues into our day. It could be an interesting spiritual exercise to try to write out a prayer as if Jesus were speaking it for you. After the ascension, Jesus has not given up on us. Jesus has not forgotten us. Jesus is not idly passive while waiting for the consummation of God's vision for the world. In Gen. 28, Jacob has a dream of angels, messengers, going up and down a ramp, or a ladder, in some translations. I love the image because it is a two-way flow of real communication. The prayers do reach the abode of God; they do not get lost in transmission. Even if the sentiment seems shopworn, I find it deeply moving to be told that "you are in my prayers." I love the old phrase, "I'll keep you in my prayers." Prayer combines speaking and listening on both ends of the channel. Even in our grief, God communicates with us in various ways. How has your prayer life changed during grief?

309) Sighs too deep for words (Rom.8:26) As Paul knows, we do not pray as we ought. At times, we are so confused or overwrought that we cannot stammer out a prayer. The same

Spirit who enables us to call god, Father/Poppa (abba) can give shape and content to our prayers. Even the very Spirit of the living God does not put everything into words. Those sighs may be the only expression available. Maybe they play for time until the words come. Maybe they create the space for the inspiration to enter the Spirit. That same Spirit intercedes for us. Within God's own being are special prayers being formed. The depth of those prayers cannot be put into words. We don't know what to say to the grieving. Part of that is anxiety. Part of it is the realization that words cannot express what we want to say. Yet, words are what we have. We may disregard the words or discard them, treasure them and cherish them. We are haunted that others do not apprehend our loss, nor can we adequately express it. So the idea that it is met with the sighs of the Spirit somehow comforts me. It is a signal to me of the caring character of God. It is also a sign that we should be gentle on ourselves for being able to come up with the perfect set of words of consolation. Even the perfect set of words may fall on deaf ears. I am consoled knowing that even heaven is rendered inarticulate in our plight at times. At creation, Gen. 1 has the Spirit hovering over the face of the waters. God creates with phrases, but here that voice is stilled. Words are healing, but they cannot heal everything. Time is required as well. Kierkegaard spoke of "the road we all have to take-over the bridge of sighs into eternity." A bridge in Venice had prisoners cross with it and Cambridge has a bridge of sighs, maybe about romance or the jitters of students having examinations. Words form bridges. They may seem shaky or incomplete, but they can still create ways of living and coming to grips with what we all face.

310) Ec. 9:4:9-12- It is a good idea for some of us to be able to have a companion in grief. It could be a spouse, a friend, a pastor, or a therapist. For others, a grief group is a necessity for them. Grief isolates, so it is wise to have some community connection. Sharing a burden helps us to feel that we do not carry it all by ourselves. Small pleasures add to the texture of life. (See new Alter translation). In The Poet's Gift Donald Capps speaks of "inviting the other-when ready-to accept the hospitality

the world offers all of its guests, most of the time" (99). Then, then, "we can receive "the world's ability to reach out and embrace us in unanticipated and unexpectedly gracious ways." (98). At first, maybe small pleasures are all we are able to absorb in bereavement. When we are able to enjoy some small pleasure is a sign that we are coming out of the deepest valleys. When did you find yourself able to start to savor the small pleasures of life again? Can you recall some particular pleasures that you were able to enjoy that were a sing that you were stepping out of the doldrums? From a therapist, I have long suggested to those who struggle with depression to have a list handy of ten things, ten small things that are easily done that almost always provide them a lift of their spirit. As I work on this section, an article in the New York Times (1/25/12) notes that the depression associated with grief should be labeled as depression and not make an exception for bereavement. For some of us, the depression that is natural and expected in grief may take a form that requires additional care and treatment. If healing can be aided by talk therapy and medicine, then more power to them. Again, it is no diminution of one's faith to see varieties of healing modalities. Again, just as Naaman in 2 Kings 5 wanted a major task for his healing to befit him, we look for a mighty task at times. Small steps can be effective, even against depression, or perhaps its onset. Small acts may well short-circuit the avalanche of doom that seems to tumble around us at times.

311) Ps. 31-Yes, this is a prayer for deliverance from personal adversaries or enemies. For our purposes, let it speak directly to death and our reaction to it as an enemy. At the same time, it speaks of a rock of refuge and a sense of the hand of God as protection; it gives voice to real concern. In many church circles this biblical prayer would be derided as showing a "lack of faith' or trust in the providence of God. So, we have a frame of trust around a most pressing lament. Look to verses 9-10-"Be gracious to me O Lord, /for I am in distress; my eye wastes away from grief, my soul and body also. For my life is spent with sorrow, and my years with sighing/my strength fails because of my misery." Yes, the pain is acute, but it is also chronic, long-lasting

struggle. It is hard to bounce back time and again. It may be wise to consider the loss itself, grief itself the enemy, the adversary plotting against your welfare. Real enemies do indeed roam about, especially death, "the last enemy." They remain inimical to human happiness. Just as those with cancer imagine their body battling the illness, we can personify or give shape to grief, in order to imagine battling against it, fighting through it, eventually overcoming it. At the cross, we have reference to this psalm, with the last words, "into your hands I commend my spirit." Into God's hand is the psalmist spirit, their very life, and also the times are in the hand of god as well (v.15). Those are beautiful words at the time of death, but they are commendable all during our life. We call the words at the funeral liturgy toward the end in letting our love done go into the presence of God, the commendation. Some folks have objected to its speaking of Christ as a shepherd and us as lambs of redeeming (BCW:925). At times, we can help others. At other times, we require a helping hand to guide us to safety andsecurity.

312) Pr. 25:20, "like one who takes away a garment on a cold day, or like vinegar poured on soda, is one who sings songs to a heavy heart." If I read this correctly, a happy song is not cheerful for the heavy heart. Indeed, it can be an act of cruelty to the mourner, even if the singing is well-meaning. The effect increases discomfort, stirs up the emotions. The constant push to be cheery or stoic in the face of adversity can often be an extra burden to people who don't feel cheerful. We try to impose an attitude on them, so that we don't feel uncomfortable. Verse 20 tells us that we need to be alert to timing, preparation, and capacity, even when we are determined to be helpful. It is an art, or a gift, to have a sense when the time is right. Maybe more to the point, we find out that our best-intentioned timing is bad only after our attempts falls flat. We try to impose good cheer on people, in our attempts to cheer them up. I saw an episode of Bonanza while on an exercise bike. Adam was beside himself in trying to care for his dying brother, and problems kept multiplying. A person kept urging him to look on the bright side, and Adam snaps that "you have an uplifting answer for every circumstance don't you.?" I

must admit that it presses my buttons at funeral visitations or family gatherings where someone decides that it is vital to evangelize the heathen with constant prattle about blessings and heaven as people are girding themselves to face hours of greeting people at a visitation. Sometimes, the blues are what folks need to hear to cheer them up, if that is appropriate to their condition, need, and preference. Indeed, some of the same could be said of our current demand to have 'celebrations of life" instead of traditional funerals. The bereaved may not be ready for that as yet. We try to impose our own disquiet for mourning on to the mourners themselves. On the other hand, that is the kind of service desired by many. It may well be the only kind of service they can imagine or even attend and be sustained by. Not long ago, I was told by a family that they wanted the words a celebration of life to replace the words, a service of witness to the resurrection in the usual Presbyterian parlance, as resurrection reminded them of death. Daniel Day Williams in a book I encountered in pastoral care classes, <u>The Minister and the Care of Souls</u> says: "the Christian is not ultimately concerned about protecting himself from suffering. ..we seek to share life, not immunity from its pain...through becoming vulnerable. Jesus was a man of sorrows acquainted with grief"(24).

313) Mt. 11- Here Jesus is an embodiment of the figure of Wisdom. (For instance, it sounds like Sirach 5). The figure of Wisdom calls out, but it is often no match for our attraction to folly, to false promises. Life is hard enough without being expected to carry extra loads, like some poor porter in an elegant hotel. "Cast your burden... My burden is light." We carry so many heavy loads. It is good to hear that we don't have to carry them at all. To know the release of a heavy burden is to know the relief of redemption. We get so chained to the past that we continue to carry the shells of old hurts or allow the full weight of an old burden to weigh us down. It is especially good to hear that Jesus has no intention of adding to our burdens. Not only is burden easy to bear, the yoke means that the burden is helped to be pulled by others. Maybe, if we are yoked to Christ, then Christ himself helps us to carry our burdens along. Some of the burdens

we bear are of long standing, even burdens of a difficult childhood and early losses. Perhaps Paul was thinking of this quote when he told the Galatians to bear one another's burdens. When the burden seems too heavy, it is good to be able to cast a burden on to the broad shoulders of God. Yes, we should "bear our own burden." Sometimes we try to carry a load so heavy that it may crush us. Our desire to try to control things, to depend on ourselves and ourselves alone, that we run into serious trouble. If we get serious with ourselves, we may not want to cast off the burden of grief. we start to think that it is the way we stay connected with the departed. Indeed the yoke reminds us that we are "yokefellows." We plow a field when joined together. It is not all up to us. Could it be that the easy yoke of Jesus means that we are working in tandem with Jesus? That easy, well-fitting yoke is so because it ties us together with Jesus adds a different twist to the passage, no? (the word for easy/well-fitting is chrestos, and I leave to the reader if we are also involved in a play on words here It is also linked to the word for kindly). We may be surprised what burdens we bear, but all of us have limits.

314) I must admit that the letter of Jude rarely comes to mind, save for its closing verses, but I am determined to get a good bit of biblical coverage in these devotional essays. It starts with a greeting that we are beloved in God the Father and kept safe for Jesus Christ. Right away, one could then be resentful for their loved one not being kept safe from the many dangers that threaten us. At the same time, we walk through life blithely unaware of what may befall us any minute. At a deeper level, we are kept safe within the life and abode of the Eternal One. Jude slips in a tradition that Moses did not die since he was not buried. That means that his letter was willing to use non-biblical material that then ended up in our Bible. For me it is a sign that the Bible is not a statue of a book but a book that lives with its time and lives into our time. That gives us a hint why Moses appears in the transfiguration with Elijah. Instead of being buried, he was assumed into the realm of God. (This takes off on the unknown grave of Moses into a tradition that no grave was needed, as he was assumed, lifted into heaven.). While he is going after various

false teachers, actions, and beliefs, he speaks of them with an arresting series of images: waterless clouds, autumn trees without fruit, wandering stars. Do the images fit your conception of mourning? All of the images pick up a sense of purposeless wandering, of chaotic movement. It closes with a lovely benediction. Hear the blessing pronounced over you, your life, and your family.

315) Is. 57:1 Rev. 14-Eulogies (good words) collect the good attributes and deeds of the deceased. Every so often, I am called in by a funeral home to conduct a service for someone who does not have a church affiliation. Often, the families are helpful and tell me about the deceased so that my anxiety is relieved. As a baby boomer, I like the sense that the service connects to an actual person and does not seem like more boilerplate. At times, the family is unhelpful, so then I station myself in the funeral parlor during the visitation and do short interviews with people who are paying their respects. What I collect mostly are stories, or fragments of them. When I hear the same phrase three times, I put a star next to it, as an indication that I have hit pay dirt in describing the deceased. Sometimes, families ask to see them and almost always remark that they never heard some of the stories or they never had an inkling that their family member was held in such regard. The best stories usually begin: don't say this in public tomorrow but...As I am reviewing this section, I did a funeral service and spoke with some grandchildren in the lounge. They spoke of Grandma allowing them to do things they did not normally do: playing in the woods, learning new card games, sailing paper airplanes in the living room, reading the polar Express every year, and most importantly, putting the whipped cream directly into their mouths. In our Bible Study, two of us lost parents when we were young. So we don't remember our parents, but we have created memories. The stories we heard of our parents, the pictures we saw contributed to a living picture of good words in our lives. We lived into their eulogies, only the eulogies were part of our growing up.

316) "Let the dead bury the dead."(Lk. 9:60, Mt. 8:22). That sounds so cruel. I worked with a pastor years ago who planned a series of sermons on things he wished that Jesus never said, and this was near the top of the list. He had lost his own father not that long ago. Why would Jesus say something so callous? The statement could be a spiritual one based on the urgency of the mission of Christ. If rejected, the call to new life renders one spiritually dead. In a way, it says each to one's own kind, the living and the dead. Even if part of us wants to climb into the grave with a loved one, we know that is not for us. Maybe the current fascination with vampires and zombies is an attempt to come to grips with life and death in the 21st Century. Many take this hard saying to be more metaphorical toward the spiritual life, where we enjoy the new life in Christ, or otherwise, we could be considered spiritually dead. That includes being called to new priorities within a new way, a new structure for life in the realm of grace. Barclay in his commentary on Matthew (314) tells that in Middle Eastern culture people did not "follow their dreams" until they had fulfilled all responsibilities to their family. In other words, the man had obligations to his family, then he could pursue the path of being a disciple. Jesus offers a radical sense of priority, especially in the pressure of events, if it was thought that the world was drawing to it close fairly soon. Are there parts of life that would be best to keep dead and buried?

317)I Tim. 5:3-15- Hebrew ethics had special concern for the widowed and the orphaned. Advice to widows in Pastoral Epistles doesn't square well in contemporary culture. After all, the Bible was written in the midst of a patriarchal culture, and that would have an effect on some of the writing. At the same time, we can keep a sharp eye out for subversive elements in the Bible toward the culture in which it was composed. We can also weigh some culturally specific material against other more egalitarian elements of scripture. At the same time, we do need to think through issues of being widowed as we live deeper into old age. I tend to think that now we need more advice on how to include the widowed in everyday life that some call secondary losses plague their lives. They're not invited to the old bridge games or lunch groups, as they were part of a couple. Nonetheless, the epistle refuses to look at widows as merely victims, as only objects for compassion. Widows do choose to act with compassion in all sorts of endeavors. They continue to extend acts of kindness, nurture and compassion into the public realm. No matter the culture, widows do suffer from "secondary losses," the loss of status, the ease of being slotted in as a couple, being part of a package. Being made suddenly single is a real transition. A community that should endeavor to embrace them often ends up excluding them. We look at couples as a unit and are at a loss when that unit is broken. We organize the card games around couples, have couples' clubs, do dinner party seating based on couples. Cruise lines routinely charge a substantial fine to those who would dare travel by themselves. Even worse, the lost opportunity for another in a cabin to spend money is called spoilage. God is with the married, the single, the divorced, and the widowed. God treasures our relationships, and God treasures the lives within each one.

318) Emmaus is one of my favorite post-resurrection vignettes (Lk. 24). Two grieving people are walking together, trying to process recent events. Their hopes have been dashed. Their image of the future is in tatters. They are going back and forth, trying to make sense of what has happened. It reminds me how we often need to go over and over aspects of the days leading up to a death in the family. They encounter a stranger, and they do not recognize him as the crucified one nor the Risen One. They were going back and forth in a heated discussion. They are astonished that the stranger does not know of the awful events of recent days. Jesus showed them that far from being immune from suffering, the Messiah was destined to suffer. Jesus, the stranger, the fellow who meets up with them on their journey, gives them a Bible study. Maybe better, he offers them a different interpretive key in reading the Scripture. He gives a different narrative framework to place different Scriptural accounts, names, and stories. Indeed Emmanuel, God with us, is with us in our sufferings and joys. Now day was ending, and they needed a place to stay. They beg the stranger to stay. Indeed,

the word is rarely used in the NT and has the sense of twisting the arm, trying to compel someone. Not until the bread is blessed and shared to they recognize Jesus. Think of that for a second. The risen Jesus offers a Bible Study, and they still do not recognize Jesus in their midst, even thought 'their hearts burned within them." One disciple is named, Cleopas, and the other is unnamed. I think that may be deliberate. Luke is inviting us into the midst of the story, and we can place ourselves in the shoes of the unnamed disciple. I think it unmistakable that Luke is saying we encounter the living Christ in worship, especially in the sacrament of the Lord's Supper. After their encounter with the Risen One in opening Scripture to them and opening himself in the breaking of the bread, they rush back the way they came to Jerusalem to tell the disciples. Back and forth, they are on the way, on the road. Journeys are marked by twists and turns, surprises and insights along the way. The journey rarely has a final destination, ultimate or complete. Emmanuel is our companion in the journey through all of our life, including the valley of grief, or the road home after a funeral. Indeed people along the way may well represent Christ to us, and sometimes we do not recognize them. The Spirit of the Resurrected One is free. Yes, Jesus stays with them for a while, but then he disappears. He appears again and again, in Scripture and sacrament, and on the road.

319) Ec. 8:6 "Every matter has its time and way, although the troubles of mortals lie heavy upon them." Time often feels as an enemy in grief. It has in fact been altered. We calculate days and years since someone died to mark the passage of time. The days are obstacles to be dealt with, survived, and gotten through, over with. Try to fill some of those empty moments with prayer. At some point, the future begins to beckon again. At some point you begin to look forward to something, instead of dreading what may come. Time does not rush us. It is our relationship to it. Time will rush by too fast once again, and we ask where did all the time go? The ever-rolling stream of time moves on, even if we feel as it it stopped, or should stop, out of respect for our condition. We wonder where the time has gone when we trudge

through days and days of numb parade. As time passes, it does not seem to lie so heavily upon our minds and souls. I take this passage to perhaps note the amount of variation in our world. Each situation has a distinctive fit in its environment, as opposed to one rigid, decisive plan or fate that runs through all activity. Instead of a rigid one size fits all policy, Ecclesiastes is showing an awareness that a fitting response that honor nuance, circumstance, and personality is often a better response. Wisdom is an ability to detect just those variations. This applies just as forcefully to our healing and recovery processes. As I am reworking this section, my radiation treatments after my prostate cancer surgery started. The very careful staff has been reliable in giving me what they call a protocol to follow for aspects of treatment. (I never imagined that I would hear that drinking a glass of water one hour before a treatment could be termed a protocol.) Have you developed a sense of a protocol for living with grief?

320) Gen. 11 is the story of Babel. We live in an age of babbling voices, not brooks. We can receive so much advice. Family and friends all know how we should grieve and how long grief should continue. The Internet is filled with self-help grief resources and chat groups. We are beset with Facebook, twitter, e-mail, voicemail. With that babble of voices is also the technological progress that Babel also notes, as God says ' there is nothing they will not be able to do." We live in a time of medical miracles .When our incredible technology fails, we want to lash out. The story of the tower tells us that we cannot build our way to becoming Gods any more than Adam and Eve could by eating the forbidden fruit. The close of the primeval section of (Gen. in ch.s1- 11) reminds us then that mere creatures of God cannot become gods. We cannot storm or build our way to the "gate of God," the meaning of Babel. Some things exceed our limited grasp. So, even words of comfort can become a babble of voices. I sometimes think that technology is a new god. We live within a technical priesthood. Some have the words for the latest devices. Some claim to have the technique and words for dealing with death, in a claim for expertise. In our need to lay a cause on, we

may well lash at at the technical priesthood, at all of the machinery that we associate not with life, but death. We may lash out at the priesthood of death, be it doctor, or coroner, or funeral director, or pastors. Genesis is filled with puns, and this story turns babel into balal, confuse. We have to deal with the babble of voices and conflicting emotions constantly running through us. Even if we speak the same language, we often talk past each other. Even if we are on the same wavelength, we may not have the energy or interest to listen fully and well. What words have helped you to get through, and what words have proved to be obstacles for you?

321) Nehemiah(1-8) feels called to help rebuild the walls of Jerusalem years after they were destroyed. He wants to make the city a proper city again. He meets with all sorts of opposition, but with planning, resources, and help, he is able to get the walls of the city rebuilt and restored to a degree. We need some boundaries, a membrane to separate us from being enveloped in the environment. I took biology ages ago, but it seems to me that like cells, our psyches need to be semi-permeable. if everything gets in, we would be overwhelmed. if we let nothing in, we would get isolated and be unable to survive. In a recent movie, Nicole Kidman plays a grieving mother in The Rabbit Hole. A couple's son dies in an accident. Both are cut adrift and are drifting apart. The mother seeks to forget with a flirtation, and the father tries to bury himself in memories and seeks solace outside. In trying to rebuild a life, rebuild relationships we do make errors in judgment; we may well act out. We cannot be completely porous to our environment. Some boundaries are necessary. We can soften the image of walls with boundary lines perhaps. As Frost said, "good fences make good neighbors." Our daughters played a computer game when they were little where they built an amusement park. As they went along, they had to keep their eye on many things to keep the park running smoothly. They learned that building, or rebuilding, requires attention and care. They learned that it was built brick by brick, step by step. They learned that plans often need to be flexible, as unforeseen issues arise constantly. At some point, we begin to

touch on the meaning and import of a life cannot be measured only in the moment of their death, as if the rest of their life matters not. To some extent, that could be the realization that helps you rebuild your own life in spite of loss, into a new future. Where have you seen that your life is being rebuilt or restored or renewed? What have been obstacles toward that process? Were they external or self-imposed?

322) Amos 9:13 looks forward to better days. In Is. 24, the lack of wine was a sign of a sad state of affairs. So, I love the image of abundance and joy that comes with wine dripping down from the mountains. It's the opposite of tears flowing down the mountainside, or an avalanche of problems threatening to consume us. Wine points to celebration. Years ago, a commercial asked us to take the plunge. Grief does not forbid better days ahead. You have already seen some better moments, better days, even better weeks. The future is always an "undiscovered country." The future of God is already hurtling toward us; it is already glimpsed in the here and now. In many was, the past is finished and gone. In Hamlet, the undiscovered country is the destination of the abode of death itself. Perhaps the picture of better days ahead makes the difficult days manageable. Yes, abundance can be yours in the future, even if it seemed absent from the past. You do not have to measure out your life drop by drop but will dive into it fully again. Part of us can be a bit afraid of a good future for fear that it too could be taken from us. We live so much of our lives in the fear of scarcity. It starts to constrict both hearts and minds. After a while we start to become emotional Scrooges or resemble the Grinch with heart three sizes too small. Eliot's Prufrock reacted to perceived scarcity by measuring out his life in coffee spoons. To focus on an image like this can break the bonds of perceived scarcity and start to look at the abundance inside us and all around us. We are people of scarcity and abundance in a constant mélange. Different types of scarcity or abundance can be wedded, such as economic and emotional pieces of the heart. They can separate easily as well, as someone rich may not have an emotional dime to spare. At this point where do you feel emotional and spiritual abundance

and scarcity?

323) 2 Tim. 1:7 God does not give a spirit of cowardice but power and love and self-discipline. We are not slaves to our emotions. We can affect our emotions with our thoughts and disciplines. All of us are victimized at times, but we do not have to become passive victims. We can respond to events; we can act. Note that love is placed in the center of power and self-control. Loving others is obvious to Christians, but we have trouble with the concept of loving oneself, as equated with egotism. To love oneself is to know that one is made in the image and likeness of God, to respect that good creation, to know that to be accepted by God is a gift against the constant suspicion of shame, of not being enough, or guilt's insistent call that we are not good enough. We may have an unrealistic picture of ourselves when we imagined that we would face grief. Then we get ashamed of ourselves for failing to live up to an unrealistic standard. While guilt asks what did I do wrong, shame asks what is wrong with me? When we try to shame someone else, we ask, what is wrong with you? Shame has a cascade of feelings (Capps Agents of Hope: 123-136). It has a sense of humiliation and worthlessness, of being foolish or stupid, or a failure. We may feel the sense of being an object of pity, of being the recipient of charity. It takes a continual renewal of courage to face grief and move on through to enter the other side. Shame makes us feel dejected and disappointed. Shame depletes the resources we need to help us regain our equilibrium and reassert a stable sense of self (see Capps, The Depleted Self). Courage is not the absence of fear. It means that we can take heart so that we can be able to face down our fears. I sometimes think that courage requires us to look fear in the face, but that means that we have to bend down very low to be able to do so, like trying to look a toddler in the face. In that sense, consider how brave you have been during this period of your life. Courage means to take heart, to find the heart to face fear. Think of what you have had the courage to face and emerge on the other side. You may have thought "I cannot face this," but you did.

324)- It is OK to question God. Recently, a faithful person recalled with fresh bitterness how a pastor refused to allow the young people in a confirmation class to question and probe the faith to which they were making a commitment. As Christopher Morse says in The Difference Heaven Makes (p.27) "a hymn of the church that contains the words, "Faith believes, nor questions how," bears false witness to the Gospel as news." In Luke and John resurrection appearance accounts feature questioning. As Paul Tillich taught, doubt is an element of faith, not its opposite. Questioning is part of a healthy relationship with God. Grief does challenge some of our most cherished or most fundamental conceptions of deity. I just heard a story how questions were forbidden in a confirmation class. That saddens me for a thinking faith is a blessing that tries to love God with the mind as well as the heart. I heard too many times that questions of faith were forbidden, as this was interpreted as doubt. Yes, we are involved in something beyond empirical proofs, but is measurement the heart of all understanding? I like to think that our image of God may grow as we grow. The great God cannot be placed in a box" but that includes a box of logic, demonstration, and orthodoxy as currently understood as well. In another book, Not Every Spirit, Morse insists that belief entails disbeliefs. Lamentations holds to some of the views that God causes pain as an instrument of punishment for evil as part of plan or intention (2:8) but the next chapter asserts that God does not willing grieve or afflict us (3:33). Sometimes, I wonder if it is a sin to be dogmatic in one's beliefs, as it moves toward an attitude of being infallible, and that is beyond most of us.

325) Elijah and the widow (I Kings 17:8-24) Elijah is in a far country. Ravens, of all creatures, brought him food. Since raven feed on carrion, they would be considered unclean, a death and life should not be mixed. Here, these creatures of death bring life to the prophet. Now he is told to go to foreign territory in Sidon. He meets a woman gathering sticks. Elijah asks for hospitality, but the widow is at the breaking point. She is making a last meal

for herself and her son. This foreign woman listens to his assertion that her hospitality would be rewarded, and she does so and makes him some food. Out of utter scarcity, some abundance returns to her life thorough her kindness to the prophet. In their hospitality to him, they are met with the gift of having oil and meal enough to survive day after day, and they live. Some time later the son grows ill and dies, and the woman wonders if Elijah has brought this on her. How could they be brought from the brink of death only to have her son now suddenly die? Was this some sort of cruel trick? Was this a sign of some of malice on the part of Elijah or even God? Elijah took the child and brought him to an upstairs sleeping alcove. His prayer is a bold one asking God why tragedy had been brought to the widow's house yet again. He lays responsibility for the death of the boy directly as God's doorstep. Three times, he lays over the child, perhaps at risk to himself, and prays that the child's life spirit would be revived. He carries the child, now alive, back into his mother's arms. Donald Capps (Agents of Hope: 30) writes "hope persists even when we have no objective grounds for trust." Sometimes, I see Fact as an idol. At other times, our delusions are idolatrous. Our lives take startling turns at times. May we always perceive a light of hope, albeit dimly, in the hard times.

326) Complicated grief (Mt.26:74-5)-As part of the "whole person' approach to my cancer treatment, I had a quick visit with a counselor. After less than a minute with me, he termed me a "complicated personality." (I think I am going to have T-shirts made.) Factors that made life difficult with someone when alive can continue to make life difficult after their death. The type of death, such as suicide, raises all sorts of anxiety within. I recently spoke with someone who half-hoped that their grief would be lessened because they did not get along with their father, nor particularly cared for or liked him. Her idea was that deep love causes deep grief, so a disturbed love, even a lack of love, would result in lessened grief. Possibly, but difficult relationships can just as likely open up a cascade of issues, guilt, what ifs, if only, and the like. The regrets about not having a better relationship can become quite wearing on the souls as well. Complicated lives

will have complication griefs. It may be just such a time to get some therapy, and work on the relationships one is capable of nurturing and changing, if need be. Naturally, we need to nurture our own health across the board: mental, emotional, physical, and spiritual. When we get run down, we are more prone to making mistakes, to accidents, to illness than usual. I would think that trauma studies would dovetail nicely into issues of complicated grief. Vietnam veterans of my acquaintance suffer from flashbacks now after forty years. Trauma survivors sometimes have a difficulty connecting with people emotionally. In part, I wonder if this could be a fear that if they grow close to someone that could increase the chance of harms befalling them. At times, I would consider the effusion of pain in Lamentations to be the result of trauma, indeed, of post traumatic stress disorder. No loss is easy, but some are definitely more difficult to bear.

327) Is. 43:1-7 is a favorite verse among a number of ministers I know who love the Old Testament. The passage gives a sense of protection even in the midst of affliction-flood waters will not sweep over you and the fire shall not burn you. Of course, it is directed at Judah and Israel but by v. 7 it is clear that individuals are included in those kingdoms. This is a God who calls, redeems, loves us by name. This is a God who forms us. It has a promise of emerging unscathed through the worst life has to offer. Lives are precious in this oracle, priceless. In the eyes of God your loved one is honored, precious, loved. Redemption is promised because it sounds as if God has labored long and hard in creating and forming us. that is no impersonal creation and forming, for we are called by name. To be called by name assumes knowledge and a connection to us as individuals, not as a number, not as a member of a class, say the grieving, or even, the saved, or the chosen ones. So deep is this love that nations count less than the few. For all of our talk about the vast expanse of creation, our god is a personal God. Out of the infinite cosmos, the Infinite One knows us as individuals, cares for us personally. Some of our evangelical sisters and brothers speak of the necessity of a personal relationship with God, but here the emphasis is on God's

personal relationship with us. That almost always pushes me to sit up straight. The creator of the immensity of this universe knows us by name. The Star Namer knows my name. Out of all of the lives ever lived, just on this blue planet, God knows my loved one. Few passages manage to try to hold the transcendence and the immanence of divinity as effectively as this passage.

328)- Some of the fuel for the book of Revelation is the issue of martyrdom (6:9-11). Like Abel, their blood cries out to heaven. For what: vengeance, justice, remembrance? Violence directed at people for no other reason than a disagreement about religious faith and practice. At least martyrs die for a cause. Part of our frustration over a tragic loss is that we find it more difficult to assign some purpose, some meaning to it. We cannot find nobility in tragedy as we do for martyrdom. It's interesting how we are willing to make martyrs of our soldiers more easily that we can conceive of being martyrs, witnesses literally, for the faith. We do not want to see people die in vain, die for nothing. We may tell ourselves that our desire for revenge is out of respect for them. We can be sorely tempted to become self-appointed avenging angels. We can also transmute those base feelings and become martyrs, in the old sense of being a witness, for peace, for justice, for reconciliation. We do face a temptation of making ourselves martyrs to an ideal of love and devotion. Even in the tumult of Rev. 19, the robe of Jesus is dipped in the blood of his martyrdom. Instead of becoming a military force, it deserves notice that the martyrs in Rev. 5beocmepart ofa vast heavenly chorus. Servants of a non-violent lamb, they form a military choir, not a groups of avengers. Know that your worship songs resound in heaven. They are echoed by a choir that knows pain all too well, but they now luxuriate in the presence of God.

329) - Remember the former things (Is. 46:9) v. Is 43:18, to remember not the former things - We have two contradictory phrases here. Part of the trick in life is to figure what to let go and what to hold on to. Perhaps part of the process of

bereavement is learning to hold these two injunctions in tension. God does not forget us. We are graven on the hands of God (Is. 49:16). When I was a boy I first heard the song, "He's Got the Whole World in his Hands." Into those hands we entrust our days. Perhaps at death we are subsumed within the memo and very life of God. We may forget, but God does not forget. We will thereby be aware of connections that we could scarcely imagine here and now. In the first passage, the Remembering One may be telling the people that they do not have to live in the past of the pain of exile. After all, the Divine Judge has already announced that the people have pain "double for all their sins." At the end of the passage, God does not remember, or call to mind, sins (v.25). That is an active decision, not divine forgetfulness. God is not mired in the past. God is fully capable of opening the doors to a new and unexpected future. On the other hand, the God of time is fully capable of continuing to have the past bear on the present and the future. Perhaps these images are demonstrations that time within the divine experience is radically different than they way we experience and perceive it. In The End of Memory, Volf reminds us that we cannot remember everything. Further, our identity is not the sum total of every experience as much as a sifting process of reflected importance or insight. Not everything should be remembered, nor should we wish to remember everything. Forgetting can be a balm to the troubled self. Some forgetting is a blessing. We don't carry memories like a computer chip with instant capacity to call them up. Yes, our lives do have a narrative, but we do have the capacity to change the narrative frame around events. We can choose to make some things central and place others in a position of less prominence. May I suggest a fine recording that reflects on beginnings and endings, Ashes and Roses, by Mary Chapin Carpenter?

330) I Cor. 11:2- At times, we can conjure up memories. These are a gift when we wish to recall our loved ones. Memory and grief are passive when a flash of memory comes unbidden. It can also be an active gift. Some folks engage in checking with their memory of a love done in terms of how they think they would react to a circumstance. We most often hear of this at something

like a graduation when someone says that your grandfather would be so proud. "If only your mother could be here to witness this." Donald Capps in his Agents of Hope (170-5) boldly suggests that we can actively adjust our memories of the past. He asserts that we may see the past as filled with problems and pain to be resolved, but it can also be seen as a source of strength and power. I am not suggesting that we can erase the past or invent a new one. i am suggesting that we can re-interpret our past and shine light on aspects of it that we have tucked away. After all, repentance/conversion means to turn one's life in a new direction. That new direction then operates to view our past with different eyes. Again, God is not bound by our past, nor is God bound by what we think is possible in our conception of present or future. Memory is not necessarily stable. Some can be relegated to the back of the mind and other can be moved to the forefront. Memory is not a perfect record of a videotape, as our mind alters the camera view and position. What memories would you rather see buried? We have it in our power to make some memories by living well, as well as being victims of circumstance or by failing or being mistaken. What seem to be the kind of memories toward which you gravitate when a loved one who has died comes to mind?

331) Rev. 7:9-17 has an expansive heaven for an expansive God. It sees heaven as a place where mourning is healed, as every tear shall be dried." It doesn't say that the tears are forgotten, but that they will be dried. they are tucked away in the past. This is often a reading for All Saints Day. I am touched by so many there, uncountable, or myriads in 5:11. 144,000 gets at the idea of the 12 tribes of Israel, but the vision blasts past that limited number, even though large, of a chosen people toward a more universal vision. It is a remarkable act of interpretation to take a huge number and try to make a limitation out of it. In the expansive love and mercy of God we can all find plenty of room. The early reformers wondered if only a small number of people could go to heaven, some small remnant for salvation. In their view, God had every right to offer mercy to whom God would choose to offer mercy. God's mercy could be limited to but a

chosen few. My suspicion is that they were caught in making God an exalted view of the justice, or lack thereof, with which they were familiar in politics, in the awful arbitrary judgment of rulers. Caught in a forensic view of salvation, it was difficult for them to accept a general amnesty program. Instead of a picture of unalloyed imperial majesty, we see a surprising figure in the throne room. I love the picture of all of these being in the very throne room of God, with Christ at the center of this enormous throne room. The image selected is the Lamb, the little lamb, the little slain lamb. That selfsame lamb died "for all." That lamb is an enthroned lamb.

332) Act 9:36-41 is the story of the raising of Tabitha/Dorcas (gazelle in both languages). She is mourned in part because she was a kind and giving woman. I bet some would call her a role model today. Also please note that mourners surround the upper room, guest room (as in the Last Supper) where she is laid. They gather to mourn together, to pay their respects. They clearly gather to share memories as well. Those memories have a tactile quality as they bring examples of her work. The keepsakes were signs of continuing attachment and honor of her. In a way, the gospels are keepsakes of the memory of Jesus. Yet, Easter accounts and the gospel of John speak of a relationship with the risen One that continues. Some folks do the same over time by wondering how a loved one would react to seeing something happen. They wonder what they would have said if we asked them for advice. My mother used the words and example of my grandmother as a fairly constant backboard for her to bounce ideas. Her dialog with her mother did not end with her death long ago. In a way, she continued her conversations with her mother and shared her observations all of the time with us, so that we felt as if we knew her. She engaged her memory for her imagined reaction to what someone would do or say, especially if it annoyed her. When someone says something on the order of what would my father have said or thought- or she would just die if she knew this happened, then people are engaged in a continuing relationship with the memory of someone near and dear to them. Keepsakes can be things or people shared, in a

way. When I scroll through songs or sports on the internet, I notice things such as ,"this singer was the only thing my father and I had in common, or this song was the only thing we agreed on, or we both loved Mickey Mantle, as the great sportscaster Bob Costas has remarked. (His recent eulogy for Stan Musial is a marvel, as well). I suppose some memories need to be treasured, but others are just as well buried.

333) Ex. 35:10, Col. 3:23-4, I Pet. 4:10-discovering skills, abilities, interests during bereavement can be a good coping mechanism. They stand as proof that not only can we survive during a period of loss, but that we can actually grow a bit through. Those skills do not have to be in honor of the deceased. It could be just for you and your well-being. Your worth has not changed. We have so many untapped resources within us. So many talents have been allowed to lie fallow over the years. Have you noticed that your capacity for relationship has changed? Sometimes we are sorely tempted to avoid human contact, because we are not willing to face the risk of pain again. So, we wall ourselves off in various ways and try, try so hard, to remain safe and secure. when we notice that we have the energy to engage projects and people, we are making some forward progress. Working on a project can provide a welcome distraction from the pressures we cannot face day after day without any break. It may be a good time to consider using some of those skills for the public interest as well as personal attention. One way to deal with private pain is to project them on to the public stage. One of my greatest prayers is that people moving through grief may start to find a sense of salvation as wholeness. Far too often, we wear so many masks to get through life that we my lose sight of our core, true self. Part of grief work is taking the shards of our lives and reworking them into a coherent whole, a new identity.

334) I Peter 1:7;2:23; 3:8-9,14; 4:1, 12 has suffering running as a bright thread through the letter, as one can see easily in this listing. Some think it to be a baptismal address that recalls that

the new life in Christ does not promise a rose garden. After 2,000 years, that warning is as fresh as ever. Indeed early Christians faced persecution, about which Americans have little knowledge or experience. Early Christians struggled through the issue of suffering just as modern Christians do. One approach in the letter is that suffering tests, refines, purifies us as an ore is refined by fire to lose the dross and reveal its true worth. Von Hugel said "radiance amid the storms and stress of life" to be indispensable mark of saints. The letter finds meaning in suffering in this way. It also reminds its readers that Jesus Christ was no stranger to suffering. Still even the marks of the lash, the stripes by which we are healed, are an awful empathy. It is as if a doctor could take on an illness to bring forth a cure for us. I need to add here that a close translation of 3:17 says if the will of God would ordain suffering. It is not a certainty, but the passage does say if we do suffer, it is better to suffer for doing right rather than a crime, but see 4:19. I've flipped through a number of printed sermons and some commentaries on this letter and am stunned to see how easily the writers speak of God's will and our suffering is accepted as if it is deserved and that it really is a good tool of character-building and education. For me, such comments stand at a remove from the experience of those in pain. For once, distance may not improve analysis. I really do not comprehend the value of this suffering as soul-making approach. I fear that people who find that they do not measure up to some aspiration of handling suffering with grace and good cheer will be further burdened if they fail to measure up to the expectation. For me, no was immune was suffering, maybe especially the good. If we can, we can derive lessons from suffering, but I still wish for a better lesson plan.

335) James 5 contains a ritual of anointing. Roman Catholics have sacraments to cover the length of life, and so the sacrament of the sick is a sign of the need for healing no matter our age. Those of us who are older know it more as last rites, or the sacrament of extreme unction. Since Vatican II a real attempt has been made for it to be oriented to healing more than consigning the person to the next dimension of our existence.

Presbyterians recovered the practice in its recent Book of Common Worship. Perhaps we could consider extending the ritual to those in mourning. Gathering some of the church elders around a mourner during different times of the year could be a meaningful spiritual response of the church. The oil was probably olive oil, originally. Gethsemane refers to an olive press. It was a healing ointment. It could be the oil that the Samaritan used for the injured man. In our time, alternative medicine advocates mention all sorts of healing properties of olive oil. As a sacramental element, we also point to inner healing, of fear and anxiety, of spiritual wounds, as well as it being spiritual medicine as enacted prayer for physical health. Some speak of a "healing of memories." I like to think that folks could benefit from pastoral counseling that would match therapeutic techniques with a real concern for religious issues. Another way could be a mix of spiritual direction and secular therapy when need be. So many factors come into play in not getting the help we need. It may be false pride. It may be fear of what could be discovered, that the secret self we try to hide could be revealed. It can be simple inertia. After a while, we get so used to feeling bad that we cannot imagine what it would be lie to be happier, so "better the devil you know than the one you don't," I suppose. the sheer social stigma of seeking therapy is powerful. I often say that we will try almost anything to deal with physical pain, but we are much more willing to try to live with emotional pain. So, we turn our backs on avenues of healing out of an obstinate insistence of "handling it myself." Where do you seek healing, right now?

336)Ps.49:15 Survivor guilt can be a nettlesome struggle. In the movie Bounce, the Ben Affleck character falls for Gwyneth Paltrow (no surprise there). She is widowed, and her husband was killed on a plane flight that he had avoided. He has to try to work through the recriminations for her side and his own guilt about avoiding that flight. In a sense, they struggle to rebuild their lives, and thye are bound by a terrible incident. In Seabiscuit, the Jeff Bridges character sees his marriage fall apart over the guilt and recriminations of having their son die in a crash. One of the inspiring things about his performance is that even as he rebuilds his life and even finds love again, the traces of loss still etch his face. Seabiscuit becomes an emblem for a struggling Depression-era country. The great army of the unemployed or underpaid can place their struggles on to the back of the poor horse and its troubled jockey and trainer. The movie shows us a community of health and healing through and from suffering that goes past human community to include that sterling animal. Doing some new things, even taking some new risks, is an entry point into rebuilding one's life. Many of us have a "bucket list" and this could well be the time to start marking off some things on the list. To avoid being and feeling stuck, a break in the routine may be the ticket to some ease and peace. Back when I was in college, or as our eldest daughter would say, in the Dark ages, I was introduced to Robert Jay Lifton in a wonderful American Studies class taught by Myron Lounsbury. Lifton introduced us to survivor guilt, the nagging sense that it was not right for one to survive in the face of loss. In the end, who deserves to live more than anyone else?

337 I Peter 1:3-5- Living hope is a great gift in the face of death. I'm not sure quite what living hope means, but I do like the sound of it. I do know what dying or dead hope looks like. I know what living despair looks like and wish to avoid it. As Springsteen sings, "is a dream a lie that don't come true, or is it something worse?" Hope does not have to die with a loved one. Even when hope is disappointed, it can blaze up again in a moment. We can have confidence that we will see our loved ones again. We will see that as living beings in a new world of God's making. Perhaps a living hope is one that grows and flourishes. Perhaps it is a resilient hope. Living hope is flexible toward means but relentless toward its goals. Resurrection then breathes life into hope. Perhaps a living hope is an active hope. In Thomas Long's fine new book, What Shall We Say, he tells of an academician familiar with analyzing texts. Getting her hands dirty at the street level of working for compassion and justice touched her prayer life. All of these contributed into a growing sense of hope within her, a growing resource for her work. Peter goes further and speaks of this living hope as being imperishable, undefiled, and unfading.

Death is he opposite of all those aspects of course. Peter sees these as protected assets of the Christian inheritance. What aspects of your spiritual inheritance would be most important to you to remain perfect?

338 Rev. 18:7 "I will never see grief." At some level, this is an arrogant presumption. Maybe it is an illusion of fear. the words are spoken by the antitypeof the City of God, Babylon. We know that the words will not remain true. Part of universal human experience as mortals means that we will see grief. Not long ago, I prepared a talk on Lyman Trumbull, the author of the 13th Amendment. He had 8 children, and only one outlived him. Death, especially of children, was a commonplace in the 19th century. As we see less of it, we can delude ourselves into thinking that it won't strike at us. No amount of faith, of positive thinking, of illusion can shield us from it. At times, all of us face a time when we have to eat our words, eat crow. The Bible opens with Creation and closes with new creation. Genesis opens with Adam and Eve being tempted to be like gods, perhaps in part to know immortality. (I am of an open mind if Eden was a place of mortality or not). Now as we draw to the close of Revelation that same arrogant position rises again that one could claim not to see grief, as if they are above the rest of us mere mortals. On the other hand it could be a great hope to be in a place where grief is put to rest. If placed into the overall framework of Revelation, it could be placed in the same set of hopes as the famous words of Ch. 21. Mortality ensures that we will all see grief.

339) Rev. 5.- In a vision of the very throne room of God, we await to see who is worthy to open the scroll. Of all things, it is a little lamb. Note it is not the Lion of Judah, not martial images from Scripture, but a little lamb. Not only that, but it is a sacrificial little lamb, one that has been slain. Going through death, the little lamb is now the victor in the presence of God. It is not a stirring powerful image. Might is what we would expect. It is decidedly not Lewis's roaring Aslan. It is a lamb who had

been slain. God can and does work for and toward good even through death. That the lamb was slain is not only a mark of it being a sacrificial little lamb, but it is a mark of memory in heaven with all of those little lambs whose lives have been cut short or struck down. They are not forgotten. Within the life of the slain lamb who is also the Good Shepherd, that those lives are remembered, honored, cherished. For me, his creates a most powerful, complex image. The Good Shepherd is at the same time the slain little lamb. In Revelation, one image morphs into another. In the end, the predatory wolves die with all flesh. In the end the wolves who will do anything to succeed, anything to advance their definition of the pack, will succumb. In the end, the sacrificial lamb finds victory, even as it seems to be of little account from a different perspective.

340) I Peter 3:13-The righteous accept suffering, but it is suffering for doing right. if Jesus could suffer, why not us? (see Is. 8:12) When Christ is presented as an example of facing suffering, the word used (hypogrammaton) has the sense of a tracing, patterning one's life with Christ as a template. The word may refer to the practice of teaching youngsters to write by having them trace the letters over and over on a pattern showing the letters to master. Of course, this goes against a big piece of Scriptural wisdom that we would be blessed for doing good and punished for doing wrong. This passage is attempting to assuage people that their suffering could be considered a sign of being and doing good. One of the deep problems that face us is guilt over the real wrongs we have done to someone who has died. Sometimes, people respond to the plaintive cry of Why me, with JFK's axiom that life is not fair, or lob the question back, "why not you?" In the Christian Century (10/18/11) Stanley Hauerwas, the distinguished ethicist, recently reviewed a new book on suffering by Eleonre Stump, Wandering in Darkness. She makes a case that suffering can indeed bring us closer to God. She makes the case by provocative readings of Abraham's family, Mary of Bethany, and Samson. Job's friends had a hard time grasping that the righteous do indeed suffer. They are determined to show Job that he must have done something, anything, to deserve that

punishment. In the movie, Unforgiven, the protagonist reminds us that "deserve has nothing to do with it." Stump is not interested in making a theological rationale for suffering. Instead, she wants to illustrate our need to love and be loved, even in the midst of suffering. Put differently, to be estranged, alienated from love is the great human tragedy.

341) Mk. 10:45- Douglas John hall frequently alludes to Tillich's notion that the great question of the classical era was about Fate and death. Is the giving of the life of Jesus as ransom for many be freeing from the hold of death itself? The great figures of the early church certainly gravitated to this concept. Ransom is a payment for release of a hostage or a prisoner. I do not see it as occupying the same symbolic space as speaking of propitiation or as a sacrifice for sin." What an incredible price to pay. Many could be read as all in this passage. What could possibly capture us more than the snares of death? In the older models of coming to grips with the meaning of the death of Jesus, the opposition was Hell, less as a place of the punishment of sin's penalty, but more as the abode for the dead. In art, Jesus leads a procession out of the abode of death. With Easter, Christ was victorious over death's eternal hold, its capture of life itself. In other words, the horror of the cross has pushed us to see it as an image that reflects the realities of the human condition in a variety of ways, and we have been mistaken in permitting it to be only a get out of jail free card in some cosmic Monopoly game.

342) Often, we use the same word in English for different senses of the word in Hebrew or Greek. A Biblical research tool, a concordance, will often give you a breakdown of the different roots of a word and where they are used in the Bible. Scripture gives us varieties of shades of comfort. One word rarely captures different shades of meaning. They may be often translated as comfort, but different words are used for effect as well as literary diversity. For instance, nacham has the sense of a sigh. For me it has that sense of a sigh when nothing else seems appropriate,

where we are left speechless in pain. In a different way, comfort is expressed in balag , to break off or desist from   grief. It may not be a total stoppage, but a break a brief cessation of mourning. That break may come as blessed relief from outside or above, but it could also be a decision we make to take a break, a ceasefire in the war of grief on us. Just as it may be a good idea for some to schedule some time for grief, to both start to manage it and to express it, it may well be a good idea to schedule deliberate breaks in mourning, to find some easy to do things to let up a bit. Paramuthemai, to relate close by, has the sense of comfort in the presence of close friends. It is the sense of wanting family and friends close by; it bears the urge to call someone when facing trouble, of not wanting to be a lone, to share troubles has a sense of easing them by having the effect distributed. Paraklesia-has the sense of being called along side as well, to comfort, to help, and to advocate like an attorney. I get the sense of someone being a helping hand. One of the benefits of comfort is eupsucheo-of good spirit/good cheer. Literally it means to be of good soul/good self. Over the preceding months, where have you found different sorts of comfort?

343) Lk.17:6 Well-meaning people will often say that your faith is strong, so you'll get through it. Some will even call on us to serve as models of the faith during trials and tribulations. I realize that these are meant as compliments and are well-meaning. The trouble is that we hear them when we fear our faith is at low ebb or may be fading away. It becomes yet more pressure. In my mind, the image of it is a castle that seems impervious to assault. I fear that such an image of faith, as a "mighty fortress" can create a rigid, defensive faith. After all, Luther's mighty fortress is God, not our faith. Jesus will refer to those of "little faith" but little faith may well be as much as we are capable of. After all, the tiny mustard seed is a sign of the kingdom as it grows appropriate for its size, but it is still a shrub. Yes, some may have faith such as to move mountains, but those seem few and far between. Jesus seems to say that just a grain of faith is plenty. Come to think of it, how many times does Jesus commend the disciples for their great faith? In Matthew's gospel he commends

the Syro-Phonecian woman who bests him in their dialogue as having great faith (15: 21-28) James has the famous line that faith without works is dead, but he doesn't speak of an amount. Instead, he sees faith in line with a single-minded focus on the love of God and neighbor. He does speak of being double-minded, torn or unfocused in one's orientation, unstable in one's internal gyroscope. One of grief's spiritual issues is that our focus keeps drifting. It is not a matter of strength of will, but it is a predictable disorientation. I have confidence that God does draw us back toward a proper focus, in due course, in due time.

344) Mt. 11:28-30, Heb. 4:9-11 Eternal rest-Some active people are put off by the term, eternal rest. To some, it sounds to be the epitome of boredom. It does sound sweet to those who are always harried and too busy. It does sound relieving to put to rest the bad news that comes at us in a swarm. To rest in God is to live within the life of God, to be enfolded into the life of God. When I lived in Indiana, I came to realize that the Hoosier work ethic was stronger even than the traditional Protestant work ethic. Hard work there is an ultimate virtue. It excuses other failings. I prefer to consider it as rest from the restless, anxious energy that often animates us but poorly. We could use rest from all the striving, all the worry, all the insecurity. It signals an end to our ceaseless beating toward the shore of autonomy and learning, like an infant, to rest in the security of the love and presence of God. In all of our anxiety, we are drawn like a magnet to the words of Jesus offering us a break, for he is gentle and humble in heart. As Barclay reminds us in the second volume of his Matthew commentary, we could translate weary as exhausted 15) That comes close to describing heaven to me. A member of one of the churches I served used to like it when I said that If I never heard the word cancer again it would be too soon. To exist where we have a rest from natural disasters and the human ones of war would be heavenly. I wonder if I would ever, ever get inured within that peaceful rest. On the other hand, the city at the end of the book of Revelation is a hive of activity, a blooming buzzing city, (ch. 22) not the silent streets of its antitype, Babylon (ch. 18). That city is restful, due to its

security. After all, the terrors of the night are banished there. Let me try it from another angle. to rest is to find rest in god, to find rest in divine Love. In Love we live and move and have our being. Our ceaseless frenetic activity is a sign of restlessness, of a frantic search for what and where we do not know.

345) John 14:16, 15:4,7,10) Continuing bonds stand against the idea that we have closure in grief, where we disconnect from their presence in our lives. Instead, grief includes the task of keeping the continuing bonds with the deceased in balance with the other bonds in our lives as we reconstruct our lives. We do accept the absence of loved ones. We do not accept the loss of love. We do not lose love. Our loves are still directed toward the departed. Our task is to change the way we love, our expression of those continuing bonds. We can deny love no more than we can deny the reality of death. In the song, "Here Today," Paul McCartney could well be singing to his murdered friend John Lennon. He wants to say that he knew him well, but guesses that the other would say that they were worlds apart. Twice he sings of what was not understood, but still he sings of presence, presence in the song. After all, all of the Beatles songs by Lennon or McCartney or both, were always simply credited as Lennon/McCartney. We renegotiate the place our loved ones have in our lives. To seek closure in the sense of letting go our loved ones completely is to devalue the continuing presence of loved ones in our lives. A possible indicator of continuing bonds is when a keepsake evokes not tears, but a smile, or a warm feeling of the person. After all, as Gail O'Day notes in her NIB commentary on John (754), "we do not emphasize the absence of Jesus," the Ascended One. We emphasize; we claim the continuing presence of the Living One, especially through the presence of the Spirit, the Paraclete/Advocate/Helper. Indeed, a favorite word of John is abide. It is linked to the word for abode in Greek, as it is close in English. "Abide With Me" is a standard in our Presbyterian hymnals. The poem was written by Henry Lyte not long before his death, in 1847, as he had suffered for years with respiratory ailments. It may have been composed near the time he delivered his last sermon to his long-time church on preparing for death.

The tune, in 1861, was composed by William Monk after the death of his infant daughter. In Greek, the word abide has a sense of remaining, of also remainder. When a lover asks, stay with me, it has the sense of abiding, of remaining with them. It has a sense of being the surviving remnant as well, perhaps, for the disciples who remain after the crucifixion. They themselves will be the abiding place for the love of Christ to find a home. Remaining, abiding in Jesus is a promise of life. To be disconnected, to become a mere remainder, is to be in death itself. Sarah Mancuso in an elegy to a friendship cut short by suicide wrote: "love abides. That is the only solace."

346) In the gospel of Mark, 3 times Jesus predicts his death for his disciples. He introduces them to anticipatory grief. For me it has become commonplace to say that knowing that death is coming for some time does not help us in the short run, but it does make it a bit easier in the long run. The reason is anticipatory grief. We start to rehearse reactions to impending loss. We start to prepare for the impending changes that we can anticipate. Utter shock and surprise fade a bit when we imagine some events in our minds eye. On the other hand, I can well imagine that the anticipation of loss only heightens the pain and anxiety for some individuals. Some evidence does indicate that sudden death is more difficult to handle over time (Volkan and Zintl p.62). We start to integrate the idea of loss into our lives. We can try to start to prepare ourselves across the board, in heart and mind, with the forms that we need, especially power of attorney, medical actor forms, financial decisions, and the like. We can learn from loved ones about how they themselves approach death. It can certainly help us with the barrage of all the things we could have said, could have done, should have said or done. I have spoken with many people who saw their loved one slip away from them in a cloud of dementia. In some ways, they have said goodbye to the person whom they loved, even thought they certainly look like the person they love. That awful twilight period is the entrance to saying goodbye, of feeling one's way into grief. Please, I am not saying that it lessens the impact of that terrible finality. I am merely suggesting that anticipatory

grief may help us along the way, down the line.

347) Dan. 8:15,Job 12, 17:4,Pr. 2:2-(See Neimeyer in <u>Meaning Reconstruction</u>)-Even in advanced secular society, religion is a primary method for coming to grips with large issues, including death. We start to cope when we can attach meaning in a loss, as that starts to make some sense of it. I think it uncovers a reason why we cling to God's plan for us, as we desperately seek to find some meaning, some sense, some rationale for a loss, especially an unexpected one. As a response to grief, some of us turn toward God's role as a controller of destinies to find some stable place amidst the mental and emotional chaos. In the movie Rabbit Hole, the mother cannot find solace in a grief group as she cannot grasp how people can say that God fated a child to die, especially her innocent four year old. She reacts in fury when people try to impose their sense of meaning on her loss. For some of us, grief changes our perspective on time radically. Some think there is no time to waste and throw themselves into projects and try to complete their "bucket list. " When we try to fit our experience of bereavement into our pre-existing categories, we may get more rigid about our world view, or we may find our world view seriously challenged, or we may realize that we have to rebuild our connections to help make sense, to help find some meaning in what has happened. I would think if one carries a narrative framework that leans toward the positive or the negative would have some bearing on the meaning we make of our experience. Recently, I went to a gathering where our presbytery (our regional gathering) asked us to consider positive features of our spiritual lives alone and together. One lady had been quiet much of the time, but toward the end, she blurted out a spasm of anxiety, fear, complaints, and foreboding. She was so taken aback that we were being asked, in appreciative inquiry fashion, to seek resources, but her radar was set to detect lack, trouble, issues, and problems. Many of us have been trained and encouraged to look for meaning in connection, but it runs against our insistence of working things out on our own. After all, to do a job well, one does it on one's own. As John Donne said, no one is an island, but Anne Morrow Lindbergh, in

Gift of the Sea did see us as "islands, but in a common sea." We may crave connections, but we contend with being set apart as well.

348)Ezek. 24:16-7,23, Jer. 16:5 Disenfranchised grief- When you hear something on the order of "well thank goodness..., or it was only or just... at least...you know you are treading in the waters of grief that lacks public sanction and support. We do not take some losses as seriously as others. Losing a pet would be a clear example, where we say things like well it's just a dog, or urge them to replace it immediately. After all, "it could be worse." Robert Parker does a nice job with the pain of losing a faithful pet in the Jesse Stone books. Jesse's marriage has collapsed, and really he carries with him, his skills as a police officer, his love of baseball, and his dog. Recently on Facebook, someone posted a series of pictures of a beloved dog with the family in different scenes. Not long ago in the office two staff members were going back over their struggles with putting pets down or being witness to their demise at home and how surprised they were at how hard it was on them I've heard the phrase companion animal being used in place of pets. Disenfranchised loss is loss that often gets minimized. Then we start to second-guess ourselves about where we are placing our emotional attachment and energy. It may well get the response, "well thank goodness it was only..." Part of the reason for this is that we do keep a bit of a hierarchy in our minds when approaching grief and do see some as worse than others. That judgment cannot look into the condition of the grieving, however. To some degree, we are mysteries to one another. To some degree, even the most empathetic person is unable to peer into the depths of someone's experience. We look at each other "through a mirror darkly." It can be difficult enough to even express feelings of loss, and they are only heightened when they feel as if they are being shortchanged or even disrespected.

349)Eph. 5:15-16 -I would think that we should be careful about giving ourselves, or others, too short or too long a timetable for grieving. It is common to speak of grieving for year. That is understandable. Part of wondering about a time frame is that we wonder if these feelings will last forever. Is it possible to feel terrible day after day? Even thinking about a time frame may well be a sign of forward movement. The cultural signals all push in favor of rushing past grief, going around it as soon as possible, not going through it. Slate's on-line magazine survey found that many respondents were in grief well past two years. On the other hand, it does seem that losing a child has a longer active grief period than other losses. Your timetable is your timetable. I think it proper to expect some easing within a year. I think it proper also to have your moments of intense grief still. If intense grief persists, please consider going to a grief counsellor for a helping hand for reflection and a hand up. I was introduced to a woman who lost her husband fifteen years before. Her conversation was only on her loss. Her very habits of life were not dominated by being in perpetual widowhood. You have changed because of loss. In innumerable ways, you have grown accustomed to living with loss, living in spite of loss, when just living is an heroic gesture, an act of defiance against Death. I do not want to make grief sound as if it would be another set of tasks we set before us that we are to master, step by step, stage by stage until we reach the completion of the goals. It has its waves, its placid moments and its storms, but we can mark some progress. We are not made to stay suspended in grief forever.

350) Ps. 90:10-13 and life review- In one of her novels Anne Tyler has a character push someone who is not demonstrating grief with "you're trying to slip through life unchanged." A number of people suggest making a loss graph of our lives noting when losses touched us during the course of our lives. My father was killed in a tanker explosion before I was three, so I have no memory of him, but that loss had an impact on my life, so I include it on my loss chart. I was an altar boy during some of Vietnam and helped bury young soldiers coming home for a final time. That too could go on the loss chart. A year after our daughter was born, my brother committed suicide. One of our

younger daughter's best friends lost her mother as a girl. Somehow our daughter could look past the anger and bitterness and saw the shining soul of her friend. With our remarkable medical advances and the advent of Medicare's provision of health care to seniors, we have seen a powerful push to seeing folks live well past the biblical 70 or 80 years. I am hearing people say that someone was young, if they died in their seventies. I don't accept that anyone can go through life with all the loose ends tied up and no regrets at all. It may be an idea to do a relationship review making a graph of high points and low points similar to the loss graph that many do in therapeutic settings. Some make "ethical testaments" as giving their learning and hopes for those who follow them. One of the good features of families helping to prepare material for eulogies is that they conduct a life review for the deceased. Preparing a life review for a loved one may also be a bit of a spur to conduct our own. In some traditions, we pray a review of the day before sleep. Graphing the course of life can be a tool for real insight for patterns that shape us still.

351) Prov. 10:9 Part of personal integrity is processing in character (Martin and Doka). I heard the grief therapist Alan Wolfelt say that we shouldn't expect an 85 year old German farmer in Iowa to react the same way as a 30 year old mother in a university town. It is wrong to expect too much of ourselves or others that we can all rise above our failures and inadequacies and achieve shining virtue in the face of crisis. God loves us in spite of our flaws and maybe even because of some of them). Looking back, what has gotten in the way of your moving through the valleys of grief? Where did you get stuck? What in your personality helped you through? When have you felt pushed to go against your personality or character type or preferences? What in your character helped you through, what resources, what assets, allowed you to move through your loss? In Kayak Morning, Roger Rosenblatt writes of his surprise at the length of the intensity of his grief over the loss of his grown daughter. A

therapist tells him that "since grief comes at a rush, we may think it will leave in a rush, but no, it is a permanent guest." As a literary person, he likes exploring the depths of character. In his grief, he realizes that that may not always be helpful or even possible. Like a kayak, sometimes it is best to stay afloat, to skim the surface. In life and on the water, it may feel as if he is not making progress, going nowhere. In his love for his daughter, in her continuing presence, he finds that her love makes "going nowhere, going somewhere." Different people grieve and cope in different ways. Some people go through the almost expected hard year of declining grief; others move through it more quickly it seems, but a substantial portion of people have a difficult time for a long period. We cannot insist that someone goes through pre-set phases in a prescribed order. Not being depressed after a loss may indicate being spared that pain, but it is not necessarily a sign of repression. Still, we struggle. We hear the words of death being part of the natural cycle. Edna St. Vincent Milay fought against it. Yes, a buried one may have it s elements caught up in the blossoms of a fragrant rose. (I think of Leo Buscaglia's popular, The Fall of Freddy the Leaf, or the Lion King's circle of life). Still, she protests "I do not approve"

352) Acts 28:26-7 Barber's Presidential Character spoke of world view as an overarching way that we approach the world. It's intended, I think, to be more far reaching than an ideology. An ideology tends to move in lockstep and tries to impose its view on everything, anomalies included. World view strikes me as more of a perceptual screen, a way of approaching and organizing experience but less prone to rigidity than ideology. As a screen, it does color our world. It can be more optimistic or pessimistic. That has direct bearing on expectations. Some of us are more surprised than others to see something bad happen to us. At our best, we do not perceive things clearly. When under stress, our perceptions can become even more unstable, or more rigid. It's been said that we do not see things as they are, but we see things as we are. When we get to the point where our ideology, our world view has become stable and far-reaching, life seems to have a way of undercutting our field of vision. When facing a

threat to our way of the world, we may grow more rigid in our adherence to it, afraid that if one piece could fall, the whole structure will collapse. Others grow more flexible in their views, as they realize that life has a way of undercutting even our most certain, and cherished, beliefs. Some feel as if the entire structure has indeed collapsed and they search for reconstruction or a whole new set of glasses to view life. I notice these in general religious terms, but perhaps most significantly in providence, God's plan, and God's control over events. I have come to see providence in a general set of patterns, but I do not see God actively using the levers for each discrete event in life. At the same time, I have a vague notion of God being involved in all of the processes of life (see process theology basics). God is engaged with our lives and responds, but does not control them as a divine dictator. Yet, some of us require that sense of a God in control as n anchor for weathering the storms of life. In the end, God has plenty of room for different ways to approach coping with largequestions.

353) Ps. 68:5 children and grief- Young children know and feel loss. We try to shield them, and that is a proper demonstration of concern. Part of our desire to shield them is to protect ourselves from their confusion, questions, and reactions. As their cognitive capacities grow, new points emerge. Magical thinking comes into play. "did my angry thoughts cause the loss?" Later, not only is it clear that they could lose someone close in death, they themselves are mortal. Children need reassurance that they will be taken care of. Different stages of development create new concerns. Always present is trying to gauge the extent to which their emotions and mental faculties are related. I admire Fred Rogers, Mister Rogers, and his long-running television program. He respected children and took them oh so seriously. Mister Rogers could take children so seriously that he was willing to allow himself to be a figure of ridicule for adults, as he tried to speak directly to them, not their parents. He both remembered and researched the thoughts and feelings of children that adults have forgotten, ignore, or laugh off. Fred Rogers was determined to respect the individual dignity of the child. He wanted them to

know that they were unique, that their life was important, to be cherished and honored. He knew that they were worried about things that we have long forgotten, like being afraid that the drain in the bathtub would take them down too. That repository of fear needs assurance. He acknowledged their feelings of hurt and confusion powerlessness. He offered ways to channel negative feelings and to talk about them with adults. If a child continues to seem very troubled by loss, play therapy, with a trained person of course, may be a good avenue when they don't yet have the verbal skills to put their concerns into words. Adults may help give them stability and security, and even guidance. Know that the Heavenly Parent is with us in the awesome task of accompanying a child in grief.

354) I Sam. 3, Jer. 1, Ec. 12:1,La,3:27-33,teens and grief- In Biblical times, when one was a teen, adulthood was assumed. We have some bits and pieces about youths. The way youth is approached would indicate the Good Book is often written from the perspective of the middle-aged, if not the elderly. In our society, teens occupy a liminal space between childhood and adulthood as they seek to forge an identity, a sense of self. They may be trying on alternative identities. For reasons that are not clear to me, teens have a sense of invulnerability, of personal immunity from trouble. They may get a 100% on a quiz about sexual behavior, but they can convince themselves that they cannot get someone pregnant or that pregnancy would happen to someone else. They may be trying to fit themselves into models that may or may not fit them. In English class, they can write poems on grief as an imaginative exercise because it seems so far from them to some extent. It can come as quite a shock that they can actually see the consequences of risky behavior, or that an accident or illness can indeed be a bolt from the blue. I notice teenage boys try very hard to keep a stiff upper lip as they try to emulate what they see of male behavior in times of grief. Death is an extra assault on their constructs, as it conflicts with their sense of personal invulnerability and immunity. Their imagined future does include their loved ones, even as they are pulling away in trying to forge their personal identities. Some folks even

now reach adulthood before they attend their first funeral. Erik Erikson places older teens in the time of identity, of taking the shards of their young lives and starting to knit them into a coherent sense of self. Its threat is role confusion. Bit by bit, we weave the pieces of into a whole we call character or identity.

355) Impassivity and God has become a theological topic again. Since the 1980s, give or take some years, the trend has been toward emphasizing the suffering of God. We pick up phrases such as Bonhoeffer's "only a suffering God can help." Now the pendulum is swinging back and trying to say in light of divinity that God is "above" suffering as we know it. Our image of God is one of power, and that image seems diminished if God is affected by our joys and sorrows. I suspect that the argument starts with our attempts to superimpose patterns on our understanding of God, Greek philosophy, with a pious yearning. Jer. 31:20 speaks of God's yearning and delight. Is. 63:9 certainly touches on a God who is "distressed by our distress" and whose spirit can be grieved (v. 10). I have some sympathy with those who fear that the suffering God becomes a passive sufferer, an impotent divinity. I recall a professor saying that he did not want God down in the ditch with him as much as he wanted God above him to give him a helping hand out of the ditch. Look at how desperate the situation of the people is in Jer. 30. God does indeed feel for them, but then God promises action, to heal and save and deliver (16-20). I am decidedly on the side of the God who comprehends suffering, but I do appreciate that we should always be careful in merely extrapolating human experience on to the Eternal and Holy One. At the same time, it is clear to me that we worship a God in relation with us and to us. If God is love, it is beyond me how that deity somehow is "above" all of what we may be tempted to term weakness and vulnerability.

356) Jamie Moyer, a pitcher who continued work well into his middle-age, has a foundation that supports grieving families in camps. American males consider great athletes to live the perfect

life, but their lives are touched by pain. Dan Marino, the great quarterback, has a child with autism. Boomer Esiason, another quarterback who went my alma mater, Maryland, has a son with the dreaded ailment, cystic fibrosis, and has a foundation dedicated to research on that disease. Such celebrities may be just the ticket to show us that no one is immune from trouble and tragedy. In high school, we read Houseman's "To an Athlete Dying Young." I did not grasp it with much depth, but I did get the sense that it is a terrible loss when someone is at their peak and then dies and got a glimpse of its melancholy spirit of elegy. Going through grief may help us to discover deep pools of compassion within us, as we see ourselves involved into a new type of community. Making a memorial gives meaning when putting a life back together after it seems broken into shards. Personal hurt gets transformed when it reaches out to others hurting, especially those in a similar circumstance. Personal hurt acquires new meaning when it is joined toward seeking to relieve the suffering of others. At times, making a memorial can be a response to the guilt feelings we have. The trouble is where we make amends when a person is gone. Memorials may be making amends to substitutes for our love ones. Hear Philip Larkin in An Arundel Tomb: "our almost-instinct almost true: what will survive of us is love."

357)Rom. 12:2 Dr. Burns approach in Feeling Good and grief-Cognitive therapies have hit their stride, as insurance is reluctant to pay for long-term approaches. Its fundamental axiom is that we can be alert not only to our feeling states but the pattern of our thoughts. Indeed, the pattern of our thoughts can be distorted over time, due to our feeling states, and then we forget how to identify and deal with distorted thinking processes. Our thoughts can affect our emotional process, just as emotions affect our state of mind. For instance, we over-generalize. We take one point and say that bad things always happen to me. We label ourselves as losers or weak or failures, whatever. Reason can help check some of the abuses we heap on ourselves. In other words, we make mountains out of molehills. We look for patterns that cohere with a damaged sense of self-esteem, or purpose or worth and dutifully ignore all of the wealth of contravening evidence. We can check our assumptions and assertion merely by asking questions. Harry Chapin sang "reality is only in your mind." In the same song he says no more sad stories comin'. In The Gift, Springsteen sings a song of gratitude to his parents for the Christmas gift of a guitar they could scarcely afford. He sings that guitar brought him so far and so "no sad song tonight, ma." Here are some simple tips. When you start saying everything is going wrong. Stop. Get clear what is going well, what is tolerable, and what is going badly. We can learn to regain some perspective. Some things are catastrophic, but not every bad event. Some things are not our fault. Events are often discrete, so they are not proof of a world in conspiracy against us, or allied in a secret plan of perfection. grief attacks our perceptions, but we can re-learn to evaluate our experiences with some level of clarity again.

358) Burton Cooper recalls a student telling him that he will need to model grief and teach them, the community at Louisville Seminary, about handling grief. I'm of two minds on such a request. I think it improper to place additional burdens on the grieving, so part of me finds another example of the grating piety of aspiring pastors. (To be more candid, if I were in the position of having lost two children to death, I fear my equanimity would vanish and I would punch out the annoying twit, or at least fantasize about it for a bit). At the same time, we do respond to events differently; we do look to others as models, as inspiration. In <u>Tracks of a Fellow Struggler</u> John Claypool quotes Myron Madden (101) "the essence of despair is relegating God solely to the past." The Creator of all, the Creator of time itself, is capable of helping us build a new future. God is fully capable of surprise. indeed, we are not condemned to a constant replay fo the past. The sense of being "born again/from above/anew" (John 3:3) is the gift of that new lease on life. A stream of books come out every year to offer advice on how to handle loss, or to speak about one's particular response to grief, less as a model and more to offer witness to one's personal struggles, good and bad, on the public stage. Some offer a lot of practical steps about

finances, and other s work at the feeling level, and some of the strain on one's thinking process through time. We should exercise caution in trying to impose our timetable of movement through different phases of grief on to others. People work through things on their schedule, not ours. I just noticed that a spouse was concerned that his wife was not weeping and wailing, as befit her introverted side around the family. Extroverts or introverts do not hold a monopoly on the proper way to grieve. The task is to learn what mechanism of coping best fits our character, our personality.

359) 2 Cor 5:7 We walk by faith and not sight. (See hope in Rom. 5) -These are bold words, when things are going well. When we are scanning our world for signs of hope amidst deep trouble, they are harder to bear. To hold on when we don't see signs of improvement can be most trying. When we looked at the body in a casket, can our mind's eye look past the evidence into another dimension? George Ile wrote: "hope is faith holding out its hand in the dark." Indeed hope strikes me as a contrary virtue, as it can look reality in the face and refuse to give it ultimacy. At its edge, I think of Elwood P Dowd in "Harvey" saying that "he had been battling reality all of his life and was proud to say that he had finally won out over it." Can we peer into the grand family reunion in the life to come? When we can joke about imagined reactions to a loved one's arrival into heaven, we are in a better place. When my sainted aunt died, her daughter in her tear-choked eulogy, joked that she her mother was already redecorating heaven. Recently, I officiated at a graveside service for a man who loved history, and someone mentioned that they hoped heaven was decorated in antiques for him to admire. In the Presbyterian Book of Common Worship, at funerals we pray "give us faith to see, beyond touch and sight, some sure sign of your kingdom, and when vision fails to trust in your love that never fails." Wendell Berry has said that "it gets darker and darker, then Jesus is born." Bethlehem was the arena for Emmanuel, God with us. Its light shines onus still.

360) Jer, 32 Here Jeremiah has been predicting impending doom and ruin. Now he is told that he has the chance to purchase some land back home and that he should make sure that it is done properly. I remember when we closed on a house that I never signed a name so many times, unless it was trying to see if I could forge my mother's signature for a school note. Making plans and implementing them is a sign of health as the future looks to be something we can affect, not as a mere passive victim of it. We can put some energy into new places. Making a decision such as this should probably not be one in the first days and weeks of grief, or maybe even the first year. Give yourself some time. As we are able to make decisions, we see that our capacity for action is not paralyzed by loss. We can welcome newness into our lives again. (We can deal with tentative options or revisiting them) Chesterton said that "hope is as unreasonable as it is indispensable." While I caution against making major decision in the first year of loss, at some point we do plan for the future again. In so doing, we announce, to ourselves and others, that the future is not to be only bleak, even if it feels that way at times. When we act in hope, we co-operate with god ushering in the new creation. Such action connects the spiritual with the concrete, the physical, the practical. As you gaze into the future, do you begin to detect any signs that God is taking some torn fabric and stitching it into something new in your life? Are you starting to see some things beckon as opportunities instead of burdens? Are you taking some steps to move into a new unoccupied future for yourself? In <u>Agents of Hope</u>, Donald Capps of Princeton Seminary lifts up hope as both psychological necessity and vital Christian virtue. He identifies shame, despair, and   apathy as obstacles to hope. He sees as allies of hope, patience, modesty, and trust. I would like to spend a moment on apathy. It is straight Greek, not caring, not feeling. How many times has someone said in disgust, "I just don't care anymore./ I don't care no more," as Phil Collins sang.

361) Jer. 8:18-9:1-Here again, it seems to me to be difficult to

discern if the prophet or God is speaking, or if we are in the middle of a conversation of different voices. I certainly can identify with the sad sense that summer is finished and gone and we are not saved. We put a due date on our feelings, and then we get disappointed when we are not "back to normal." We find a difficult matter, is there balm in Gilead? The question is answered by the old hymn, There Is a Balm in Gilead. Yes, there is a balm in Gilead that heals the sin-sick soul. Grief affects us at all levels, even all the way to the very depths of the self, the soul. Hoping for heaven, holding to the communion of saints can be a balm. Sometimes our spirits get refreshed out of nowhere, as if the hand of God has consoled us. As we move through grief, we start to notice that we don't fly off the handle when a usual incident befalls us, such as someone cutting us off in traffic. Sometimes, we crave that experience and it does not come when bidden. For a public grief that can mean investing in a continuation or a project. In the movie, We Are Marshall, we see the devastating impact of the plane crash that took almost the entire team and coaches. The college president determines that the football program needs to continue. His position is undercut by a board member who lost a family member in the crash. His malice emerged from grief. The president was right that the football team offered restorative balm to the community, even as it was a painful reminder for the board member. Of course, nothing can replace the lost one, and something nothing we offer can soothe a soul. So, the very thought of heaven is a restorative balm for the grieving. Over time, where have you found some healing balm? Are there areas where you feel as if the summer is past and winter approaches, but you have miles to go yet? "Sometimes I feel discouraged/and think my work's in vain/but then the Holy spirit/revives my soul again/ there is a balm in Gilead/to make the wounded whole/there is a balm in Gilead/to heal the sin-sick soul."

362) Ps. 121-This is a travelling psalm, a pilgrimage psalm, and it fits when we end our time here and journey to the next world. Our travels place us into the valley of the shadow of death and the radiance of the mountain top experience. God is with us in

our going out and our coming in. In a late Beatles song, Let it Be, we hear "when the night is cloudy/there is still a light that shines on me/shine on 'til tomorrow/let it be" Sometimes, this is a difficult psalm because we feel the promised protection against blows by sun and moon has failed us. I always see birth and death as holy moments where I am in the presence of the God of life. Yes, it fits the travelling motif of going in and coming out as a plea for protection. Day or night we seek protection on the road. If we see life itself as on the road, I imagine God ushering us into this life and ushering us into the next dimension of our existence after we die. We can make it a daily pilgrimage too. God is with us in or rising to consciousness after sleep and our falling into sleep at the end of the day. It just dawned on me that Hebrew ethics are most concerned with the widow, the orphan, and the sojourner. In a broad sense, are we not all sojourners here, passing through. I have a tape where James Taylor remarks that as one writes songs in the music business, one starts to accumulate a lot of road songs. Off the top of my head, I think of Midnight Rider by the Allman Brothers and Turn the Page by Bob Seger, or the Beatles" Long and Winding Road.. If you are approaching a year since your loss, it is a good thing to look back at how far you have come. Time has established a more regular pattern again; every minute doesn't seem to tick away forever, like sitting thorough a terrible math lesson in third grade. Has the pain softened over time? Consider marking the journey of this past year. Where are the mile markers you would jot down? Have you kept circling back to certain times in memory? Were detours more or less frequent in this journey?

363) Mt. 1:23 Emmanuel-God is with us, with us in everything. In a way, Matthew uses that title as a theme for the entire gospel. Given that declaration, we cannot then we left stranded, abandoned, alone by God, ever. God is with us in grief. God is with us as we emerge from its shadow. God is with us in all of the in-between moments. God's own self did not dip a toe into the human experience and test the temperature of the waters. Jesus Christ lives as God immersed in human life, just as we hold that he was immersed in a God-filled life. We can even shade the

meaning of with a bit and claim that God is indeed on our side, as Paul has God saying Yes, Amen, to the human race. As a little kid, the nuns would take us in the cafeteria during Advent and we would sing songs of the season. I always like O Come, O come Emmanuel, even as its mournful key did not fit the cheery Christmas music. Later, I think I liked it because it had a "Jewish" mournful, longing sound to it. Look back on your experience for this past year. Where have you noted God with you? Please note well that God is with us in the moments of crushing grief, when those moments become less frequent and less deep, and in signs that we are recovering through and in the midst of loss. God is not only with us in the deepest cave, but God also takes us be the hand as we start to emerge from its depths. God relentlessly leads us toward the light. What doe sit mean to you to say that god is with you in your grief? Has your sense of God's presence changed in this year? Has a sense of God's seeming absence then affected you when you do sense the presence?

364) Living into our own eulogies (2 Tim. 4) I saw a movie, Get Low, where the Robert Duvall character wants to have a funeral, but the catch is he wants to be able to witness it and to hear what people have to say about him, what stories they want to share. It is true that we wait until it's to late to tell someone how much they mean to us. If we had the chance we may well know how they would want to be remembered, what stories capture their attitudes the best. Julian Barnes tells of a type- A corporate leader who was given but a few months to live. He had a decision to make if he would apply the same attributes to his remaining life or not, similar to Jack Nicholson's character in the bucket List movie. I saw a moving eulogy recently where the spouse at the funeral used objects that spoke of his wife's life and then he deposited them as they were no longer needed, such as her oxygen tank. A eulogy literally means good words. I heard about a minister who opened up the funeral service for the first time in that congregation, to the remembrances of family and friends, as he couldn't think of anything good he had to say about the deceased. Sometimes we hear so much about the good of the person we start to wonder if we walked into the wrong funeral

chapel. In a new position at a church, I was honored to see a family start to collect stories, attributes, and memories of their loved one. They were able to present a sheaf of papers filled with snippets that describe a good life well-lived form the perspective of husband, children, grandchildren, and friends. As I was reviewing this, our younger daughter, knowing my admiration for Mr. Rogers, alerted me to a book by Tim Madigan, I'm Proud of You. Those were words that the author longed to hear from his own father, and Mr. Rogers provided them in every note he sent, even abbreviating it, IPOY. Allow yourself to hear the words you needed to hear from your departed loved ones. Let yourself say the words to them they you want them to hear from you.

365) I Sam. 20:6 Est. 9:21- The one year mark after loss does not have some magic potency. Yet, it is a significant marker. I don't know if we ever come to closure in grief. We continue our attachments with those who have gone before us. We continue to create and hold and work with relational space, yes, even with the dead, as part of being human. Those attachments do change. I don't know if magic descends after one year of loss. At least, we don't go through first holidays of absence any more. In some traditions, a candle is lit on the anniversary of a loss. In others, the gravestone is laid. After twelve months of mourning, the rabbis tell us to continue to speak of one's parents with the introduction, 'may their memory be a blessing."
Look at how far you have come. Yes, you have miles yet to go, but the psychological distance travelled is immense. There were days when getting through another minute seemed hard to imagine. Recall Robert Pirsig's words toward the end of Zen and the Art of Motorcycle Maintenance: "Trials never end of course. Unhappiness and misfortune are bound to occur as long as people live, but there is a feeling now that was not here before, and is not just on the surface of things, but penetrates all the way through. We've won it. It's going to get better now. You can sort of tell these things."

David J. Crowley is the Designated Pastor of the first Presbyterian Church in Alton, Illinois. Previously he served churches in LaGrange and Greensburg, Indiana. Prior to the ministry he taught political science. He is the justifiably proud father of two daughters, Saralyn and Jocelyn